BEHIND

THE TALL WALLS

BEHIND
THE TALL WALLS

Azar Aryanpour

Rutledge Books, Inc.

Danbury, CT

The author/publisher gratefully acknowledge permissions to reprint lines from *Odes of Hafez*, published by Mazda Publishers, 1984, by Abbas Aryanpur; and lines from *Rudyard Kipling's Verse Definitive Edition*, published by Bantam Doubleday Dell Publishing Group, Inc. reprinted in 1989. They also acknowledge credit for using verses from *Rubaiyat of Omar Khayyam* translated by Edward Fitzgerald, published by Doubleday & Company, Inc., 1952.

Rutledge Books, Inc.
107 Mill Plain Road, Danbury, CT 06811
1-800-278-8533

Manufactured in the United States of America

Library of Congress Cataloging in Publication Data
Aryanpour, Azar
   Behind the Tall Walls: From Palace to Prison
     ISBN: 1-58244-000-X

      1. Iran—Revolution—1979-
      2. Women—Iran—Autobiography
      3. Exiles—United States—Autobiography
      4. Feminism—Iran
      I. Title.

305.4 / 092   98-066997

To the people of Iran
And to my grandchildren,
Kayvan, Kamron and Kimya

And I only escaped alone to tell thee!
The Book of Job

Preface

Iran is one of the oldest civilizations in the world. It gets its name from the Indo-European race or Aryan tribes who came from the regions north of the Iranian plateau around 2000 B.C., and settled in the country known as Iran today. The Persian Empire founded by Cyrus the Great, was based on humanitarian ideals and religious tolerance. Darius I extended the Empire to its farthest boundaries, and promoted Persian culture which, along with the ancient Greek and Egyptian cultures, formed the basis of Western civilization. Despite subsequent invasions, Iran has retained its independence and a distinct homogenous culture. Persian language, arts, sciences, and philosophy have dominated the Islamic civilization, and have influenced other nations as well.

I was born in Iran/Persia, the land of the great poets, beautiful palaces and magnificent mosques.

My father belonged to the Nayebis, a courageous tribe from Lurestan, which fought for half a century against Iran's tyrannical governments — and were eventually exiled to Kashan and its leaders executed. My mother's family was aristocratic and prominent within the literary community. My maternal

---

grandfather, Abdul-Hosain Sepehr, a recognized historian, actively promoted the Constitutional Revolution of Iran. My grandmother—Hamideh Kalantar Zarrabi, was an accomplished poetess.

After high school, I married Shoja Sheikh, a young, bright and socially conscious physician. Together, we left for the United States to continue our education.

Five years later, we returned to Iran to face the challenges of obtaining jobs and raising children in a rapidly developing country. With a graduate degree in education, I started teaching and writing children's stories and poems. My husband, an American trained orthopedic surgeon, established a private practice and eventually founded the National Iranian Society for Rehabilitation of the Disabled. Later, Shoja became Minister of Health and Social Welfare under the Shah, and further contributed to his country's welfare.

At the beginning of the Iranian uprising in 1978, we witnessed a revolution not only in our country, but in our own life—a revolution that came to involve the United States, and nearly destroyed us.

The story you are about to read, comes from my life!

ACKNOWLEDGMENTS

I am equally grateful to all those who have graciously supported me in writing *Behind the Tall Walls*—family, friends, and colleagues.

Lori Van Decker, my good friend, worked patiently with me for days as I verbally translated the Farsi version of my book into English, and she transcribed and lightly edited it. Her sense of humor and her intelligence made this project more enjoyable.

A special thanks to Donald MacLaren for his professional editing, judgment and insights in guiding the manuscript along and giving it more life.

I owe a very special appreciation to the brave people of Iran who have proved themselves resilient and inspiring through the centuries. A part of me will always remain in my beautiful homeland.

I am also grateful to my new country, America, which made it possible for this story to be told.

INTRODUCTION

In telling this story, I have referred to several people by pseudonyms in order to protect them. I have also tried to recall the conversations that took place many years ago as accurately as possible.

This socio-historical book is an attempt at chronicling the tumultuous events of the Iranian Revolution of 1978 that affected my life. It covers a thirteen-year period which includes the overthrow of Shah Mohammad Reza Pahlavi; the rise to power of Ayatollah Ruhollah Khomeini; and the Iran-Iraq war.

Behind the Tall Walls could not have been published sooner because it would have endangered certain lives.

It is fair to say that, in the last few years, Iran has slowly but consistently shown progress in many areas of life. However, the lack of political freedom still remains an issue.

CHAPTER ONE

The story of love's sorrow is only one,
Yet told in countless ways!

Hafez (Fourteenth Century)

I had no idea how much my life would change as I flew away from Dulles International to my destination in my beloved homeland, Iran.

Something precious was left behind as the 747 jet sped its way in the sky. It was my two eldest children, Roxana and Ramin. They were almost as fascinating and beyond my reach as the white clouds floating outside the cabin window. After a short visit with them in the States, I was heading back to what I believed to be the safety of home. There, my husband, Shoja, and our youngest son, Babak, were waiting for me.

I hated being separated from Roxana and Ramin who had grown to be responsible, independent university students. It was not a simple decision to send them to school in the United States. But Shoja and I wanted our children, like us, to have a good education in a more liberal and challenging environment. Yes, Shoja and I had dreams. We sent our children abroad, hoping that they would come back to build the future of their country. And, in the confines of our own home, where the Shah's secret police could not hear us, we deluded ourselves into believing that they would have a turn in helping Iran become a real democracy!

Whenever the plane jostled in turbulence, my mind clicked back to my present reality. I automatically reached for my stomach to protect what seemed to be a newly conceived child, still so recent in my womb that its existence had to be officially confirmed. A new life! How did this happen? Was my husband ready for a fourth child? Here's a case where the doctor's wife has a surprise for the doctor! A smile crossed my face as I tried to imagine Shoja's reaction to the news.

Two months ago, Shoja had resigned as the Minister of Health and Social Welfare under the Shah. He had risen to that position only to be thwarted by the treacherous intrigues of SAVAK, the Shah's secret police, and other greedy power brokers around him. Instead of persisting in that conniving type of cesspool environment, he finally chose to go back into private practice as an orthopedic surgeon. I felt sad, as I sat on the plane, thinking about how recently my husband's idealistic dreams of helping to improve the medical conditions of his country, Iran, had come to a stop. Still, it was a relief to know that after several years of politics, our lives were getting back to normal. We no longer had to socialize for the sake of Shoja's position. No more dull receptions, formal dinner parties, or pompous galas with the Shah and the Queen and their guests where our every minor gesture was being monitored. We could now do the simple things that we both dreamed of doing for years, such as traveling across Iran, along the vast central deserts, following the caravan routes where the mountains and the valleys merged together under the bluest sky. Or discovering the dense northern forests where we could go camping with the children during their holidays.

Our future seemed to belong to us!

At 8:00 p.m., Thursday, September 7, 1978, the Mehr Abad Airport bustled with activity. Several international flights had landed at once.

Shoja's warm, kind face beamed through the crowd, as I walked into the terminal. He appeared to have gained a few pounds during my absence. There was no one at home to remind him of his tendency to overindulge. When we greeted, he, like most Iranian husbands, refrained from public display of affection, and only squeezed my hand gently to assure me of his love. However, he noticed the pink stylish linen suit I was wearing. "You look nice. Where did you get that smart outfit?" Shoja said as he took the luggage from me.

"Neiman-Marcus," I answered, smiling.

Babak, dressed in a freshly pressed shirt and jeans, showed less inhibition and embraced me. "Hi, Mom! Great to have you back," he added with a broad smile.

I looked at my son with pride. "You've grown taller in the last few weeks, sweetheart."

Babak raised his head proudly to appear even taller. He had not yet gone through that "awkward age" that most fifteen-year-olds endure. His skin was smooth, even though light patches of downy hairs appeared here and there on his young handsome face. And his luminous, brown eyes! How much they reminded me of my father's.

We exited the terminal and walked leisurely to the parking lot. As was usual for Tehran at this time of year, the weather remained very warm. Tourists from around the world were directed to special buses to begin their visit in the history-rich Iran. They would usually start their tour with the all-mirrored Golestan Palace in Tehran, built in the eighteenth century, where the Shah crowned himself on the bejeweled peacock throne. Then, they would visit the historical cities of Kashan and Isfahan, both with architectural masterpieces. Shiraz, the city of poets, and its nearby Persepolis, the ancient ruined city of the Achaemenid period, would highlight their tour. Of course, the tourists would not be disappointed in the Iranian night life—perfect imitation of the Western countries!

"So, love, how was your trip? Had a good time?" Shoja asked.

"It was all right, but not much of a vacation without the two of you. The kids and I spent a lot of time searching for a moderately priced apartment close to their university. They finally agreed on sharing a studio apartment. It's small but more convenient than their dorms. Shoja, I really wish you would reconsider buying a townhouse in D.C. It would make their stay and our visits to the States much easier."

Shoja's relaxed facial expression changed slightly. "Azar, by now, you should know how I feel about investing abroad! We don't intend to live in America. So please, let's not go into it again, love."

I sighed. Perhaps, he was right. If we had intended to live in America, we would have done so many years ago, when we finished school. Back then, Shoja could have established himself as an orthopedic surgeon, and I would have had no trouble making a career of teaching. At that time, America was an attractive place for two young professionals to plan a life together. Now it seemed too late for us to start over.

"Hey, guess what, Mom? Dad's got a new car—a nice, blue Buick with all kinds of electronic stuff. Wait till you see it! It's right over there," Babak pointed.

Just as I spotted the car, two husky men in black suits and ties appeared in front of us, almost blocking our way. I reacted spontaneously by clutching Shoja's arm. Babak moved closer to his father on the other side. The five of us stood there frozen for a long second. The men looked squarely in Shoja's eyes.

"Excuse us," Shoja addressed them nervously, as he edged us and my luggage past them. The men remained silent and threatening for a few more seconds before allowing us to pass. How strange some people can be! There was no logic to what had just happened. Perhaps they were just SAVAK agents. Nothing new in their stupid attempts to intimidate people!

"Where is Rajab?" I asked Shoja as he put the luggage into the trunk. Our chauffeur would normally handle such tasks.

"I dismissed him early today. There's been some unrest in parts of the city, and he wanted to be with his family. Things seem to be getting out of hand," he said with an apprehensive voice.

"It's hard to believe. How does the government explain what's happening?"

"As always, by evading the truth and blaming everything on the leftist terrorists," Shoja responded grimly with his eyes on the road.

I listened anxiously. Since last January, Tehran and several other cities had witnessed antigovernment demonstrations and riots, some even quite violent. The Shah's unrealistic development programs, extensive arsenals, and ostentatious displays of wealth had resulted in excessive inflation and corruption. People were demanding an end to the social injustice, political suppression, and economic instability. It was the kind of environment that spawned the extremists.

On the drive through Tehran, we passed the Shahyad Monument, standing tall and magnificent in the center of a gigantic circle. It was at the foot of this monument which marked the 2500th anniversary of the Persian Empire, that the Shah or his Prime Minister greeted foreign heads of states. Now, in the surrounding park, the carefree crowds were enjoying the scenery. I rolled down the window to get some fresh air.

"Isn't the car cool enough for you? I can turn up the air," Shoja asked with a puzzled look.

"No, it's fine. The movement makes me queasy. That's all. You know, a twenty-one-hour trip could be very exhausting," I assured him, resting my hand on my stomach. It was not time to tell him I suspected I might be pregnant. After all, I thought with an inner laugh, he might crash his new car into the curb!

We passed rows of modern concrete high-rises, which held no aesthetic or indigenous appeal. In his haste to produce a Westernized city, Mohammad Reza Pahlavi, the Shah of Iran, had destroyed most of whatever represented Iranian architecture. The beautiful, low, brick houses with small windows and majestic ceilings had been progressively replaced by an eclectic mixture of European styles, which fit neither the Iranian climate nor the culture. Nevertheless, I felt a mental grip with this city. It was mine!

"Dad took me with him to his hospital a few times—even into the operating room! It was neat, Mom! I think I'd like to be a doctor someday, like Dad," Babak broke the silence.

Shoja and I smiled. As a child, our youngest son wanted to become a fireman and a pilot. Now he wished to be a physician. His career choice had certainly improved. What was it that Ramin, our sensitive son, wanted to be when he was younger? He rarely talked about the future, although he was passionately interested in sports and social issues. Roxana always wanted to work with children and, of course, have her own.

"Azar," Shoja called to catch my attention. "I'm planning to go to the States in *Now Ruz*—the Iranian New Year—and spend some time with the kids. It's the same time as their spring break. We'll have some fun together. I've really neglected them over the past few years."

"They'd be thrilled to spend the holidays with you," I said with excitement. My husband had finally admitted to neglecting his family. That was a positive change!

We entered Shemiran Road heading north towards the Alborz Mountains. Shemiran, the former suburb of Tehran, was famous for its cool weather. Almost like gypsies, the rich Iranians used to move from the heat of Tehran to the mountain breezes of Shemiran every summer. Within the last twenty-five years, as Tehran grew, it rapidly absorbed Shemiran into its bulk. Now, it was part of the city.

We drove a few miles in busy traffic along Shemiran Road before turning right to our quiet residential neighborhood. Two symbolic powers featured our neighborhood: a small mosque with a blue mosaic minaret and a large army camp, called Heshmatieh, behind a stretch of white walls.

We made a short left turn and stopped. At last, we were home—a white stucco house with a red roof, rose garden, and a turquoise pool shaded by old tall poplar trees. Like all Iranian houses, it sat quietly on property surrounded by high walls that provided both privacy and security. It felt good to be returning home to my family, my garden and my teaching job.

Friday started like any other Iranian Sabbath. Shoja had gone to the hospital to check on his patients. With my body sluggish from jet lag and queasiness, I began tidying up the house. Our housekeeper was away for family problems.

Around noon, my sister, Aryan, telephoned. "Azar! How'd your trip go?" she exclaimed cheerfully.

"Not bad, except for a lot of running around," I commented while taking a momentary break from work.

"I tell you what. Come over for lunch and tell me all about it."

"Sounds good. Now, let me get back to my work. I'll see you around noon."

"Listen!" Aryan who never camouflaged her emotions, continued. "Did you hear about the recent violent clashes between the military and the people? SAVAK blames it all on 'saboteurs', but the demonstrators come from all walks of life—students, merchants, working class, and clergy. You name it. Rumors are that another large demonstration is planned soon. I just hope the army doesn't kill hundreds of innocent people," Aryan reported with concern.

Being aware that our telephone might be tapped by the SAVAK, and this innocent conversation could be manipulated the wrong way, I quickly changed the topic. "I haven't even unpacked my suitcase, Aryan. You know how fussy I am about getting things done quickly! I'll see you as soon as I finish straightening up here."

Since I lived only a few houses away from Aryan, we could resume our discussion later, in person. I popped into the player a tape Ramin had given me in Washington, D.C., and resumed my work as John Lennon sang: "Imagine there's no country. . . ."

Babak rushed into the room. "Mom, turn that music off. The radio just announced martial law—effective immediately!"

The last time we had martial law was fifteen years ago when, in the holy city of Qom, a group of religious men, seminarians, and citizens staged a protest march under the leadership of a high-ranking clergyman named Ruhollah Khomeini. Among the issues that instigated the protest were the Shah's so-called reforms or White Revolution, and a new law giving United States military personnel and their dependents extraterritorial capitulary rights. This law took away the power of the Iranian courts to hear complaints against Americans. It fact, it was a flagrant violation of international rights. As a result, there were several bloody confrontations with the armed forces, and the opposition did not cease until Ayatollah Khomeini was extradited to Iraq.

Most certainly, some ominous event in the city had warranted such a reaction from the Shah's government. Under martial law, gatherings of more than three people were not permitted in public, and a curfew went into effect an hour after sundown. Aryan's luncheon was canceled. I called Shoja at Pars Hospital to warn him to come home.

"I can't leave now! The emergency room's full of patients. They were injured during a demonstration today outside the Parliament," Shoja answered with an exhausted voice.

"Have any been killed?"

"More than you can imagine. I'll tell you later. For now, you and Babak stay put. No one can predict what might happen next. I don't know when I'll be home."

An eerie mood took over me. Had the military actually shot our own Iranian citizens?

The media was oddly silent. I turned on the television and listened as General Oveissi, the Commander of Ground Forces, and Administrator of the Martial Law, officially ordered the civilian population to observe the curfew. Then, as usual, the rest of the broadcast focused on "His Imperial Majesty, *Shahanshah Arya Mehr*"—the King of Kings, the Light of Aryans—and his "great reforms." Obviously, the SAVAK still kept close control of the news media.

Around 4:00 p.m. the phone rang.

"Your husband will be dead soon!" a strange throaty voice rasped.

"What? Who is this? Hello? Hello?"

How bizarre! Was this a prank call? Wrong number? People must be crazy to get a kick out of harassing others.

Then, the phone rang again. I waited for it to ring several times before answering. This time it was from Dr. Torab, Shoja's surgical colleague. I had met him at several hospital parties. He was a nice person, but not overly friendly or demonstrative.

"Just called to see that everyone in your family's well," Dr. Torab explained in a harried tone.

"Why? We're all fine. Shoja's still in the hospital. Did you want to talk to him?" I asked, surprised by his unexpected call.

"Oh, no! I just wondered how you are all doing. With the city in terrible turmoil, one worries. Give my best to Shoja. We'll talk soon." His tone was not convincing.

I contacted the hospital again to make sure Shoja was all right.

"Could you please tell me if my husband, Dr. Sheikh, is still in the hospital?" I asked a nurse.

Shoja's family name—Sheikholeslamzadeh—was considered very long even by Iranian standards. So, everyone called him Dr. Sheikh for short.

"Dr. Sheikh's on his way home." The nurse set my mind at peace. I went into the kitchen to prepare Shoja's favorite dinner: sirloin steaks, mashed potatoes and salad.

During dinner, Shoja talked animatedly about the day's events. "Apparently, the announcement of martial law didn't reach the peaceful demonstrators at Jaleh Square in time for them to disperse," he said. "From what I heard, the military opened fire on defenseless people, killing hundreds and injuring many more. Some were literally trampled to death in their attempts to get away. The whole situation is disgraceful!"

I listened with dismay. This could be the beginning of civil war in Iran. Though we were living in uncertain times, surely the military's actions were beyond the people's understanding of what was tolerable.

A sense of wanting to protect Shoja came over me and without mentioning anything about the bizarre phone calls, I warned, "Please, Shoja, be extra careful."

He put his arm around me. "Nothing's going to happen to me, love. Even if, against all odds, a revolution occurs in Iran, it won't affect us. I'm no longer involved in politics. And when I was running the Ministry, everything was aboveboard."

The word revolution was too strong to use. It implied radical change, anarchy, renunciation of the existing regime. We were not prepared for that. "Sweetheart, let's go away for a while," I pleaded.

"No! Whatever happens, we'll face it together," Shoja replied confidently.

In the morning, Babak started tenth grade at the Iran Zamin International School. Run by an American superintendent and an Iranian principal, this top private school taught in both English and Farsi.

I still had a couple of weeks before the fall semester began at the College of Shemiran and the National University where I had been teaching philosophy of education and children's literature for several years. As a part-time instructor, I had tried to challenge my students to appreciate their ancient history and literature and become acquainted with the Western culture. It was fun and fulfilling to teach young enthusiastic students.

I drank some coffee and went outside to do some late-summer gardening. The extensive landscaping that we did two years ago was flourishing exquisitely.

Shahri, our humble gardener in his late forties, greeted me. He wore his tan shirt and dark pants.

"*Salaam, Khanom*—Good day, Madame. Hope your trip went well, *Inshallah*—God willing."

"Yes! Very well, thank you," I said, bending down to admire the latest rose bush with delicate pink white roses.

"Surely the house isn't the same without the children."

"You're right about that, but the garden looks wonderful, thanks to you."

Shahri was flattered. "God bless this house, and your family." Then, aware of the SAVAK's hidden ears, he lowered his voice. "*Khanom*, is it true that thousands of people were killed yesterday outside the Parliament?"

He took me off guard. The underlying social paranoia that we lived in began to take over. As much as I trusted Shahri, he could easily misquote me.

"Where did you hear that?"

"Oh, *Khanom*, everyone's talking about it. They are calling it Black Friday in honor of so many who died. The Mullah at our Mosque has declared a *Jihad*—Holy War!"

I frowned. Those were startling words for me. If thousands were killed, not a few hundred as Shoja had suggested, then the government had created war on its citizens. Or, could the numbers of the dead be exaggerated by the clergy to generate hatred and invite Iranians into a war?

"I hope it doesn't come to that," I said quickly. This was not a safe conversation in such times. I put on my gardening gloves. "By the way, should we plant a few mums over there, near the porch?"

"Sure, *Khanom*," Shahri said. "I'll get a dozen pots tomorrow." He folded his hands and looked at me shyly.

"Is there something I can do for you?" I realized that he had a personal request.

"*Khanom*, I wondered if you could pay me this month's salary in advance. I need to stock up on supplies for my family in case of a civil war. You know, basic things like kerosene for heat, sugar for tea, and, of course, rice."

"You're worrying a little too much. But, I don't see why you can't have the money now. I'll speak to my husband," I said decisively. "Now, let's get to work before it gets too hot. We have got a lot of weeding to do."

At dinner, I discussed the gardener's request as I had promised.

"Things are bad," Shoja exclaimed, "but a war? Honestly, some of the people's fears are based solely on rumors. If the truth weren't kept from the public...! I don't understand how the government can keep silent about yesterday's event. By now the international press has probably publicized it all over the world. Anyway, I'll pay the gardener tomorrow."

"Did anything new happen in the city today?" I asked, looking over a dozen red roses in a crystal vase—my homecoming gift from Shoja.

"Not that I heard of. I had three operations, over twenty patients to see, and a telephone that rang continuously."

I sighed with relief. Thankfully, Shoja had left politics to be simply a busy doctor. I must stop worrying about him.

Babak brought a letter and gave it to his father. "Dad, please send this express mail tomorrow. I promised Roxana and Ramin that I'd write about the first day of school. I'll really miss chatting with them."

Babak and I cleared the table and did the dishes. Shoja, exhausted by his work, went to bed early. When I entered the bedroom, he had already fallen asleep with Nehru's autobiography lying on his chest. I removed the book, turned off the light, got undressed, and climbed into bed next to him.

My mind circled around the recent events, and kept me from falling asleep. I rested my hands on my stomach. At thirty-nine, in a country with an uncertain future, having another child was a big decision. How would Shoja react? With everything that had happened, I never found the right time to tell him.

The moon shone through the window on Shoja's face as he slept innocently. The strange phone calls came to my mind, and the subdued fear surfaced. I leaned over and placed a tender kiss on my husband's cheek. The warmth of his skin and his steady breathing comforted me. I laid back gently, shut my eyes, and tried to let go of my concerns. In the garden, a bird called to its mate with a melodic cry.

CHAPTER TWO

September 10 started with a cool morning. Through the open window I heard the gardener watering the roses, spreading their light, sweet fragrance into the air. Shoja had finished his shower and was getting ready for work. Though half awake, I was aware of his every movement. He returned to the bedroom to dress quickly, with his customary opening and banging of closet doors and drawers. He left the bedroom, only to come back immediately to retrieve his wallet, which he had forgotten.

"I'm late," he mumbled as he exited.

Every day for the last twenty-one years, I had heard the same statement, but he was never late. I opened my eyes and glanced at the clock on the bedside table. The red digital numbers showed 7:30 a.m. I knew Shoja would be at work in less than thirty minutes.

Before he reached the yard, I called, "Shoja! I'm going to your hospital for an exam this morning. Could we have lunch together?"

I planned to surprise Shoja with the news after the doctor confirmed our new baby's existence.

"Okay," he said, without exhibiting any curiosity. I heard

him talk with the gardener, and a while later, the gate closed behind him.

Suddenly, the house seemed very quiet. Although not very large, it had taken us nine years to get this house exactly the way we wanted—simple but elegant. The furniture was an eclectic combination of Persian and French contemporary, and antiques. Shoja, being a busy professional, had left the entire interior decorating to me. I had tried to select and arrange each piece carefully to create a comfortable and pleasant home.

I made myself a cup of coffee and started the process of waking up. Through the kitchen window, I gazed at the house behind where my parents had lived for many years until my father's death. Now, it was vacant. Out of her grief, Mother had moved on to live a block away in an apartment. Their home was a silent reminder of many happy days. Beyond that house, I glimpsed the majestic, snowcapped Alborz Mountains. They were like a diamond tiara crowning Tehran.

At 8:30, our driver was standing motionless by my car, a light green *Paykan*—an Iranian assembled car with English parts. With deep blue eyes and silver-blond hair, Rajab, looking rather out of the ordinary for an Iranian, appeared even more pale this morning. When he opened the car door, I noticed that his hands were trembling.

"Aren't you feeling well?" I asked.

He mumbled something that I did not understand. Rajab had been in our household for a long time. We had assisted him with the down payment on a house. Shoja also helped three of his nine children find jobs. Five years ago, when Shoja joined the government and a car and chauffeur were assigned to him, Rajab quit, because he wanted to be the "Minister's Driver."

Eventually, he agreed to return and remain solely the family's driver—certainly a demotion, in his opinion. We were never able to explain to Rajab that the new driver had probably been cleared by the SAVAK and most likely assigned to spy on us.

I got into the car and instructed Rajab to take me to Pars Hospital.

"By the way, Ramin has sent you a letter. I hope you can read his scribbling," I said, handing the letter out to him.

Although Rajab was friends with Ramin, he showed no interest. He did not even turn the car engine on.

"What's the problem? Something's wrong?"

"It's—it's *Agha*," he stuttered.

As it was common in Iran, he addressed his master by the formal term of *Agha*—Sir.

"What about him? He left for the hospital this morning, didn't he?" I asked apprehensively.

"No!" Rajab pointed to Shoja's Buick parked further down the street.

"Where's my husband?" I demanded, fear beginning to simmer inside me.

"As *Agha* was getting into his car, two men in police uniforms grabbed him and forced him into their car. *Agha*, quite puzzled, went along," Rajab managed to express in words.

Blood froze in my arteries. "What do you mean? Where would they take my husband? What kind of car was that? Police car?"

"No. Just an unmarked white Chevy."

"Did anyone else witness this?"

"I don't think so, *Khanom*. The street was quiet, and the gardener was still inside the house. He left just a few minutes ago."

I folded my hands in frustration. It made absolutely no sense that Shoja, who had been a Cabinet member only two months ago, could be arrested. On what charges? It was impossible. I had Rajab repeat the morning's incident over, hoping to discover some clues as to Shoja's abduction. None emerged.

"Why didn't you inform me right away?" with uncharacteristic rage, I yelled.

"*Khanom*, I was too shocked. Besides, I didn't want to worry you, in case it turned out to be no big deal."

"I understand, Rajab," I said, taken aback by my own yelling. *Stay calm. There must be a logical explanation for Shoja's disappearance*, I kept thinking as I hurriedly went back to the house to telephone the hospital.

"Dr. Sheikh has an operation scheduled in half an hour, but he hasn't checked in yet. Where is he? He's never late," the nurse asked.

I gave a quick answer, and then called Shoja's father, a lawyer, hoping that he had heard from him.

My father-in-law was out, and my mother-in-law had no news from her son. "Shoja hasn't visited us for some time," she complained in a drawl.

"Please, if you hear from him, have him call me at once," I ended the conversation quickly.

Fear gripped my body and I held my stomach. What if Shoja was kidnapped? Why would anyone come after my husband, who was no longer a cabinet minister? If they were looking for ransom, Shoja was not the ideal target, my mind kept telling me. In fact, while in office, he had used most of our savings to supplement his low government salary. No! There must be another explanation for his disappearance.

I walked back to the car and found Rajab standing where he was. We both looked up and down the street, but there was no sign of Shoja.

"*Khanom*, do you wish me to ask around about *Agha*?" Rajab inquired kindly.

For the first time, I considered the scandalous side of the situation. How could I explain Shoja's kidnapping to others?

"No, no! Why worry everyone when my husband may be returning soon? I don't need the car any longer. You may leave now. Just don't forget to pick up Babak from school. And please, don't mention anything to him, or to anyone else!" I said with some authority.

I returned to the kitchen and sat down by the window where I liked to think. My head was filled with a confused buzzing sound.

During his term in office, Shoja had made many enemies. In his efforts to improve the health and welfare system of Iran, he refused to concede to the intrusive manipulations of the SAVAK. Eventually, he preferred to resign. Shoja assumed that once he was out of the government, his life would be normal again. So did I. Obviously, we were both wrong.

I picked up the telephone. "Dr. Asad Aram, please. It's urgent."

Dr. Aram, Shoja's former deputy at the Ministry of Health and Social Welfare, was ambitious and shrewd. He now worked in the private sector.

"He's not in the office, and I can't get hold of him," the secretary informed me.

Where could he be? Where could they all be? Who else could I call? Of course: Reza Neqabat—another former deputy under Shoja who currently worked at the Ministry.

"What's happened?" Neqabat asked when I reached him on the phone. He sensed trouble in my voice.

"I can't go into details. Please, come to see me as soon as you can." I deliberately withheld information because no telephone conversation was safe, particularly on a government line.

"It'll be a while—not till afternoon," Neqabat said and we hung up.

How could I wait that long? I tried different departments in the hospital several more times, but no one had seen Shoja.

The phone sat mutely on the desk. Why didn't it ring? Why didn't Shoja come back? Over a hundred times, I looked out the front door. No sign of him!

In the afternoon, Babak and Neqabat arrived at the same time. Babak was stunned by his father's kidnapping. Neqabat did not appear very surprised. A rather short, fit man of forty, Neqabat wore a finely trimmed mustache which added to his respectable demeanor of a Deputy Minister. He believed Shoja had been detained in a political arrest.

"What makes you suspect that?" I asked in a baffled voice.

"Just a feeling," he said thoughtfully. "Our history's full of such arrests in politically tumultuous times. This is probably just a gesture from the government to appease the dissidents. I assure you, Shoja's life is not in danger."

"My father's arrest can't possibly have something to do with Friday's massacre, can it?" my teenage son asked anxiously.

"Oh, by the way, I couldn't reach Dr. Aram. Could he be arrested too?" I added.

"We'll find out soon enough." Neqabat began rubbing his chin with his hand. His pretended confidence had disappeared. "I may also be detained," he anticipated. "We all worked together as a team. If one is targeted, the others are not immune."

"What charges could they bring against any one of you?" Babak asked.

"Under martial law the government can arrest anyone without charges, if he is perceived as a threat to national security," Neqabat explained.

"My father, a threat to national security? Insane!"

"I know, but politics is unpredictable." Neqabat sighed. "I better go home. The police are probably waiting for me at my front door," he said sardonically and got up to his feet.

Later in the evening, Jaafar Sharif-Emami, the current Prime Minister, appeared on television and for the first time publicly acknowledged the massacre on "Black Friday." He blamed the demonstrators for ignoring the curfew and denied that his government had any responsibility for the incident. The Prime Minister went on to request public restraint and obedience to the law. To our disappointment, Sharif-Emami did not make any reference to Shoja's arrest.

Babak and I stayed up all night, pacing and praying. Shoja did not return.

At 8:00 a.m., the radio reported: "Dr. Shoja Sheikholeslamzadeh, former Secretary of Health and Social Welfare, and his two deputies, Dr. Asad Aram and Reza Neqabat, have been arrested and charged with creating discontent among the populace!"

I gasped. So, my husband had indeed been arrested. Shame on the government! Shame! But creating "discontent?" What did this mysterious word imply? He was not the one to go to the political rallies to make speeches against the government.

Within a short time of the announcement, two of my brothers, my sister, and her husband rushed over for a family meeting. My eldest brother, Amir Hosain, and his family, along with my mother, were spending the summer in England.

My brother, Amir Ashraf, fifty-one, tall, slim and rather stiff, adjusted his wire-rimmed glasses. "Why didn't you inform us sooner, Azar? What's a family for? Shoja's our brother-in-law. You should've told us right away," he scolded.

My other brother, Amir Hushang, two and a half years younger than him, had a softer look, a gentler approach. "How can I help, Sis? I could try to arrange a meeting with General Oveissi. He's the one who ordered the arrests."

People often commented on Hushang's handsome resemblance to Marcello Mastroianni, the Italian actor.

Aryan, my forty-three-year-old impulsive sister, thrust her attractive head upright and said, "I know who's behind it all—SAVAK! They'll kill Shoja!" In our family she was known for her fiery nature.

Aryan's husband, a reputable pediatrician several years her senior, whom by respect we called Doctor, was more prudent. Despite his lean physique, he was like gravity to our family. 'Doctor' was a good listener without being judgmental.

"Please, Aryan! Let's not speculate before we know the facts," her husband protested. "The whole thing might turn out to be nothing but a misunderstanding."

"Still, I think I should call Mother in London and tell her

to come back right away, before it's too late," Aryan said offhandedly.

"Aryan, please," I reacted strongly. "Don't say anything to Mother until I hear something more substantial about Shoja. This is her first trip since Father passed away. I don't want anything to interrupt it. In fact, don't discuss this with anyone!"

Unfortunately, the bad news had already struck Roxana and Ramin in Washington. They were both shaken.

"Mom! We want to come back and be with you at this time. We could take a leave of absence from school. It's no big deal," Ramin and Roxana said on the telephone.

"No! Stay put. We'll manage here," I told them firmly. "I'll keep you posted if I hear anything on your father. He's going to be just fine, sweethearts."

I realized that coping with Shoja's imprisonment might be particularly hard for our son, Ramin, who was extremely proud of his father. With Shoja's arrest, our lives would never be the same.

Strangely enough, some members of the Cabinet called and expressed their surprise and concern. Amir Abbas Hoveyda, the present Court Minister and the former Prime Minister under whom Shoja served, divulged no information regarding the arrest. Instead, he promised "to speak with *Shahanshah* about this situation."

Hushang Ansary, Chairman of the National Iranian Oil Company, also pledged to discuss my husband's arrest with "His Imperial Majesty." In addition, Abdul-Majid Majidi, Chairman of the Queen Farah's Cultural Foundation, gave his word to bring the case to the attention of *Shahbanou*—Her Imperial Majesty—when she held court.

Nice gestures.

Shoja's arrest, and those of his deputies, had made the headlines in all the daily papers. Not much was written about the nature of the charges against them. Obviously, the media waited to receive comments from the SAVAK.

One week after Shoja's arrest, my living room was full of visitors, including some high-ranking government officials who came out of sympathy, concern, and curiosity. Although mentally exhausted, I received them with traditional hospitality. On the outside, I gave the impression of being calm and composed; on the inside, I was shattered.

"Was Shoja being treated like a common criminal? Tortured? Why weren't you told of his whereabouts?" The same questions kept coming from everyone. Nobody seemed to believe that I didn't know any more than they did

The visitors offered a plethora of contradictory opinions and each took appropriate turns in the conversation. Shoja was not an enemy of the Shah, surely, or was he? One related Shoja's arrest to the political upheavals. Another blamed his "corrupt deputies" for the ordeal. Still a third suggested that Shoja's detention was just a political charade and, soon, he would be rewarded by the Shah!

After they left, I felt more confused and unable to unravel the mystery of my husband's arrest. Later, Dr. Torab's appearance at the door added to my fear and confusion. The gray-haired surgeon did not accept my invitation to enter the house.

"I can't stay more than a few moments," he said, looking around him. "Azar, I tried to tell you the other night on the phone that Shoja's in danger," he confessed confidentially.

I grew increasingly irritated. "So, you knew what was going to happen all along? Where did you get your information?" I asked with alarm.

For an instant Torab seemed to be debating with himself. Then, he shook his head. "Please, for my sake as well as yours, don't ask me to give any names. I can only tell you that according to a reliable source, there had been a plot to assassinate Shoja at the airport, on the night of your arrival!"

I listened to him with my mouth wide open. He paused and leaned forward. "For some unknown reason, that plan had not materialized. Instead Shoja was arrested!" Torab added in a hushed voice.

My mind flashed back to the strange encounter with the two men in the dark suits. "My God! Who would ever want Shoja killed?" I asked in terror.

"I don't know. I just think you should watch out for yourselves. You could all become targets!" Dr. Torab warned me. "Now, I must go. Please, don't mention my name to anyone!"

I nodded helplessly as he left and shut the door behind him. Suddenly, the significance of the news struck me. I felt aghast! A plot to assassinate Shoja? My children? Myself? This was beyond my comprehension. What was I to do now? How could I protect my family against a mysterious enemy? It felt as if I was caught in a sudden hurricane with winds blowing over 150 miles per hour. I leaned against the hallway wall as a sharp pain like a chisel hit me in the belly. Slowly and painfully, I managed to walk back into the living room. Something was terribly wrong inside me.

By midnight, I began to hemorrhage. A few hours later at

Pars Hospital, I had a miscarriage. I lost a child that Shoja never knew anything about. Our first victim to a mad situation!

Two days later, I was still weak and very despondent when Pazani, our loyal, hardworking thirty-five year old housekeeper, returned to work. He had not heard about our troubles, having been preoccupied with his own.

"*Khanom*, my household is a mess. It's like my eleven-year-old son is possessed. He acts so strange," Pazani disclosed with a strong Azeri accent. Like Shoja, he came from the Azerbaijan province, near Turkey's border, where everyone, in addition to Farsi, spoke in a Turkish dialect

"What do you mean by strange?" I asked with concern.

"Ayah! The boy wakes the neighborhood at night, wailing. When we rush to help, he locks himself in the bathroom. It all started after the circumcision. My son had just reached his eleventh birthday. As a Moslem, I couldn't forgo the ceremony."

"Of course you couldn't! Did a doctor perform it?"

"No, *Khanom*! Just the usual tradition. I sent for the barber. He was busy, so I sent for the butcher to do the job. We planned a big family gathering—even hired street musicians for my only son. But all the boy did was scream and carry on. He hasn't stopped since," he said.

"Listen! He must be hurt, physically and emotionally. At eleven, it must be unbearably embarrassing to go through such a thing, especially with a large audience! Perhaps you should consult a doctor. Unfortunately, my husband isn't available."

The doorbell rang and Pazani shuffled off his hardy frame to answer it. He returned with an unexpected visitor—a tall, gaunt figure in a military uniform. Once in the living room, the officer took off his cap and introduced himself as General Tabatabai, deputy to the Minister of Defense.

"I am a personal messenger sent by His Imperial Majesty, *Shahanshah Arya Mehr!*" He claimed in a self-glorifying tone.

I rose to my feet and shook hands. "General, please tell me what you know of my husband's arrest. Where is he?" I immediately pleaded.

"*Khanom*, His Imperial Majesty has commanded me to assure you that your husband's arrest is a small sacrifice which will be recognized by our great leader."

I looked at him with disbelief. "What is the connection between my husband's imprisonment and proof of his loyalty? Where is he now? As his wife, I have a right to know!"

The General evaded my questions. "*Khanom*, you needn't be worried. Trust me! Your husband faces no danger. He will come back to you soon. Just be patient. In the meantime, if you need anything, I am at your disposal," he said haughtily.

"All I need is my husband!" I uttered. "I hope you understand!"

The General, still holding on to his cap, nodded and retreated quietly. Pazani walked him to the door. I sank heavily into a chair and held my aching head between my hands. The situation had become much more complicated than I could ever imagine.

Sometime later, I heard from a certain source that Tabatabai was not what he claimed to be. Who was he? An impostor? A spy? Who sent him?

Despite the curfew, opposition forces had not stopped demonstrating across the country. As usual, the authorities blamed others for the unrest.

The day before, Congressman Esfandari had openly

addressed the Parliament: "The people are revolting because of the corruption of a few. As long as opportunists like Dr. Sheikh rob the nation blind, one cannot expect a safe and orderly society. Cut the hands off these thieves so the people can enjoy the bounty bequeathed by our Great Leader!"

My world began to crumble. So far, the charges against Shoja had been that he contributed to public discontent. Now this liar was accusing him of corruption. The regime was planning to save itself by deflecting the dissidents' anger to others. Shoja had become a convenient scapegoat.

My father-in-law, Agha Joon—Dear Sir, as he was called respectfully—came immediately to see me in a frenzy and vented his anger at me.

"How far will you let these slanderous accusations go before you decide to help your husband?" he yelled.

"What is it that you want me to do for Shoja?" I yelled back from my own pent up fear and anger.

"Go see the real thief—the Prime Minister! Ask him what proof there is to accuse my son of corruption!"

"I tried, but the Prime Minister wouldn't see me. And I was denied an audience with the Queen. No one seems to care."

"So you sit back until they completely destroy your husband's reputation?" Agha Joon boomed.

"Shoja won't be damaged by any of this. Those who know him remember all the honorable things he's done for his country," I offered in a softer tone.

"I'll deal with those bastards personally," Agha Joon said.

This was the first time that I heard him use such language.

"Agha Joon, if they give me visiting permission, would you come with me?"

"I will never visit my son in a prison!" the despondent old man answered emphatically as he stomped out. Babak ran after his grandfather and said, "Agha Joon, you left your hat behind." He stooped, put on his hat, and gave his grandson a pat on the shoulder. I could not help making a mental comparison between Shoja's appearance and his father's. Both men were rather short and broad, with thinning hair and fine features. Father and son had the type of face that evoked warmth in the people around them. Their personalities were also similar. They were men of principle—honest, and forthright. But while the father was more authoritarian, the son took a more gentle approach to people.

Suddenly, I imagined Shoja's generous smile, and longed for him.

Ten days after Shoja's arrest, a man called and introduced himself as Dr. Azodi. It was 11:00 p.m. I was told I could visit my husband—alone—tomorrow at the Central Department of Police in Sepah Avenue. In a gruff voice, the man instructed me to take a minimum of personal belongings to my husband: two changes of underwear, soap, toothbrush, and toothpaste, but no shaving equipment.

"Make sure to do just as I told you, Lady!" Dr. Azodi concluded rudely.

With a paradoxical mix of apprehension and anticipatory excitement, I began to pack Shoja's things. This was the first time in my life that I was about to enter a prison.

Since childhood I had frequently heard stories of Iran's heinous prisons, torture chambers, and persecutions. My paternal great-grandfather, the leader of a prominent tribe from

Lurestan, was first exiled to Kashan. Later, he and his son—my grandfather—were both captured and hung, as a result of the tribe's long warfare against the oppression of the Qajars—the previous monarchs.

During the Pahlavis' reign, the Shah's police often invaded my parents' home, looking for forbidden literature to use against my brothers. They were considered "intellectuals" and, therefore, threats to the government.

Now, I was extremely nervous. What might happen to me?

At 6:00 a.m., wearing a plain black dress and tinted glasses, I drove myself to the Central Department of Police, an impressive old building situated in the heart of the city, opposite the Ministry of Foreign Affairs. This morning, the Ministry's building was not as spectacular as it had been on the evening that Shoja and I attended a gala for King Hussein of Jordan a few months ago.

I approached the prison with a small travel bag and much humiliation. People around the country were beginning to make false assumptions about Shoja without really knowing the truth. It was hard to fight for the truth when the whole system seemed orchestrated against him.

In the front entrance, a guard checked my I.D. against his list of scheduled visitors and sent me into a small waiting area. Fortunately, there was no one else in the room except a sullen-looking officer, who searched the carryall and phoned for my entrance permission. Nervously, I waited.

A listless orderly with an impoverished, unkempt appearance came to escort me inside. I began to feel uneasy. Why wasn't he wearing a proper police uniform?

In a large lobby displaying pictures of the police officers recently killed in the skirmishes, we were stopped by another guard, who had difficulty reading my long name. After his approval, we continued down a stairway and into a courtyard.

The orderly handed me to another man in civilian clothing. Silently, this man led me to a shabby room off the court, furnished with a filthy, tattered sofa, a broken table, and a worn-out rug with a musty stench. The room was lit dimly by a twenty-watt bulb that hung naked from the ceiling. The place would have made a perfect set for a spy movie, except it was for real.

My attendant, hollow-cheeked and skinny, perhaps a junkie, ordered me to sit. I refused. He came up to me, stood directly in front of me and, with lustful eyes, stared. I turned my head away, fearing this man, this place. He grabbed my carryall and hurled it to the floor, exhibiting his petty power.

"But, it's already been searched!" I exclaimed.

He knelt down and pulled everything out onto the disgusting carpet. I restrained myself, pressing my nails into the flesh of my palms. The man scrambled up to his feet, took a cigarette from his pocket and put it in the corner of his mouth. His hands trembled as he tried to strike a match. In frustration, he flung the cigarette and match across the room. Again, his eyes rested on my face. I dodged away from his stare. Suddenly, the man's damp, sweaty hands moved quickly, grasped my arm, and pulled me closer. I tried to escape, but he yanked me back and attempted to brutally kiss my mouth. I screamed at the top of my voice.

The door opened with a loud noise and a guard entered. The junkie tossed me aside. He had bruised my arm but I was relieved to be rescued. The guard gestured for me to follow him. I smoothed down my hair, and followed him instantly. Grateful for his sudden entrance, I forgot to pick up Shoja's belongings that were scattered on the floor.

The guard and I walked across the courtyard into a building with offices on both sides of a wide corridor.

"First door on your right," the guard said grudgingly.

Cautiously, I walked into a neat, bright room—quite a contrast to the previous one. Beyond the attractive furniture, a huge man sat behind an imposing desk, taking time to scrutinize me. I proceeded slowly. Suddenly, the man let out in a piercing scream, "You insult our men and refuse to obey their orders?" The junkie must have reported me to him.

"That is not true!" I objected in a meek voice which disappointed me for I had intended a bolder response.

"Now you call us liars, too?" The fat man stood up to further terrorize me. A giant! Six feet and close to three hundred pounds. "You act so arrogantly! Think you're still the wife of a Minister? Your husband's no more than a prisoner," he spat his words venomously. I was in the presence of the king viper.

"Prisoner? More like a sacrificial lamb held without justification! You will have to free him, soon!" I said with more courage.

"Go on living with that hope!" the man hissed as he walked towards me.

"No matter how lawless this country may be, people cannot be held without charges," I asserted, believing in a higher law than he or his junkie cohorts represented.

His face reddened. He brought his index finger up and pointed it in my face and shouted, "I was told you're impudent.

But, I see you're insane as well to speak to me like this. I'll show you who's the boss here: Your visit is canceled today!"

Angry and frustrated by his power play, I turned to leave. Was it worth seeing my husband under such demeaning circumstances?

I had not quite reached the door when a section of the bookshelf in front of me slid open to expose a handsome young face. Could he be part of the police?

"Dr. Azodi, please let this woman visit with her husband. She promises to behave!" the young man said on my behalf.

Azodi? He must be the man who called last night.

I turned my head in surprise. Azodi motioned for me to sit down. He went back to his desk where he swallowed two green capsules, perhaps tranquilizers, before shouting, "Bring in the prisoner!" He kept one eye on me and the other zeroed in on the door.

I perched on the arm of a sofa, scanning the bookshelves and avoiding Azodi's menacing stare. Most of the books were Persian translations of such famous works as Gorky's *Mother*, Steinbeck's *Grapes of Wrath*, and a few Iranian novels. All contraband as far as Azodi was concerned, and most likely confiscated from the homes of so-called "Communist intellectuals."

Shoja was escorted into the room, blindfolded! An absolute shock! He wore prison stripes, shaved head, unshaven face.

"Remove the blindfold," Azodi shouted.

Shoja blinked twice with the light, saw me, and forced a smile. The deep shadows around his eyes attested to his lack of sleep. I started towards him, tears streaming down my face. "What have they done to you?" I asked with confusion.

His lips tightened.

"What have you done to deserve this?" I asked again as I took his hand.

"I can't think of anything," he answered in a quivering voice. Then he straightened his shoulders and added, "Don't worry. Things will be cleared up soon. How are you and the kids?"

"We're all fine, except for being concerned about you. Why are you detained at police headquarters?"

"Police headquarters?" he said with a grim smile. "Not this part of the complex. This is SAVAK!"

I felt like I had been kicked in the ribs. Instantly, my mind teemed with the horrifying rumors about this place—burns from cigarettes and boiling water, electric shocks, rapes, threats against prisoners' families, endless days of brooding silence in dark cells, starvation rations and a slow, painful descent to death.

"Why? Why would they bring you here?"

"Perhaps for revenge. During my five years in office, I didn't bow to their whims or pay them kickbacks."

"This is not your bedroom that you coo to each other!" Azodi shrieked. "Speak loudly enough so I can hear you!"

Shoja pressed his lips together but did not say anything.

"Don't let these people intimidate you. You're innocent. We both know that you haven't committed any crime." I intentionally raised my voice so Azodi would hear. "Your father's a lawyer. He'll file suit against them for false arrest."

The room reverberated with demonic laughter. Ho! Ho! Ho! "No lawyer's been born yet to file such a suit against SAVAK. We make the law!" Azodi boasted.

Shoja and I exchanged glances helplessly. He was nothing like my proud, strong husband.

"The visit is over!" Azodi announced.

The guards blindfolded Shoja and rushed him out.

"Look, lady! No more visits for you. Get it? Now leave!" Azodi shouted.

The truth was worse than anything I had ever imagined. My husband was not just a prisoner; he was a prisoner of SAVAK where even the most basic human rights were nonexistent.

CHAPTER THREE

Along with malevolence came a hundred masks
To conceal the truth and reality from all sights

Rumi (Thirteenth Century)

Gossip had begun to run rampant. Friends' remarks had taken on an accusatory tone. Without referring directly to the congressman's allegations against Shoja, they discussed the "exceedingly high corruption in the government." Even my girlfriend Mina, normally easygoing and discreet, alluded to the possibility of unethical conduct: "Poor Shoja! He's become a victim of his thieving deputies," she sympathized in an odd way one day.

Her husband, a rather subtle man, also warned: "Shoja should try to distance his case from theirs."

"I really thing you should stop condemning people until they are proven guilty," I objected.

Mina, obviously surprised by my sharp response, turned to her husband.

"Honey, I think we should leave," she told him. "It's been a long day for Azar. I'm sure she can use the rest."

As soon as they were gone, Dr. Memari, another visitor who had been listening to the conversation, turned to me. *"Khanom*

Sheikh, I wouldn't pay much attention to what that couple said."

"They didn't mean any harm. Simply offered advice," I defended.

"I hate to say it of your so-called 'best friends,' but they are both informers for the SAVAK. Who knows, they may even have spied on Shoja. This has come out from a reliable source. You must keep away from them," Memari advised.

What he said was repulsive. How could our close friends betray us? Friendship and trust had to go together, for me.

Mina and her family left Iran shortly thereafter. I knew I would always miss this friend who shared my passion for traveling.

Two days later, Amir Abbas Hoveyda suddenly came to visit. He had been the Shah's Prime Minister for fifteen years, and was demoted to a Court Minister since last summer. Shoja had served in Hoveyda's Cabinet for over three years, and under Jamshid Amuzegar, Hoveyda's replacement, for more than a year.

Hoveyda, a slightly taller version of Winston Churchill, was courteous and distinguished looking. Whereas Churchill had an omnipresent cigar, Hoveyda wore an orchid in his buttonhole.

Even though he and Shoja had a friendly relationship, I was surprised to see him. After all, Hoveyda still worked for a regime that had turned against us. While serving tea, I asked, "Please tell me why my husband is in jail. More than anyone, you know his work, how honorable he is."

"Shoja is a good person and does not deserve jail," Hoveyda said kindly. "Frankly, I have no explanation for his imprisonment, though I expect that once the unrest is quieted, he'll be freed. If something happens to him, I'm to blame. Shoja was a successful physician, serving the people. In fact, the Iranian Rehabilitation Society would never have existed without his ambitious vision. I was the one who introduced him to the government. Have I ruined his life?"

"When you offered Shoja a post in your Cabinet, you didn't know that things would change," I said politely.

"One should always expect change. The only thing that could remain unchanged is one's honor," Hoveyda mused philosophically, fingering the fresh orchid in his buttonhole.

"What will happen to Shoja?" I asked.

"Nothing, *Inshallah*. But if something does, stand behind your husband. He's a decent man who truly loves you."

Hoveyda's words intensified my underlying fears. Did the old politician know more than he let out? He did not tell me enough.

I decided to take a bolder step by consulting with General Hosain Fardoust, Head of the Imperial Inspectorate and probably the most powerful Iranian four-star general. His organization was one of the several intelligence apparatus that the Shah had at his disposal. I knew the General's wife from our school days and she arranged a meeting. My brother, Hushang, volunteered to join me. In Iran, women were not well received alone at government offices.

The Imperial Inspectorate's office, a nondescript building, was located in central Tehran. General Fardoust, a man of small stature, was not behind his impressive mahogany desk, but rather engulfed in a large leather armchair in an attempt to give an informal appearance to the visit. This was the first time I had seen him in person. This enigmatic General, who hardly ever appeared at social events, looked different from what I expected. He was not at all the tall, massive, imposing presence of my imagination.

The General rose slightly and stretched his plump hand out to my brother, who shook it and introduced himself. Fardoust remembered Hushang from the time he served as an Admiral in the Navy. The General then turned to me, and I became self-consciously uneasy as he assessed me with a mischievous sparkle in his eyes.

"No need to blush. Have a seat. I was just observing whether you measure up to what my wife had said about you. Ha! You know how she likes to babble and brag about her friends. Ha! "

Uncomfortably, I sat forward in my chair. "General, I'm here to find out about my husband's arrest. As you may know, he has been held at the SAVAK prison for several weeks now."

Fardoust's demeanor became serious. "How would I know who has ordered your husband's arrest?" he snorted. "Ask him! He makes all the decisions!" He pointed above his head to the picture of the Shah dressed in Commander-in-Chief regalia.

Was Fardoust implying that our great enemy was the Shah?

"But, General, my husband has done nothing wrong."

"The authorities are holding my brother-in-law without legal charges, and are not bringing him to trial," Hushang added.

The General ran his fingers through his dull black hair and grunted with approval. "Dr. Sheikh was an honest and dedicated Minister. He really stood up to his first name, 'Shoja', which in Arabic means brave. Ha! Before him the Ministry had fallen asleep for years. He came in, shook up the system, and with it a few people. Of course, those people won't forget. In any event, at this point, it has been decided that Dr. Sheikh should remain behind bars. There's nothing anyone can do. Wait and see what transpires," the General said in a commanding voice.

I complained about Azodi's ban of my visits to the prison.

"I've heard about that," Fardoust said abruptly. "You have got to watch your mouth in the presence of the SAVAK's chief interrogator. Ha!"

So, the SAVAK had kept the General well informed! Although the Imperial Inspectorate's office was a separate entity and reported to the Shah directly, it kept close contact with the SAVAK.

"General, they were treating my husband like a criminal. It was terrible," I protested.

"Oh, stay calm! Nothing upsets me more than a woman getting highly emotional," the General said disapprovingly. "Look, you need to understand how politics enslaves us. I grew up in a modest home. My father, a low-ranking officer, sent me to a military school where, by chance, the Crown Prince Mohammad Reza—our present Shah—was also a student. Later, I was selected to go with the Prince to Switzerland for further education. Do you think it was easy for me to be away from my family, especially in a foreign culture? But I had no choice. Ever since, freedom for me has been nonexistent. I have only lived to serve my Commander, and, of course, my country. The same applies to your husband. Once in politics, there is no way out. One must accept anything that happens—Ha!"

"Anything?" I asked in bewilderment.

The General ignored the question. "Anyhow, I will arrange

for you to visit with your husband," he said, rising in his chair. Hushang and I realized that we were dismissed.

General Fardoust kept his promise. Soon, I resumed my visitations at the SAVAK prison. Nothing was changed. Azodi, whose organization was in charge of arresting and torturing the political dissidents, was his own boss. He would not completely yield to the Imperial Inspectorate's office. He admitted me but took every opportunity to mentally torture us. Sometimes, he allowed us merely a few minutes together before sending me away. Even then, we had no chance for private conversations, as strange men frequently entered the room, mumbled secretly to Azodi or handed him notes. Their faces were masks—expressionless.

Having no access to news media, Shoja once asked me about current events.

"It's a vicious circle," I said. "A round of government attacks, a round of public demonstrations, then—"

Azodi jumped from his seat and roared, "Woman, you are not allowed to discuss these things with a prisoner!" He then turned to Shoja. "Don't read too much into what she says. One of these days we'll beat the shit out of those Communist rabble-rousers! Just wait and see."

Shoja told me how much he missed the children. Azodi interrupted: "Right! Like you're the only one with a family. How about me? I hardly ever leave this room because of those f—ing Communists and Mullahs! Now this old reactionary Khomeini thinks he has become the leader of a revolution. From exile, no less! He won't live long enough to see how we parade his lice-ridden Mullahs through the town, turbans removed and beards pulled up to expose their true identities. Damned foreign agents! That day will come soon! I'll be here, waiting!"

More and more, the name of Ayatollah Khomeini was heard in connection with the country's uprising against the ruling regime. The Ayatollah's old animosity had flared up against the Shah when a slanderous article about him was printed in the main Iranian newspapers last winter. He was described as a "mad, foreign agent with homosexual tendencies." Within hours, the holy city of Qom reacted violently to the article. Other cities soon followed. Now Ayatollah Khomeini had emerged from exile as the unrivaled leader of the opposition.

The charges against Shoja and his two deputies were escalating out of proportion. The media accused them of all sorts of horrible, unimaginable crimes. Zokai, a former Ministry employee, added more confusion to the existing accusations when, during a press conference, he demanded that Dr. Sheikh and his deputies be given the maximum punishment for "deception and extortion!"

Another accuser, Nabi, a veterinarian, claimed that Shoja had spent over 45,000 touman ($6,000) for one evening in London with a high-priced call girl, while he was in office!

How on earth could anyone make up such lies? Shoja's last trip to England was eight years ago with me!

While in office, Shoja had, apparently, stopped this veterinarian from practicing medicine on people. Now Nabi had found an opportunity for revenge.

My kind and serene mother, who had cut her trip short to

London to be with me at this difficult time, tried to downplay the impact of recent attacks.

"Azar, don't lose your mind over some false slanders that will only reflect poorly on the accusers. Shoja would want you to stay strong for him," she said.

I rested my head on her delicate shoulder and cried. "Mother, They're going to ruin us."

She patted my back with her lovely fingers. Her dark brown eyes gleamed with sadness under a strand of gray hair as she spoke.

"Calm down, my dear. Everything is going to be just fine!"

My eldest brother, Amir Hosain, a well-established sociologist and scholar, had also returned with Mother. He was short but fit. He had been Iran's number two weight lifter years ago. Beyond his physical strength, my eldest brother had the skills of an orator and the charisma of a magnetic leader. Amir Hosain, only sixteen years younger than Mother, was the pride of our family.

"The people will not take seriously the last delirious comments of a decaying regime. Shoja will be fine," he verbalized his support intellectually.

Indeed, Amir Hosain, with his exceptional political foresight, had predicted a few years ago that the regime would collapse with a revolution. For some reason, we were in a daze, unable to perceive the forces that would lead to the current changes. It was too late to regret.

My father-in-law was outraged by the new accusations, but he had no power to help even as a lawyer. His petitions to present his son's case had been rejected.

My mother-in-law, Shazdeh Joon, a distant Qajar Princess,

was physically and mentally distressed. She suffered from painful kidney stones. She had also been manifesting a gradual and growing loss of memory since the sudden death of her eldest son, Zia, four years ago. Her large, dark eyes were filled with tears when I visited her.

"Have you heard anything from Shoja?" she implored.

I kissed her cheek. "He's all right."

My mother-in-law crossed her thin arms across her narrow chest, sat back in the bed, and sighed. "God took my eldest son, and the Shah is taking this one!" Then, she closed her eyes and called out to God for help: "*Ya Bab Al Havaej*"—Oh, Lord, Gates to all needs!

Visits from friends became less frequent. If the strikes, demonstrations, and curfew did not keep them home, our deteriorating social standing turned them away. Fabricated stories of our life appeared in all the notorious tabloids. It had become fashionable to defame cabinet members of the Hoveyda era.

Zari, a close friend and an executive at the Blood Bank of Tehran—a significant position for an Iranian woman—used to visit me almost every weekend. Having an unhappy marriage and no children of her own, she had found solace among mine. Since our ordeal began, she had distanced herself. What kept her away? The rumors? I missed her vitality and her sense of humor.

Another longtime friend and schoolmate, Azarm, a teacher, had unexpectedly left Iran without saying good-bye. Her departure was most surprising, since she belonged to that mercantile class of Iranian society known as Bazaari who had historically supported any political movement led by the clergy. However, like many Iranian women of my generation,

Azarm was caught in the clash between modernism and tra-
ditionalism, not knowing exactly how to make the two com-
patible. Her college education had inspired her to believe that
a woman should search for her identity, express her thoughts,
and cultivate her potentials, just as a man did. At the same
time, her strong traditional upbringing prevented her from
committing wholeheartedly to change.

It was hard to accept that my friends had abandoned me at
this troubled time.

One month after Shoja's arrest, Azodi was nastier than ever.
Following the detention of me for two hours in the guardroom,
he ordered me to leave and return in the afternoon. Even then,
I had to wait an additional three hours before being admitted. I
saw no other visitors. It was known that SAVAK deprived most
prisoners of all human rights, not even permitting family visits.
Had my meetings with Shoja been arranged through pressure
exerted by Fardoust?

Azodi's phone rang constantly, and he mumbled abruptly to
the mysterious callers. His entire sordid existence was being
threatened by the inevitable change, and he seemed distracted
and worried. Shoja also looked more sullen. Azodi had shown
him the defamatory articles, telling him, "Hey, don't expect your
wife to show up after finding out about your affairs in London!"

"Nothing would change my faith in you, sweetheart," I
assured Shoja.

He remained low-spirited. I discussed my new anxiety with
him, "All colleges are closed because of strikes. I have no job, no
income. My savings are almost used up. Please, sweetheart,
sign a check for our living expenses."

Shoja refused. "I'm sorry, but until my name is cleared, I will not touch our money. I don't want to be accused further."

"Perhaps you'd better use some money from your Swiss accounts," Azodi interjected, smiling ambiguously.

"How can you say something that is so false?" Shoja protested. "We have no money outside this country."

"Ho! We'll see."

"Don't let this man upset you, Shoja," I said, squeezing my hands. "Since the SAVAK is losing its hold on people, its members have nothing else to do but fabricate stories."

Azodi pounded his fist on the desk and roared, "Shut your mouth, you slut! Now, get the hell out of here. And don't come back! Otherwise, I'll do something to you that will make you hide from shame!"

Out in the street, it was dark and almost time for the curfew. I ran towards my car as fast as I could. How defeated, humiliated, and frightened I felt. Azodi was capable of any crime!

The Shah's fifty-ninth birthday went by without fanfare. Even the media, still under his control, made only an honorary mention of the occasion. What a contrast to the previous celebrations! Perhaps the media was restraining its adulation of the Shah in order to assess which way the national movement would head.

Last year at this time, Shoja and I had been among the dignitaries present at "His Majesty's" birthday celebration in Arya Mehr Stadium. We were seated two rows behind the royal couple in their pavilion. Drinking tea from a gold cup, the Shah, with his third wife, Queen Farah, and his heir son, Reza, reviewed the parade and the lavish fireworks with such arrogance as if he were a supreme being. This spectacular public celebration was followed by a private but ostentatious party at the Queen Mother's palace in Sa'd Abad.

Within the past year, everything had changed.

Seven weeks had passed without news of either Shoja's trial or release. Banned from the prison by Azodi, I heard about Shoja only from Ellen, Dr. Aram's American wife, who now had visitations with her husband. Although she had enjoyed living in Iran and had adjusted well to our culture, the growing anti-American sentiments had made Ellen concerned for her family's safety. She was planning to leave Iran as soon as her husband was released. Ellen conveyed Shoja's request to seek General Fardoust's assistance again in regard to resuming our visits.

Fardoust's secretary informed me that the General would dine at the Iran Javan Club around six o'clock, and I could speak with him there. How strange of this enigmatic General to receive me in a private club, only two hours before the curfew.

It was a rather cool evening with autumn still lingering in the air. For the occasion, I wore a beige cashmere suit, simple but stylish, and arranged my shoulder-length hair into a chignon. Although I was never too fashion conscious, I cared to look presentable. This evening, neither the suit nor the hairdo did anything for my looks. I had lost considerable weight, and looked tired and haggard.

Since Rajab had called in sick and I was afraid to drive in that area of the city, I called a cab. The only traffic on the streets was from those rushing to get home before the curfew. All night entertainment—restaurants, cabarets, and movie houses—had ceased. The General and his wife were the only guests at the club. Fardoust was listening to the BBC news on a shortwave radio. I apologized to Mrs. Fardoust, a pretty blond woman, for imposing on their family dinner. Confidentially, this old schoolmate told me that she too was leaving for the States, soon. If the General wanted his wife out of the country, the situation must be getting grave.

BBC reported more skirmishes between the army and the people, this time in the city of Tabriz near the Soviet border. There had been many casualties.

"General, how do the demonstrators dare ignore the curfew?" I asked as I tucked back a couple of stray hairs.

"They get their courage from above," he replied, sipping his whisky.

I was not sure whether he referred to the Ayatollah's spiritual leadership or the superpowers' presumed support of the uprising. Although a man of constant conversation, he chose his words carefully tonight.

I seized an opportunity to discuss the reason for my being here.

"Did you go to the jail again and defy Nasseri?" Fardoust scolded.

"Nasseri? You mean Azodi, or rather, Dr. Azodi?"

"His real name is Nasseri, but at the Agency they call him Dr. Azodi so the inmates will not know his true identity. Ha! In his position, he could make many enemies," the General disclosed.

I reflected for a few seconds, digesting this incredible piece of information. Why would Fardoust reveal such information about the SAVAK's clandestine agents? Wasn't he once himself its chief organizer? It seemed to me that the General was trying to further distance his organization from the SAVAK's.

"General, I'm scared for Shoja's life," I said.

"Now, calm down. I'll arrange for you to see your husband again. Just avoid any confrontations with Nasseri. Otherwise, we may all regret it. Ha! He can sometimes get out of control. Understand?" Fardoust warned.

Dinner was being served. I grabbed my purse and got up to leave, not wanting to impose further, and concerned to make it home before the 8:30 curfew. Babak was at home alone. Azodi's —or Nasseri's—bloodthirsty look came to my mind, and I shuddered. What if he had my son kidnapped, or worse?

"Sit down. I'll have a military driver take you home," the General ordered.

I made poor company for the rest of the night. The General, content and warmed by his drink and food, stroked his face and began his characteristic chatting. "Do you know about Chile? One of these days, Iran will be a second Chile! Some unknown, ambitious colonel, after drinking two bottles of straight *araq*— vodka—will stage a coup d'état! Before anyone realizes, one million will be massacred. One million! Ha! The country will be calm then! No one would dare think about—let alone breathe a word of—protest! Ha!" the General said in a swaggered tone.

A coup d'état? What was he trying to tell me? Was I being used for his political ambitions? Was the General plotting against the Shah?

"Do you know why a colonel always starts a coup?" the General continued with amused eyes. "Because when one reaches a higher rank, one becomes conservative and resists change. But colonels are more gutsy. Think of Colonel Qaddafi in Libya, for example."

The latest news report on BBC caught his attention and he tilted his head to listen, raising his hand in a command for silence. BBC reported that the Prime Minister Sharif-Emami and his Cabinet were being replaced.

"Ha! That's some news," the General remarked as he slipped into deep thought.

We left the club one hour past curfew. The General sat in one car which drove away, with police escorts at both front and rear. Mrs. Fardoust rode in a second car, and I in a third. I had heard from her that the General and his wife lived in separate homes—perhaps for security reasons?

Once a city of lights and noise, Tehran was now dark and desolate. We were the only car traveling northeast. Around Abbas Abad—an affluent neighborhood—the shrill of a police siren brought our car to a stop. An armed soldier jumped out of the police car and pointed his gun directly at us. Instantly, the driver displayed his military identification. The soldier carefully examined the card and motioned us to proceed. I had forgotten to breathe. The driver calmly explained, "If we didn't have the proper I.D., he would've pulled the trigger. Last night, a man driving his wife to the hospital to have a baby ignored the siren. Instead of the hospital, he ended up in the morgue!"

By November, Iran was being tossed and turned on the political ocean like a wrecked ship. The Shah, seeing his Peacock Throne in danger, admitted against his will that there had been wrongdoings, but blatantly placed the blame on the government administrators. To silence the opposition groups and to save face, the Shah took an extreme measure: he replaced the short-lived administration of Sharif-Emami by a military government. Hoveyda was also removed as Court Minister. All through his reign of thirty-five years, the Shah typically changed top government officials whenever there was social unrest in the country.

By the Shah's order, General Nematollah Nasiri, a previous SAVAK director, and many other former Ministers, were arrested. General Gholam-Reza Azhari, the new premier, promised essential reforms, such as democratic elections and freedom of the press. To appease the clergy, Azhari also ordered the ban of all "immoral" activities: cabarets, casinos, liquor stores and sexually explicit movies. None of these superficial reforms seemed to stop the country's slide towards revolution.

Once again General Fardoust kept his promise and visitations resumed. Many of Shoja's former colleagues had joined him at the SAVAK prison. Fortunately, we no longer met in Azodi/Nasseri's office. For the first time, we met in a large conference room which was most likely bugged, its mirrored wall a two-way device. Still, it felt less threatening without Azodi's loathsome presence. A few other inmates and their families were in the same room, talking in hushed voices.

Mansur Rouhani, former Minister of Agriculture, appeared haggard. Even his wife's presence did not help to raise his spirits. Neqabat and Aram, Shoja's former deputies, were also wary. Dr. Aram's usual carefree air of self-assurance had disappeared, making him seem older than his late forties. All of the detainees had come to a desperate point of embarrassment by becoming scapegoats for the Shah. We exchanged brief greetings.

Shoja pulled a chair out for me next to himself.

"Hello, sweetheart," I said. "I see that some of your old colleagues are here, too."

"Speak more softly," Shoja pointed his index finger to his lips. "Yes, it's become quite a melting pot, here. The prison population now ranges from Communists to Moslem fundamentalists, to Nationalists, not to mention the members of the previous Cabinets," Shoja whispered. "These arrests will only heighten the resistance. In our case, especially, everyone knows that the government officials couldn't act without the Shah's approval."

Quietly, I informed Shoja that the Queen had gone to Iraq, evidently to negotiate with the Iraqi government about repressing Ayatollah Khomeini, who lived in the city of Najaf.

"Seems too late for negotiations." Shoja rubbed his temples. His formerly shaved hair had grown into a short, unkempt style.

"Do me a favor, love. Arrange a meeting with the martial law administrator. He was the one who ordered my arrest. He would be the one to release me. Also, find out what Hoveyda and Ansary know about the Shah's plans, I mean in regard to my situation." Shoja still felt confidant that these people would help him.

"I doubt they would discuss such sensitive matters with me, but if that's what you want, I'll do it."

"Thanks. And tell the kids that their father's an honest man who has committed only one crime: joining the government!"

"They already know, sweetheart," I said, squeezing his hand.

After several attempts over weeks, I was finally granted an appointment with General Oveissi, martial law administrator.

Hushang was busy that morning and could not accompany me.

A thorough search of my purse was made before I was allowed into his ostentatious office. General Oveissi, a medium-height, slender figure, also held the position of Commander of the Ground Forces. He greeted me with a cunning smile, and cold eyes, while playing with his prayer beads to present a religious image. All at once, I knew that I was looking into the face of the enemy, and felt contempt. If it were not for his administering martial law, my husband would be a free man. I refused his offer to sit, and demanded that Shoja either be freed or tried immediately.

"*Khanom*, it was unfortunate that your husband and the other government officials were arrested. But, it was His Majesty's decision. I could do nothing else except obey my Commander's wishes." Oveissi tried to justify his action formally. "As long as the unrest continues, there will be no time to hear their cases. All we can do is pray that under His Majesty's auspices and God's protection, this political crisis will be resolved soon and our enemies destroyed. Only then will we have time to attend to less serious matters," he concluded.

Oveissi's phone rang. He picked it up and listened for some time, then shouted: "Do as you are ordered. Do not hesitate to engage in necessary confrontations. Destroy them! Report the outcome immediately." He turned to me, continuing his frown. "You see, *Khanom*, we have many other problems, top priority. Your husband's imprisonment is insignificant in comparison!"

Before I had time to react, he faced the portrait of the Shah above his desk, held his chin up and hailed, "On my soldiers' honor, I will defend my *Shahanshah* with my blood!"

I realized the show was over.

As Shoja had requested, I also went to seek advice from Amir Abbas Hoveyda. After his recent removal as the Court Minister, Hoveyda—a divorcé—had moved from a government mansion to an unpretentious apartment on the West side of Tehran. Although he was no longer a public figure, his apartment was still protected by security guards. Hoveyda who had previously served the Shah as a Prime Minister for fifteen years, greeted me amicably in his well-stocked library. Then, he quickly wrote on a piece of paper: "Watch what you say! The apartment may be bugged!"

Were the guards actually spying on the Shah's old confidant?

"Sir, I'm here to ask for your help." I proceeded. "Certainly, you are still aware of His Majesty's decisions. Is it presumed that my husband, along with a few other detainees, are solely responsible for the existing corruption and unrest? If they have any concrete proof against Shoja, why has he not been tried?"

Hoveyda responded by writing, "Discussed matter once or twice with His Majesty—no satisfactory response. Trial will not happen soon. Wait to see what transpires."

So the guards might glean something from their eavesdropping, the old politician spoke loudly: "Don't worry about Shoja. He's served the country well and will survive all this adversity. As the saying goes, an innocent person may get to the foot of the gallows but won't be hanged."

"I hope you are right, sir," I said.

"Well, Azar, what do you think of your husband's affair with the British beauty queen?" Hoveyda humored me. "I hope you're not jealous! He's not that kind of a man."

I smiled. "Who knows Shoja's integrity better than I?"

A servant served coffee. We drank in silence. Hoveyda's eyes had a faraway look in them. He seemed concerned for his own fate.

"Tell Shoja we'll be seeing each other soon!" Hoveyda said portentously, as we bid farewell.

Chapter Four

Due to nationwide strikes by customs workers and the petroleum industry, cooking fuel, gasoline, and food were in short supply, resulting in long lines at the stores and gas stations. The cold winter, typical of the Iranian plateau's extreme continental type of climate, had arrived. Fearing a civil war and famine, Pazani, our longtime house-keeper took his family to the village, where they could live on the bare minimum. Rajab, our driver, also quit.

Babak's school had been closed by employee strikes. The two of us spent much time in the house alone.

By the middle of November, I had no money. The children had also run out of their savings in the States. Shoja still refused to sign a check for me. In desperation, I sold my diamond engagement ring, a family heirloom passed down from my mother-in-law, for 35,000 touman ($5,000). I transferred $3,500 to the kids immediately, and used the remainder to pay house-hold expenses.

While I was planning to sell more stuff to support my family, Dr. Boomand, a friend and colleague to Shoja, came with shocking news. His deep brown eyes, under a prominent fore-head and over a thick mustache, had a look of alarm in them.

"Look at this list, Azar," he said, holding a paper to me in the privacy of my den. "It was made public today by the 'Society of the Central Bank of Iran.' They claim these people on the list have transferred vast amounts of money to banks abroad. Shoja's name is among them!"

I glanced quickly at the long list to find our last name with a figure of 48 million touman (7 million dollars) next to it. "Forty-eight million touman?" I gasped. "I don't understand!"

"Listen! Carefully," Boomand said, with a tug on my arm. "Shoja's accused of sending this large amount. It implies that you must have had this money to transfer to foreign banks. True or not, frankly, people will believe it and wonder how anyone on a government salary or a physician's income could have such savings!"

"But we never had that kind of money. This is preposterous." I pressed my clenched hands against my chest. "Look! The date on this transaction is after Shoja's arrest. How could he have arranged this transfer from jail? I had to sell my diamond ring just to pay our bills and to send money to my children. And that was only $3,500. Perhaps the name on this list isn't ours? No first name is given. Besides, there is no such thing as the Society of the Central Bank of Iran. It's a sham."

"Still, the list will be used to confirm Shoja's alleged abuses," Boomand warned. "They are building a strong case against him."

Suddenly, the truth dawned on me. "I know! The government has set us up," I shrieked. "It wasn't long ago at the SAVAK that a man, whose real name is Nasseri but calls himself Azodi, gave us a hint when he suggested that we use money from our Swiss bank accounts. He knew what they were scheming!"

"Azodi? A notorious torturer! Perhaps one of the most ruthless in the history of mankind." Boomand pulled nervously on the sides of his thick mustache. "As a Nationalist, I had the pleasure of meeting him in prison once! I wouldn't put past him or his organization any hideous crime, including the publication of this list."

For a few seconds I could not focus my thoughts. Then, the significance of the matter began to sink in.

"I'll write to the chief prosecutor on Shoja's behalf and protest the validity of the published list," I said defiantly. "Surely, there will be an investigation to clear our name. No one in their right mind would believe this list!"

When I visited the prison the next time, I found out that Azodi had tormented Shoja by giving him a copy of the 'List'. He had told him mockingly how our 'secret wealth' had been exposed!

"Azar, this is my death warrant!" Shoja moaned. "Don't you see? They have condemned me before my trial. The whole nation thinks I am a thief now!"

I put my hand on his. "I've already written to the authorities, and demanded an immediate investigation. The truth will surface, Shoja. Our bank records will speak for themselves," I said with foolish optimism.

"You don't seem to understand. They will use this false list to confirm the previous charges of embezzlement. No matter what I try to do in my defense, it won't clear my name entirely. SAVAK's devious propaganda weighs much more than the truth. I'm ruined." His brown eyes showed genuine despair. Suddenly he seemed older.

"Don't let them see you defeated, sweetheart. You are innocent!"

Gloating, Azodi barged into the conference room, his huge body swaying from side to side. He came up to our table, reached into his pocket and pulled out a cigar. While toying with it, he gazed at us. His head began to nod, and his lips pursed into a vile smirk.

"Bring a cup of tea," he screamed to a soldier. "And some cake too!"

We watched him in silence as he sat down and took his time to drink his tea, never lifting his gaze from us. The SAVAK's torturer was celebrating our demise!

"I told you to use your fat Swiss accounts, didn't I? SAVAK is aware of your every move. Ho! Ho! Ho!" Azodi laughed like a hyena.

Unnerved by the whole affair, I shouted frantically, "You must be the one behind the List. Your scheme won't work. Soon you and your system will go under. Your days are numbered!"

My boldness shocked Shoja. He patted my arm to keep me quiet. Azodi abruptly stood up. His scornful laughter vanished. Blood surged in his eyes. He took a step forward, shaking both hands in the air. "Don't forget, they call me 'The AZODI'," he roared. "One more outburst will be the end of you. Got it?"

"Your real name is Nasseri! You are a torturer!" I attested.

Azodi/Nasseri went berserk. His true identity had been revealed to a stranger, and he could not let it go. In a flash, like a wild beast, he lunged his huge body at me. Shoja, in an automatic reflex, threw himself between us. "If you touch my wife I won't leave anything to chance," he warned, white with rage.

SAVAK's torturer pushed him aside forcefully, grabbed me by the shoulder, and pinned me to the wall. His nails pressed hard into my flesh. I tried to pull free but his huge hands enclosed my throat. I struggled helplessly. Shoja screamed. Suddenly a window opened in the opposite wall, and a man's voice was heard: "Dr. Azodi, my dear friend! Don't poison your blood over a woman! Let go of her, please. She is not worth it!"

Panting, Azodi/Nasseri stared at him for a second and, then, disengaged his hands and backed away, that insane look still in his eyes. I resumed breathing. The secret window closed, hiding the man who had saved my life. Perhaps, in this psychological prison drama, one of his roles was to be a petitioner, just like the man who once came out of the bookshelf.

"Go home, Azar, and don't come back as long as this maniac is around. Do you hear?" Shoja implored.

My hands came up to my bruised throat, as I nodded in silence and left the SAVAK prison.

The 'List' had instantly overshadowed all other accusations against the government officials. It included the names of most Iranian top-ranking politicians, rich power brokers, and a few members of the royal family, with the exception of the Shah. I had no doubts that some of the people on that List had indeed transferred enormous amounts of money abroad. Many were wrongly accused. The conspirators behind the List had succeeded beyond their wildest expectations. The public opinion had turned permanently against us.

More immediate action was needed. This time, I pleaded to Hushang Ansary, Chairman of the National Iranian Oil Company, at his mansion on the scenic hills of Niavaran.

Perhaps, he could provide the help where others had failed.

Ansary was a middle-aged man of five feet four who had been holding cabinet positions for years prior to taking over the oil company. He was very powerful and rich by all standards.

I entered a magnificent library filled with the finest artifacts. A servant served tea in silver cups. The NIOC Chairman was cordial and impeccable in appearance. I inquired about Mrs. Ansary and was told that she and their children were visiting the States. Mr. Ansary asked about Shoja.

"Physically, he's fine. Emotionally, he's frustrated!"

"*Khanom* Sheikh, I am troubled by Shoja's situation and have already spoken to His Majesty several times," Ansary said candidly. "I particularly intend to discuss his case in today's audience. Hopefully, by this evening, I will have some good news for you."

"I appreciate your confidence," I said. "Shoja has also requested that you speak with the president of the Central Bank regarding the so-called List. As you know, its effects have been explosive. In the public's mind, Shoja and many others have already been found guilty. If I am not mistaken, your name also appeared on the infamous List—for 480 million touman," I added with a wry smile.

Ansary's cold stare implied that he did not enjoy my humor. He looked at his watch and said, "I'm afraid it's time for me to leave for the Palace. One can't possibly keep His Majesty waiting! You will hear from me soon. Please say hello to Shoja."

Ansary never called. The morning newspapers reported that the Chairman of the National Iranian Oil Company, because of a "sudden heart problem," had left for the States.

Apparently his meeting with the Shah had not gone as well as he expected.

Most people who had the means and the insight had already left the country. Shoja had been left behind to answer to the raging public.

On November 22, Shoja turned forty-six. As a birthday present, I wrote a poem for him:

> *Midnight moon,*
> *My only companion.*
> *How lonely, terribly lonely I am:*
> *My man,*
> *Behind the tall walls,*
> *Inside the steel fortress,*
> *Is kept a prisoner!*
> *Deprived to behold the tender dawn,*
> *The capricious sunset,*
> *The carefree dance of the trees,*
> *In the morning breeze.*
> *From the court of despots,*
> *My man's crimes are grave:*
> *He cared for all children as his own,*
> *Eased the pain of the disabled,*
> *Held the hand of the sick.*
> *His biggest sin?*
> *Defying the tyrants,*
> *Feeding the seeds of contempt in their hearts.*
> *As long as integrity is a crime,*
> *My man will remain,*

Behind the tall walls.
The land where honor's a virtue;
And justice more than a word,
Is far, so far away!
There are no lights,
No friends,
On the road to freedom!

I could never present this poem to Shoja. If found by Nasseri, it would be confiscated as contraband.

My fortieth birthday followed Shoja's, within three days. I had been born on a Thanksgiving day, and was named Azar by my father for my Iranian birth month. Azar also meant 'fire' in Farsi, something that my father had assumed I would add to the warmth of his large family.

I always dreaded this particular birthday as the devastating end of my youth. With my husband in prison, getting old did not seem to matter now.

Since our name had appeared on the damned List, we had become something of a public spectacle. Almost everyone had begun to doubt us. Dishonest people were using this opportunity to take advantage of me. A few days before, a burly man had come to my home, introducing himself as a representative from the Buick car company. He claimed that our car payments were overdue and he had come for the money. Shoja paid cash for the car; there was no debt!

Another time, a total stranger stopped me on the street and asked for 1,000 touman. When I refused, he started cursing: "With all the money your husband robbed this country of, you can't afford to give me a little?"

And, of course, there were those threatening telephone calls to blackmail us. The greedy opportunists were out there to make our life hell. Could it become any more helpless than this?

For security reasons, all the official detainees, including Shoja and his two deputies, had been moved to a prison within Jamshidieh garrison. The SAVAK prison had become over-crowded.

The garrison looked like any other military base: flat build-ings sprawling across a vast area. According to the strict regu-lations, Babak and I and other family members might visit on Sunday afternoons and Thursday mornings only. We were allowed to bring a set of clothing to exchange for the prisoner's dirty laundry.

On our first visit, Babak and I passed through the security gate, and entered a respectable waiting room, which opened to a yard. Major Sharafat, the officer in charge, sat under a portrait of the Shah in full military regalia. He was a solemn man with fine features, and courteous manners. The families of political prison-ers waited quietly, like schoolchildren in the principal's office.

Unlike Nasseri, Major Sharafat seemed indifferent to what went on beyond the compound, as if his life began and ended in the garrison. He assured everyone confidently that, "As long as we have the Shah, there is no need to worry about the future!" Hearing his informal use of 'Shah', one would think that the two were the best of friends.

At ten o'clock sharp, a soldier called the names of three fam-ilies: Sadri, Majidi, and Sheikh. Mrs. Sadri, the charming wife of the former chief of police, stood up flaunting her black lambskin coat, as if she were joining her husband in an officers' club. In comparison, Mrs. Majidi, the wife of the former Chairman of the Queen's Cultural Foundation, was conservatively dressed and seemed sad.

In the small visiting room, the families sat at separate tables. An officer holding a newspaper stood nearby, watching but not eavesdropping as they did at the SAVAK. Shoja, no longer in prison stripes, was especially excited to see his son. He gave me the usual warm nod, and hugged Babak.

"Dad, you look good."

"Yeah? What's up, son?"

"Not much Dad; school's closed."

"And how are things with you, Azar? I haven't seen you in a while."

"Well, it hasn't been easy, but we've managed. We often have no water, gas or electricity. The house is cold. Yesterday I bribed someone with 200 touman in return for a few liters of gas for my car. You can't imagine the number of people waiting on lines for both gasoline and kerosene, and the situation is getting worse! The workers are trying to paralyze the government by strikes."

"Maybe you should go live with relatives for a while. I'd feel more at ease," Shoja said.

"No! We can't leave our home and go somewhere else to live. You'll be coming back any day. This is a temporary situation, right?"

"I don't know, love. I just don't know. But I think you should sell the carpets for cash. The proceeds may last you for a few months. I may be here for a long time," he said broodingly.

"Please, Shoja. Don't be so cynical. You'll be released soon. Everyone that I contacted advised us to be patient."

"Never mind about me. How are Roxana and Ramin?" He changed the conversation abruptly.

"Okay, I guess. They've sent you a letter which I handed to prison authorities for inspection. I hope you'll answer it."

"Do you think I wouldn't want to?" He threw up his hand in the air. "I simply don't know what to write."

I was wrong to think that the change of prison would make a difference in his morale. Shoja had been disappointed. He expected to be released, not to be transferred to a new maximum security prison.

"Azar, please, tell my father to come and see me," he added in a disquieting voice. "I need to talk to him."

"I've asked him several times, sweetheart, but he stubbornly refuses to visit you in the prison. I'll ask him again."

The officer announced, "Visiting hours are over!"

Shoja turned to me. "Forgive me for snapping at you."

I nodded.

"It was good seeing you, son," Shoja said to Babak.

"You too, Dad. Hang in there."

He waved at us and left the waiting room with the other prisoners. Our visit at the new prison lasted thirty minutes. At least, we were treated like human beings.

At night, by candlelight, I wrote a letter to Roxana and Ramin:

My beloved children,

Your father's present prison atmosphere is more tolerant. He seems healthy, and is allowed to read books. (Perhaps, the only benefit of a prison is that one is never short of time!) However, a prison is a prison, and one never gets used to it.

Your father often asks about you and wants you to continue with your studies. There is no news of his trial yet. The government is too busy fighting the revolutionaries to find time for other affairs. At the beginning, people were demanding more freedom and asking the government to rule by the constitution. Now, they speak of changing the regime!

Despite your grandmother's persistence, we have decided not to leave our house and live with her. Money is tight, but we manage.

Babak helps me in all matters. He has become more serious and responsible than he usually is. Yesterday, he was a fifteen-year-old teenager. Today, he is acting like a young man!

Your brother and I have become avid readers. Babak is now enjoying Dickens, and I am reading a book about the French Revolution. Quite timely!

My dearest children, these tenuous and sad times will pass. We shall get to know ourselves better, and appreciate more what we have. In these momentous days, you must remain strong for your family and think of your country.

Love, Mom

In Iran, the military government's attempts to reconcile differences had failed, and the wave of opposition increased rapidly. Side by side, groups of people from diverse political, religious, and social beliefs were fighting for the downfall of the ruling regime. The Shah, who perceived Ayatollah Khomeini as the main force behind this movement, appealed to the government of Iraq for help. The Ayatollah was forced to leave Iraq for

France, where he found access to state-of-the art communication facilities to broadcast worldwide propaganda against the regime. Now the world knew him as the orchestrator of the Iranian Revolution. While in France, the Ayatollah and a few faithful disciples drew the plans for Iran's future ruling government.

Rattled by the news, the Shah ordered the arrest of Hoveyda, his loyal friend and supporter of many years. Another scapegoat in the Iranian political arena! Hoveyda's arrest, as "accessory to corruption," sent shock waves across the country. Many saw it as an act of betrayal. The Shah had not shown mercy for even his most faithful servant. Others, fearful for their lives, fled the country. This was the final blow. All my hopes for Shoja's release vanished. Things could only get worse for him.

I immediately arranged another visit with General Fardoust, my last tie to the regime. He still seemed to be a major player in the Shah's politics.

On the way to the General's private club, the taxi passed overturned cars, ablaze, stinking of burnt rubber and plastic. A small crowd of demonstrators worked its way down the street, shouting in hysteria. The driver took a detour, ignoring the stoplight, and nearly smashing into another vehicle. The brakes shrieked; the car jerked; I was thrown forward and then sideways. Finally the car reached its destination.

At the club, the General and his wife were dining alone. In fact, the club had remained open exclusively for them. They both seemed intact despite what was happening outside. Mrs. Fardoust was leaving Iran the following day.

"General, with Mr. Hoveyda's arrest, I'm really afraid for

my husband's fate. Would you kindly take this letter to Her Majesty?" I asked, handing him a letter. "As a wife, the Queen may relate to my worries."

"I doubt she'll have the time to read it. Too many of such letters these days." Fardoust raised his eyebrows.

"Then what do you suggest I do, General?"

"Nothing. Just be patient, Ha! I'm as anxious about the future of the country as anyone else," he said with some resentment.

The General did not hide his happiness about Hoveyda's arrest. "He was the source of all the corruption in Iran! His favoritism made it very difficult for the legal system to work. The Shah has also been soft when it came to the transgressions of his family. No wonder people are revolting!"

I could not believe what I had just heard. Was the Head of the Imperial Inspectorate openly defying his Commander? Had this mysterious, powerful four-star General turned his back on the Shah?

Alarmed by the tone of the conversation, I decided to leave the club early. It was obvious that I could not expect more help from Fardoust.

CHAPTER FIVE

Did you hear of the Persian Kings
Who exercised oppression against their nation?
That grandeur, that kingship did not endure:
Nor did the tyranny of their reign.

Sa'di (Thirteenth Century)

It was the first day of the Moslem month of *Moharram*, commemorating the martyrdom of Imam Hosain, the prophet Muhammad's grandson, at Karbala in the seventh century. Throughout the entire month of *Moharram*, especially on the holy days of *Tasu'a* and *Ashura*—the ninth and the tenth—pious Shi'ite Moslems dressed in black, and marked the event with extreme piety and mass processions. The Bazaar closed and all commerce stopped. In brief, all social activities ceased.

Since childhood, my family had observed *Moharram* quietly. The only happy activity during this time seemed to be the cooking of traditional *Sholeh Zard*—saffron rice pudding—which Mother prepared meticulously, and sent to the mosque to be distributed among the poor. Mother would also have a separate small bowl for me, but instead of garnishing the top with the words "Imam Hosain", she would write "Azar" in cinnamon, making me feel special.

This year, the military government had banned public mourning to prevent enormous gatherings. The Ayatollah, from his new exile in France, had encouraged the public to disregard the curtailment. He had also asked the soldiers to join their Moslem brothers in observance of the holy month, and in defiance of the regime.

At night, I woke up with the sound of chanting. Shivering, I wrapped myself in a blanket and went to the window to listen. *"Allahu Akbar! Allahu Akbar!"* The mourners repeatedly shouted: "God is great."

Babak ran to my room, huddling his arms close to himself and trying to keep his teeth from chattering in the unheated cold house. "Mom, what's happening?"

"Just the religious people marching down the street, by the mosque. They are mourning for Imam Hosain's martyrdom."

"But, their voices seem to be coming from around the army camp. What if they attack the place?"

"These people wouldn't do such a thing, sweetheart."

"But, it's ten o'clock. They've already broken the 8:00 p.m. curfew."

"I know. Let's hope they scatter before the army reacts."

As the worshippers' rhapsodic spiritual sound of *"Allahu Akbar"* neared, it drew the neighbors to their roofs and balconies. Like a musical canon, the chorus of rooftop voices added to the exuberant chanting in the frosty bleak night. Suddenly, we heard an unsettling sound of Tat! Tat! Tat! It was followed with screams. Then, another sound of Tat! Tat! Tat!

"My God! The army!" Babak yelled alarmingly. "Move away from the window, Mom. I'll go check the front door!"

"It's locked and bolted, Babak!" I yelled back. "Nobody's going to attack our home!" I tried to reassure both of us.

"*Allahu Akbar! Allahu Akbar*! " the believers revived their chanting. The verve of the voices were stronger than the soldiers' machine guns.

Tat! Tat! Tat! Another round of gunfire made a surreal atmosphere. The cacophony of noises became garbled—people chanting, more shots, people running up and down the streets, shouting, followed by faint screams. Over and above these sounds, a cannon blasted with such a roar that overwhelmed all living sounds. A deadly silence took over the neighborhood.

Shattering the quiet, the phone rang maddeningly. I stumbled in the dark looking for the phone.

"Hello?"

"Azar! Come to our house at once," my brother-in-law, 'Doctor', demanded. "We want you and Babak safe with us."

"No! Not tonight. It's too dangerous to be on the streets. Perhaps, in the morning. We're okay," I tried to sound calm.

By the morning, a much exaggerated broadcast report of the previous night's massacres, both in our neighborhood and in other parts of the city, shook citizens throughout Tehran. Pictures of the martyrs were displayed everywhere. At the Mosques, the Ayatollah's newest manifestoes were distributed to further civil disobedience. Revolutionaries armed themselves for the future confrontations with the army. The fear of a civil war created an impending famine scare. People ravaged stores, hoarding supplies off the shelves.

Babak and I decided to leave our home and stay with my sister, for the time being. Mother also joined us there. It would be safer for all of us to live together. She took the family room. Babak and I occupied the empty bedroom of my nephew, Mehran, who was studying sociology in the States. My sister's other son, Armin, was a first-year medical student.

While unpacking our few items of clothing, I briefed Babak on the rules for living in our temporary home. "We must live economically, sweetheart," I said. "We may turn the heat on at night, but only if it's below freezing. You know how hard it is to find fuel. We may shower every other day. Whatever food they serve us, we will eat. These are hard times, not just for us, but for everyone."

Babak quietly hung a picture of his father, Roxana, and Ramin on the wall.

Later in the day, I went to clean out Shoja's office so that another physician could use it. Shoja had personally assigned this unpleasant mission to me. Under the circumstances, he had no choice but to temporarily give up his precious medical practice, to which he had dedicated years of hard study and training.

On Shoja's desk, a beautiful portrait of our family reminded me of the happier days. I started emptying the drawers, as he had instructed me, feeling bad to go through his private belongings. A yellow folder with my name on it had been tucked into one of the drawers. Hesitantly, I opened it to discover Shoja's will, dated three years ago. He had made me the sole inheritor of his estate and guardian of our children. Also enclosed were his life insurance policies, naming me as beneficiary. For a second, I felt proud that my husband would entrust me with such responsibilities, which was contrary to Iranian customs. Then I thought of his possible death and hurriedly returned the papers to the envelope.

With all Shoja's papers and books packed, I took one last look around the room. Many times I had waited in this office for him to finish working so that we could go out for an evening together. Sometimes the children had come along to see their busy father in between patients. His patients would also miss his professional expertise and his human touch. Shoja really loved his work as an orthopedic surgeon. Would he ever return to this office? To us?

Night after night, growing crowds of people ignored the curfew and chanted *"Allahu Akbar"* in the streets of Tehran. It had become a revolutionary credo by now. Everyone anticipated that on the ninth and tenth of *Moharram*, the demonstrations would reach their peak.

One morning, our gardener came to my sister's home, where he also worked. In observance of *Moharram*, he had not shaved and was wearing a black shirt. "Shahri, you look like you are ready to join the mourners," I said.

"I try to be a good Moslem," he answered, folding his hands.

"I'm afraid I have to end your services at my home," I threw the bomb at him. "With no income, I'm forced to cut expenses. You understand, don't you?"

Shahri's face dropped. "Oh, *Khanom*, I understand your situation. Just last night, I was telling the mother of my children that I worry for the Doctor and his family. But you also realize, *Khanom*, that I'm the sole supporter of a large household. First, you don't need my services and then your sister may follow. Soon I'll be in need of bread."

I explained our financial situation to him again. "I know it's going to be hard for you and your family, but I have no choice. Ask around. You may find other neighbors who are looking for an experienced gardener like you."

After an awkward pause, Shahri conceded and handed me the key to our house. "I'll always remain your humble servant," he said with a sigh. "Ayah! The Doctor had a heart of gold. He did a lot for my family. Of course, you were equally kind and generous, *Khanom*! God bless you both."

Something in his voice stirred me. I could not fire that poor man. I handed back the key to him. "Here, keep this. The garden belongs to you. I'll pay you somehow," I said.

On December sixth, a typically cold winter day, I managed to get some gasoline to visit the prison alone. Babak was in bed with a flu.

Not anticipating what was happening, I turned the car to Arya Mehr Street when a group of several thousand people with clenched fists approached. I pulled over and stopped to prevent an attack on the car. A few hundred feet away, close to the Inter-Continental hotel, a military jeep was ablaze. The dark acrid smoke was tossed by the wind. Suddenly, from the opposite side, the crowds were confronted by military convoys carrying troops with loaded machine guns. It would not be long before the two groups converged and the bloodshed began.

I quickly abandoned the car and started running around the soldiers, joining other frantic pedestrians on the sidewalk. The demonstrators, chanting revolutionary slogans, reached their target—the headquarters of the Iran Novin, which later became Rastakhiz, Iran's only official party. Rocks and Molotov cocktails smacked against the building. Glass crashed. Shouts of

"Death to One Party For All!" rang through the air. Soldiers used tear gas, bayonets and the butts of their guns on the crowd. The people counterattacked. Shots were fired.

I continued running, completely out of breath, my eyes burning from the tear gas. A man darted by, shouting: *"Marg Bar Shah!"*—"Death to the Shah!"

Since the 1952 coup d'etat during which, with America's help, Mohammad Reza Shah's dictatorial reign was reinstated, no one had dared to say those three Farsi words. Saying it was equal to suicide. It still was. The man who had desecrated the idol fell to the ground with a gunshot. A stream of blood came from his mouth. His eyes began to cloud. Cold tremors of fear shook my knees, and I almost forgot about myself. Screams, sirens, and a roaring fire snapped me back to my senses. I resumed running.

In a short alley with no outlet, a young woman and her child had taken refuge. The three of us huddled under the overhang of a house and coughed from the fumes. The dead man's bloody face appeared before me, and I vomited violently, as if my guts were being torn from my body. Helplessly, we waited.

An hour later, an eerie quiet indicated that the combat was over. The street looked like a deserted battlefield: shoes, pocketbooks, blood, bodies—all left behind. Military convoys had remained throughout the street for surveillance. Making no attempt to find my car, I ran towards the prison garrison, some two miles away. I did not look back for fear of being shot.

As usual, Major Sharafat was sitting quite composed behind his desk in the waiting room. "What was going on out there? I heard shooting," he asked nonchalantly.

Panting, I described what I saw.

"When people go looking for trouble, they find it!" he said in a low, raspy voice. Despite his callous reference to the demonstrators, his tone lacked vengefulness. He handed me a glass of water. I was the only woman who had ventured out to visit the prison today.

"*Khanom*, I promise you that in a month's time things will be normal again," the Major said firmly. " If not, I am not my father's son but a bastard!"

Shoja was happy to see me. But when he heard what had happened, his excitement vanished. "You shouldn't have come today. I don't want you to risk your life for me," he said.

"I'm fine. Really," I assured him.

Shoja looked around him furtively and in a hushed voice told me, "One of the officers, a former patient, informed me confidentially that the Shah is fleeing Iran and doesn't plan to release us. It's rumored that the Shah may have us all executed before his departure so that we can't betray him if we go on trial."

As I listened in horror, he leaned closer and whispered, "You must get me some money. I might need it, if things reach that point."

I held his hands in mine. "I promise to get the money, no matter how."

The nearby officer interrupted me sharply. "*Khanom*, the streets are not safe. Go home now!"

Out in the street, the significance of Shoja's words hit me hard. What if the Shah really has Shoja and his colleagues killed to save his own neck? Hasn't he used them as scapegoats already?

I came to a dead stop. Then, remembering the officer's warning, I began to run towards my car.

The car was exactly as I had abandoned it, except for several dents on the fender and one on the roof. Before I could jump into the car, a young man approached quickly, carrying an injured woman.

"Take us to a hospital. Hurry!" he ordered. On the way, the woman cried constantly.

On *Tasu'a*, the ninth day of the Arabic lunar month of *Moharram*, we were all sitting around the traditional *korsi*. It was a low square table covered with quilts and blankets, under which there was a brazier heated by coal. Mattresses and cushions surrounding the *korsi* provided seating. We stretched out our legs underneath to warm ourselves. With no fuel left in the house, this traditional heating system seemed to work, although the rest of the house remained frigid. My sister had drawn the thick drapes over the windows to keep out the cold. We had a simple dinner—meatballs and yogurt. What was Shoja having for dinner?

My brother-in-law passionately believed that tomorrow— the tenth day of the mourning month—would be an historic turning point for Iran. We should all join the *Ashura* demonstration, and show our unity with the revolutionaries. Mother, a Nationalist at heart, welcomed the idea. Aryan was fearful of the consequences. When only seventeen, my daring sister was expelled from high school because she had once joined a demonstration against the Shah. Her photograph had appeared in the newspapers, labeling her a traitor to the "patriarch", the Shah! My brother-in-law, a politically liberal physician, happened to see and like the picture and decided to ask for her hand. Luckily, the marriage worked out well.

Despite Shoja's situation, Babak and I decided to join the rest of the family, and participate in *Ashura's* demonstration, Why should we remain loyal to a regime which did not, in turn, give loyalty and support? Didn't we long for a real change, a democracy, that would free the Iranian nation from the yoke of a dictator? It was time to determine our own future.

This *Ashura* morning was clear and unseasonably warm, a good omen according to the believers. Mother had been cooking the traditional *Sholeh Zard* since dawn. By eleven o'clock the saffron rice pudding, which due to shortages in food supplies was not as colorful or tasteful as the previous years, was delivered to the Mosque for the poor.

Close to noon, we prepared to leave for the city. Due to a gigantic traffic jam, we were obliged to park the car and walk the remaining two miles to the demonstration site on Shah Reza Avenue.

The sight was breathtaking! At least two million people of all genders, ages, and social classes had joined together to either march in or observe the event. Each group represented in the procession was distinguished by its placards. One read: "*Allahu Akbar*/Khomeini Rahbar"—"God is great/Khomeini is the Leader!" Another read: "Victory Belongs to the Workers and Peasants!" And, of course, the Nationalists' slogan was: "Constitution Above All!" Then, a new slogan: "Down with the East, down with the West! The Islamic Republic is the Best!"

Unlike any other *Ashura*, nobody mourned Imam Hosain, the prophet's grandson, who was killed by Omayyad Caliph, Yazid. Instead, people called for the demise of Mohammad Reza Pahlavi: "Death to the Traitorous Shah."

The crowd was noticeably organized, and the military absent. Any confrontation with this enormous mass of people seemed incomprehensible. Women offered food and drink for the hungry and thirsty. Men held out stacks of paper money to those who had lost income due to the strikes. No one took the money.

First-aid stations had been set up at regular intervals. An elderly spectator who had fainted was carried hand-by-hand overhead to the nearest ambulance. Such solidarity, in a nation that usually lacked it, was inspiring. It seemed that all Iranian people had found a real sense of national identity, regardless of belief or ideology.

An old man, his grandson on his shoulders, said with awe: "Child, watch carefully. Remember this day always!"

Someone pointed up at the sky. "Look—helicopters! What if they start shooting?"

Voices shouted: "It's the Shah! It's the Shah!"

Tens, hundreds, thousands, even millions of fists were clenched upward, roaring *"Marg Bar Shah!"*—"Death to the Shah!"

The choppers ascended, disappearing quickly in the sky. The Shah—and the world—had witnessed the people's victory.

We woke up one frosty day to find out that the oil tank at my sister's home was empty. There was neither heat nor hot water. Due to continuous strikes by the oil workers, chances of getting fuel soon were slim. Babak and I, who had not washed for several days, decided to use a public bath. This was his first time.

Public baths in Iran were used mostly by those who did not

have private bathing facilities at home, but they also provided steam baths and massages. When I was growing up, few people could afford the luxury of having their own shower. Even though Father's home had one, we used the public baths in the winter, because our heating system was poor. Our nearby facility contained many shower cabins and was beautifully decorated with floral mosaics. The proprietor—who was called *Hadji* because he had made a pilgrimage to Mecca—knew our family and favored us with the best bath cabin.

The bath was opened from dawn to dusk every day of the year. As soon as a cabin was evacuated, the janitor would clean and prepare it for the next customer. Nevertheless, Mother would always send our maid to disinfect the area before we entered. Once we were in, we had the privacy of the entire cabin for a couple of hours at a fixed rate. The cabins consisted of two sections: a large dressing room with a long mosaic bench on which the maid spread a rug and placed our carryall containing towels and toiletries. The second room was the actual bath, with a hot tub—which we never used—and a shower. There was also a large marble bench for relaxing while we washed ourselves.

Taking a bath was not much fun for Aryan and me. Mother would show no mercy to us in performing this twice-a-week ritual. She would begin with washing our hair with a very harsh soap, which ran down our faces and made our eyes sting. Next, she would use the rough scrubbing mitts to wash our small bodies. Our tender skins would turn red and painful. The final stage was a succession of hot shower rinses which seemed to last forever. As Aryan and I almost choked with the steam, I feared we would be sucked into the large drain along with the suds.

Once convinced that her daughters were thoroughly clean, Mother would send us back to the dressing room where the maid helped us get dressed. There was also a pitcher of cool lemonade waiting for us. Our reward for being good girls!

Sometimes, Mother would call in the *Dallak*, who made a living bathing women. The *Dallak*, a scrawny little woman, would enter the bath cabin in a loincloth. Although she was not as rough on our skins as Mother was, my sister and I disliked her. She smelled of henna and mildew. It was rumored that the *Dallak* was also a matchmaker.

One day as the *Dallak* was scrubbing Aryan, she said to Mother, "*Mashallah*—Praise God—this pretty young lady is starting to bud. It's time to find her a husband. If the Grand Lady would allow me, I'll look among my other customers for the right suitor."

"My daughter's much too young!" Mother snapped back. "Don't mention such things again. Just do your job!"

I was upset too, but for a different reason. The Dallak never commented about me!

Today, the public bath looked nothing like the one I remembered as a child. Even worse, it was closed. "No fuel!" a sign on the glass door read.

Back at Aryan's house, Babak and I heated water on a kerosene stove and gave ourselves sponge baths. As I was towel drying my hair, Mother called from downstairs, "Pick up the phone, Azar."

A man introduced himself as Mir Ashrafi, publisher and editor of the weekly *Atash* newspaper.

"Lady, perhaps you should know. Our next issue will have an article about your very private life," he warned.

My heart sank. Mir Ashrafi was the most notorious journalist and his newspaper the worst rag publication in Iran.

"Mister, I don't care what you write," I said, trying to sound cool.

"I bet you'd care, if you knew what I'm going to write."

"Are you blackmailing me?"

"Think of it as a contribution to my newspaper," the reporter coaxed. "Come to my office tomorrow, and we'll reach some agreement."

"You and I will never reach an agreement. Print whatever you want to! No one will believe your lies," I shouted.

"Hey! Watch it! I know, for a fact, that just a couple months ago you spent thousands of toumans on a diamond ring. Considering that your husband is in prison, that's quite a purchase," the infamous editor haunted me. "You also participated in the *Ashura* demonstrations against the Shah. The former Minister of Health's wife has become a revolutionary. Ha! Ha!"

I paused to take time with my answers. The SAVAK must be spying on me. How else would this man know about my activities, wrong as the impressions were? They accused me of buying jewelry when I had been selling it.

"Listen! There's still more," the reporter added. "Rumor has it that your good looks helped your husband to power!"

This was outrageous. I could not possibly allow this shameless, immoral man to go on harassing me.

"Go ahead! Fabricate whatever stories you want. I'm not afraid." I yelled and slammed the phone down.

The truth was I was terrified. The public would devour any slanderous gossip this low-life journalist printed about a fallen member of the upper classes. I might end up in prison!

On the day the article was to appear, Mother burst into my room, waving a copy of the paper: "Rejoice! There's nothing about you here!"

Obviously, my overwrought mother had listened in to my phone conversation with Mir Ashrafi. What had prevented that opportunist from trashing my name?

By mid-December the whole country was on strike. In solidarity with the people's movement, all government offices, industries, banks, airports and bazaars were closed. Production had ceased, thereby crippling everyday life. The coalition of all opposition groups and the entire country's civil disobedience indicated that thirty-five years of Mohammad Reza Pahlavi's monarchy was nearing an end.

The Shah, in a last-ditch effort to save his throne, established a moderate government. He appointed Nationalist Shapour Bakhtiar to replace Azhari's military government and announced his plan to leave the country for a brief vacation. To gain popularity, Bakhtiar, the Shah's proxy, ordered the termination of the SAVAK. He then secured freedom of the press and released all political prisoners—except those who had served as government dignitaries over the last fifteen years. "Priority will be given to trying those officials and punishing them severely for their crimes," he declared. To further prove his credibility to people, Bakhtiar prohibited these prisoners and their families from conducting financial transactions.

Bakhtiar's order came too late. The rich had already transferred huge amounts of money abroad.

Money became a problem for me again. With only a few

thousand touman obtained from selling a carpet, I was destitute.

"My children will be living in poverty soon," I confessed to Mother. "We are not even permitted to sell our own house."

"I will sell mine, Azar, if we have to," my compassionate mother offered.

So far, our abandoned house had not been looted, but the walls surrounding it were stained in red graffiti: "Death to the traitors! Death to the rich!" The windows were also broken. People had vented their animosity towards us. It was not safe to enter our own home.

How ironic! We had built physical walls around our house for privacy. Mentally, we had lived behind a Chinese wall to shut out the world. We had enjoyed our own secure comfortable world, not realizing that around us our ancient land was spinning out of control. The invisible walls between the upper and lower classes were shifting.

Shoja's parents' lives were interrupted by the social changes. I was visiting them one day when the landlord suddenly brought an eviction notice. Only four years ago, my in-laws lived in a large home in Tabriz, a city some three hundred miles away, in the Azerbaijan province. They moved to Tehran after their son, Zia, along with his wife and daughter, died in a car crash. The sad parents needed to be near Shoja and their youngest son who hardly ever visited them.

"Why are we being evicted?" Agha Joon asked the landlord in confusion.

"You are the father of that corrupt Minister, aren't you? I won't have the wrong kind living under my roof. Can't afford to get into any trouble. If you're not out by the end of next week, I'll report you to the authorities!" he said heartlessly.

My father-in-law's face turned purple. The veins in his neck protruded as if ready to burst. "How dare you insult my decent son and threaten me with the law!" Agha Joon screamed. "Who are you to tell me to leave? Even the Shah cannot until my lease has expired. Now get lost!"

The landlord did not budge his fat body. "This place must be emptied by the end of next week. Got it? Your disgraced son is in prison. You got no more connections. You can't bully poor people like me!"

Apparently, this rich developer had become a revolutionary overnight!

"Either you take back what you said about my son, or I'll kill you now," Agha Joon exploded. With both hands, he lunged towards the man. "No one can defame my son before my face!"

The two men got entangled, wrestling and tearing at each other's clothes. I screamed. My mother-in-law rushed into the living room, looking pale and panicky. At the sight of her husband combating a mad stranger, she raised her frail hands towards the ceiling and cried: "*Ya Bab Al Havaej*—God, help us!"

The two stubborn men kept wrestling.

"It's all right, Shazdeh Joon," I rocked her gently in my arms. ""Nothing to worry about. Let me take you back to your bed. You don't look well."

The poor woman clung to me like an infant as I led her back to her bedroom.

"It hurts. . . so bad," she pointed to her sides.

"I know. Here. Take this medicine for your kidneys. It will help."

When I returned to the living room, the fight had stopped. The landlord's nose bled. Agha Joon's ankle was sprained. More than anything else, the old man's pride was wounded. "I will not stay in this place another day!" he declared.

With the strikes, finding another home within a short notice would be impossible. Mother came to the rescue. She offered my in-laws her empty house, the one adjacent to mine.

At night, I had my first nightmare. Our entire abandoned house was wrapped in flames. The raging fire and dark thick smoke filled the rooms. All windows and doors were locked. Shoja and the children were trapped inside. I tried frantically to open the gate and rescue them. The scorching heat seared my skin. The fumes began to suffocate me. I struggled and woke up to the sound of my own gasping.

Babak was asleep. The unheated house was freezing. Mother, whose chronic asthma had been acting up, coughed in the next room. I got up and put another blanket on her. Fear of having another nightmare kept me awake all night. What would become of our country? Of our family? My children?

I had not heard from Roxana and Ramin in three weeks, and wondered if they were all right. Calls to America were expensive, and I did not wish to impose more on my sister's generosity. How lonely Christmas holidays must be for Roxana and Ramin away from home.

Shoja's situation seemed far from settled, and although a trial date had not been set yet, I decided to seek the services of a lawyer. Matin-Daftari, a well-known attorney and a friend of Hushang, trusted in Shoja's innocence and was willing to take his case—with one condition: Shoja must disclose everything he knew about the Shah's crimes. Matin-Daftari was convinced that Shoja's trial would instigate much publicity and propaganda, and only a first-class attorney like himself could handle it. He was the grandson of Dr. Mohammad Mossadegh, the Prime Minister who had nationalized the Anglo-Iranian Oil Company. Eventually, because of his immense popularity, Mossadegh was considered a threat to the monarchy, and after the 1952 coup d'état, exiled by the Shah.

Like his grandfather, the grandson had a passion for the political arena. He would fly into a rage at the mere mention of the Shah's name; he had been arrested on several occasions for opposing the dictator.

I could not accept this acclaimed attorney's condition. Shoja could not afford to further jeopardize his position by warring against the Monarch openly. The Shah was still Iran's supreme ruler. I turned down the attorney's offer.

The next attorney, Mr. Hosaini had less social status, but, on the surface, appeared to be hospitable. He offered us tea and cookies, and let us know right away that defending a former Minister could be considered an antirevolutionary act. He would be risking his profession in case the revolutionaries came to power. He had to work on tiptoes in the handling of this political trial.

I listened anxiously.

"I will only take Dr. Sheikh as a client for a fee of 20 million touman ($3 million dollars) in cash—10 million in advance!" Hosaini concluded.

"What? My entire family couldn't raise so much," I said, placing the half-finished cup of tea back on the table.

The lawyer cackled, "*Khanom*, if you don't have the money, then who does? If not to spend on your husband's life, then for what?"

That damned infamous List! Even this lawyer believed that we were billionaires! Finding Shoja an attorney would be impossible.

CHAPTER SIX

1979 arrived without a happy beginning. Shoja was still kept a prisoner at Jamshidieh garrison.

My brother, Amir Ashraf, invited the family to his house for New Year's Day. I did not feel much like socializing, but, because of Babak's insistence, accepted the invitation. Perhaps, a day away from home would help me to snap out of my depression.

Amir Ashraf and his family lived in downtown Tehran and no matter which road we took, reminders of the recent disturbances were evident. Despite the new Prime Minister's efforts, the people's resistance had escalated, resulting in deadlier confrontations. The city was falling apart.

My sister-in-law, Pari, was an opera singer, now unemployed since Tehran's opera house, the Rudaki Hall, had shut down. Amir Ashraf had a Ph.D. in musicology from Vienna. After living many years abroad, he, along with his wife and their only daughter, had returned to Iran to work. Amir Ashraf had been teaching arts at the University of Tehran, and writing his regular musical columns in newspapers, before the strikes ended both activities.

After having a delicious lunch of white rice and *Qormeh*

Sabzi—a Persian dish of beef and herb stew—we all joined in the den to have tea, and to listen to one of Amir Ashraf's classical tapes: Beethoven's Pathetique Sonata. That was among my favorites.

This relaxed time did not last long. Soon, my family got into a heated discussion of current politics—something that could not be avoided these days. Everyone turned to Amir Hosain for answers. A man of extensive insight and knowledge, Amir Hosain was our ultimate personal source in every matter. He had been forced by the SAVAK to retire early from teaching because of his liberal social and political views, and his great popularity among the university students and the intellectuals.

Amir Hosain predicted that the change of regime would be followed by a spasmodic period—quite bloody at times—leading to an uncertain future.

My youngest brother, Hushang, shared his view but was more optimistic. "Surely, Iranians would not allow themselves to be deprived of their last chance for freedom," he said. "Iran would have a democratic government, after all."

Hushang also was not spared from the Shah's dictatorial abuse. He had reached the rank of Admiral in the Navy, only to be forced to resign; Hushang had exposed his commander's one-hundred million dollar embezzlement, which might have been linked to the Royal Family. Currently, he owned a small shipping company,

Amir Ashraf, more of a conservative, was planning to leave Iran before the situation got out of hand. He did not wish to raise their daughter in an unstable environment.

I listened to their discussions intently, but did not participate.

As a child, I had learned not to openly disclose my political views, despite our family's resentment of the regime. I did not wish to end up like my sister who had been expelled from school for expressing her views.

Sitting quietly in my brother's den, I recalled my distant childhood. How innocently hopeful I had been about the future.

A studious young girl, I had decided to excel in my studies and eventually pursue a career in literature. Having been discouraged by our society from candidly revealing my feelings, since age ten, I had turned to writing. There, in the solitude of my poems, I freely portrayed my aspirations.

My three older brothers had expected me to be their protégé. Amir Hosain, with his commanding authority, provided both Eastern and Western reading material, usually the classics. He also demanded that I speak and write Farsi flawlessly. He was non-forgiving with any grammatical mistakes. As an adolescent, I never admired nor feared anyone as much as I did my eldest brother. Still, I would sometimes sneak my friends' romance novels into the house, hoping that Amir Hosain would not find me reading them.

Amir Ashraf, a devotee of music, had arranged for me to take piano lessons. He had also encouraged me to join a choir at fifteen, and even perform at a few concerts. Sometimes he would make me spend several hours at a time listening to Bach or Mozart. Of course, in the middle of these sittings, I would often lose concentration and start day-dreaming about things more interesting to a teenager, such as boys who were beginning to pay attention to me.

Hushang, more of a friend than a teacher, had the most

impact on my social development. However, due to rather great age differences between my brothers and I, our relationship was rigidly structured and formal. Even with my sister—only three years older—I was friendly but not intimate. My upbringing required that the youngest child always obey the older ones.

I did not have close contact with boys except for interaction with my male cousins or my brothers' friends, and then only with a chaperone. My upper-middle-class family had all the contradictions and tensions that come from trying to reconcile the cultures of the East and the West. We were exposed to Western ideas, yet bound by centuries-old Eastern traditions. My parents were neither narrow-minded nor fanatical, but lived according to established social values and ethical principles. Through them, we learned early in life that family was the most important core of our existence. Together, as a family, they taught us, we were indestructible. Alone, we could not survive!

Despite all restrictions, I believe that I was very privileged compared to most Iranian girls.

During my senior year of high school, I met Ahmad Madani, a true gentleman, one of Hushang's friends from the years at the Royal Naval Academy in England. I cannot think of what he found in me that prompted him to ask my parents for my hand after a few formal meetings.

Delighted by Madani's qualifications as a prospective husband, my parents consulted with Amir Hosain, who was doing his graduate work in sociology at Princeton. He told them that the final decision was mine to make. They assigned Mother's eldest sister to talk to me.

Blushing, I told Aunt Mahin Banu that I was not ready for marriage yet, and that I wanted to continue with my education, and to get to know myself before making any decisions in regard to a future husband. My aunt, a sophisticated woman for her time, agreed with me. But she also believed that Madani was too good to let go. "My dear child, one can always continue an education after marriage, but a suitable husband doesn't come around every day. I am not just referring to Madani. There are other good suitors to consider. At your age, it is expected of you to select a prospective husband."

In those days, it was inappropriate for a young girl to argue with her elders, so I kept silent. My aunt interpreted this as a positive response and secretly informed my parents that preparations should be made for a wedding!

When Madani left for America for more training, I stopped thinking about the matter altogether and continued with life as usual. A few months later, I graduated from high school with the highest honors and was chosen to receive an award from the Shah at a graduation ceremony. My prize was a scholarship to study abroad. That was the ultimate of my dreams.

This was my second time in the company of royalty. The first was at age twelve when I was selected by the school to recite one of my poems on the Shah's birthday. At that age, I perceived the Shah as a divine father. At eighteen, I had learned enough to have a different assessment of him. He was no longer transcendental, but a dictator.

I also had the honor of an audience at Sa'd Abad Palace with the Shah's second wife, Queen Soraya—an extremely beautiful woman. Soraya was not a warm personality, and her marriage was in serious trouble. She had not been able to give the Shah any children. The Shah's only child was a daughter from his previous marriage to Princess Fawzia of Egypt.

In a society where most privileges were given by favoritism, my success in attaining the scholarship made my parents proud. Nevertheless, Father, who always hoped that one of his five children would study medicine, seemed disillusioned, for I planned to continue my education in literature.

During that summer, I fell in love for the first time. What a wonderful, mesmerizing feeling! It felt like I was set free to fly through the air, and unfold the entire universe.

I knew Shoja through his friendship with Amir Ashraf. Shoja came from Azerbaijan—a northwestern province—and was in his final year of medical school at the University of Tehran. He, a baritone, also belonged to the same choir as I. Shoja was not tall or particularly handsome, but he had a charming face and kind eyes. His overly friendly, unceremonious manner contrasted with my formal, and perhaps more genteel, behavior. Yet, his abundant self-confidence, unending energy, and ability to lead attracted me. Those were the qualities that I lacked.

Our choir went on an excursion to the outskirts of Tehran one day. The pristine scenery of mountains, my recent academic success, and the possibility of exchanging my sheltered life for an independent experience abroad made me feel in love with the whole world. Shoja, who was hiking beside me, began singing a ballad in his native Azeri dialect. Although I could not understand the meaning of his words, at that moment, I desired to spend the rest of my life with this strong, cheerful, young man. Love's magical power disregarded our differences. He would make me happy. I thought.

That same month, my parents started to plan my upcoming wedding, and the graveness of the situation struck me. With my flourishing love for Shoja, I had totally forgotten about Madani and his proposal. What was I to do?

I confessed my love for Shoja to my aunt. "I could not marry anyone else!"

"Is this young man in love with you too?" she asked, restraining her shock.

"He's never said anything to me in that respect," I expressed. "But I think he likes me by the way he looks at me."

"Dear child, open your ears and eyes. Don't mistake infatuation for love or you may live to regret it!"

"Please, let me find out for myself," I begged my aunt. "Don't make any further plans with my parents before I'm certain as to what I want. And, please keep this a secret."

I decided to take the initiative and talk with Shoja. I had to know his true feelings. My future depended on it.

Against all conventions, I went to the rental apartment that Shoja shared with a few classmates—something that a "decent" girl would never have done! Shoja was stupefied to see an unattended young female standing at his door. Stuttering, yet determined, I told him that I had something very important to discuss. Reluctantly, he let me into the all-male apartment, and then to his room.

Every word was a struggle to utter, but I managed to tell Shoja about my marriage proposal.

"Is he a good man?" he asked casually.

"Yes!"

Shoja seemed puzzled. "Then what's the problem?"

"The problem? Uh-eh—well, I love someone else!" I confessed shyly.

Shoja darted a sharp glance at the door to make sure it was

closed. This was not a confession for his roommates to hear. He then turned to me.

"So, who is the lucky guy?" he pried.

I blushed till my skull tingled. "You know him," I said quietly.

"Ha! Does this other man love you in return?"

"I don't know. That's why I'm here," I blurted out, avoiding his eyes.

Shoja was taken off guard. He looked at me in surprise. I was about to die from embarrassment. He didn't, couldn't, love me, I thought. What would he think of me now?

To my great relief, after a long pause which seemed an eternity, Shoja started to show some emotions. "Azar, I care for you too in a very special way. In fact, I care for you a lot, but I'm not ready for marriage. I am planning to do my residency in the States."

I jumped with the comment. "That's wonderful! We can go together. I've just received a college scholarship, so I wouldn't burden you financially."

He was at a loss for words for a few seconds. Waiting for what I wished to hear, I gazed steadily at his mouth.

"I just wouldn't want to see you regret it later," Shoja said, weighing every word.

Was he speaking his mind, or putting me in a difficult position to test my conviction?

"I won't marry anyone but you," I said confidently.

Shoja smiled and took my hands. "In that case, you'll have to wait until just before we leave for the States. I can't provide a home for you now."

It was not a conventional marriage proposal, but good enough for me.

"I'll wait, even if it takes the rest of my life," I said.

We stood close to each other, holding hands and feeling wonderful. The desire to kiss was there, but the predominant tradition required that we wait for our first kiss until we were officially married.

I left Shoja's apartment, the luckiest girl in the universe. Of course, my parents would have died if they knew their 'good' daughter had secretly met with a man!

If revealing my feelings to Shoja was difficult, discussing them with my parents was impossible. The short happiness was followed by a sense of guilt and fear of disapproval. Mother, specifically, would not understand. She had never discussed puberty, or love with me. And, sex was a forbidden word—a taboo—for her. How could I explain a romantic love to my mother? My parents would never forgive my rebellious conduct, I thought.

It was only through Aunt Mahin Banu's clever intercession that my parents finally accepted my decision. Of course, once they got to know Shoja, they were very pleased.

On January 30, 1957, Shoja and I were married. My parents gave us a small, simple wedding in their home. Neither one of us wanted anything fancy. We preferred to save the money for our education in the States. Shoja's parents traveled over 300 miles to give us their blessings.

For the first few months of our married life, I remained at my parents' home, and Shoja at his apartment. Oddly enough, we started dating! He would come to my house, take me out to a restaurant or the movies, then bring me back home, and kiss me goodnight at the front door. That was our limit!

In June 1957, we left for the United States. We finally had a honeymoon—a glorious week in Paris and an unforgettable cruise on the Queen Elizabeth to Ellis Island in New York.

Our years in America were difficult but instrumental in structuring my adult life. It was there that I became a woman, a mother, and a professional. The familiar sheltering walls of my home began to expand, giving me a view of the world beyond. However, unfamiliar invisible boundaries took their places. For a while, I struggled frantically to live between different times, different places. Being separated from my parents was quite painful, as I had never spent even one night away from them. In addition, there were the adjustments to married life, our extremely tight financial budget, and most of all a shocking alien culture. I knew America only through the eyes of Hollywood. But it also seemed that Americans knew Iran solely through images of old Persia: exotic bazaars, lovely oriental rugs, fluffy cats. A classmate actually asked me once, "Is Iran where you worship cows?"

Financial responsibilities were totally new to me. In Iran of that time, a young, upper-middle-class woman living with her parents never bothered to think about where money came from. For the first time, I opened a checking account, paid bills, and worried about the rent money.

My love for Shoja and my zest for learning helped me mature, and I began to assume more control over my life. Using the scholarship from the Iranian Government, I studied English literature at Western Reserve University in Cleveland, while Shoja began his internship in a hospital.

Shortly after we had settled in America, the Iranian Government stopped scholarship payments to students in areas not deemed "useful to the future of the country." To my dismay,

I had to switch my major to education. Eventually, the government's financial assistance was cut off, and I was obliged to depend on my father's generosity to continue through college.

Early in December, I discovered I was pregnant. The thought of having my first child was an unparalleled joy. Nine months later, our daughter was born. We named her Roxana, after the ancient Persian princess who married Alexander the Great. Roxana means "dawn", but our child became so much more to us—the sun, moon, and stars all in one tiny package. If my marriage was the most important event of my life, my daughter's birth was the most cherished. To be able to spend more time with this wonderful baby, I rescheduled my classes from morning to evening, leaving her with Shoja on his nights off, and a kind neighbor when he was working.

A year after Roxana's birth, as part of Shoja's residency training, we left Cleveland for Philadelphia. I attended classes at the University of Pennsylvania. Despite the hardships, our life was gratifying.

Unexpectedly, Mother, inflicted with cancer of the uterus, came to the States for treatment. Always thin and small, but dynamic and forceful, she now looked worn down. The thought of losing her darkened my happiness. After weeks of radiation therapy and a very slow and painful convalescence, Mother recovered from the terrifying disease.

As if caring for a sick mother, raising a child, attending school, and looking after a busy husband were not enough, I found myself pregnant again. When it came to family planning, Shoja was irresponsible.

From Philadelphia, we moved to Akron, Ohio, where our first son was born on June 7, 1960. We named this healthy, handsome boy Ramin, after the romantic hero of an Iranian lyric. One look at him, and I forgot that he was unplanned. Shoja had offered the first grandson to his family!

After five years, we left the United States. Shoja had turned down a good position there as an orthopedic surgeon. He had already planned our life in Iran.

At Tehran airport, my parents met us. Mother was more or less back to her old self. Father, once erect and tall, was now rather stooped, and gray. He had retired as the chief accountant for the National Iranian Oil Company.

Tehran had gone through many alterations in those five years. The northern section of the city had developed tremendously with new high-rises, hotels, shopping centers, amusement parks, and roads busy with modern cars. A new upper-middle class was expanding as a result of the enormous oil revenues. They boasted that Tehran competed with any modern capital. Nonetheless, the hunger for things Western was so great among Iranians that many of them lost no opportunity to travel to Paris or New York to shop. Nothing like the real thing! For the *nouveau riche*, money and position seemed all that mattered.

The rest of the city had remained the same, if not more impoverished. The gap between the rich and poor had grown out of proportion. It was as if two separate nations coexisted within one city, without knowledge of the other.

My parents had sold the Shah Avenue house, the one in which I had spent the greatest part of my childhood, and moved to the suburb. The new house was equipped with modern conveniences. Television, a recent phenomenon in Iran, was also added to their furnishings.

Amir Hosain and his wife, Homa, lived in a house nearby.

My two other brothers were abroad. Amir Ashraf and his family were in Vienna. Hushang resided temporarily in California with his wife, Parvin, and their two daughters. He was working for a graduate degree in mechanical engineering. Aryan and her husband and their two sons lived one block away from my parents in a new house that they had just built.

We stayed with my parents and occupied the second floor, which had been recently added to their house for us. Shoja actively sought a position with Tehran's medical schools, but was rejected. Most medical organizations, affiliated with the universities and funded by the government, were staffed by older, French-educated Iranian physicians. They did not appreciate American-trained newcomers. Shoja decided to join the prestigious Pars Hospital, staffed by American-educated physicians, and start a private practice. With a graduate degree in education, I started a part-time job at the School of Social Work, and our kids began preschool.

Our second son, Babak, named after a brave Persian warrior, was born on July 26, 1963. He completed our happiness. I stayed home for the next six years to care of our three children, and spent whatever spare time I could find to write lyrics and stories for a children's program at the Iranian National Television. During this time, I also translated two books on the history of mankind from English to Farsi for which I received good reviews. Meantime, with the money that my parents had put aside for my dowry, we bought a piece of land next to theirs and built our own home within a year. Eventually, Shoja, along with his successful medical practice, established and directed the first Rehabilitation Society of Iran, a major achievement in his ambitious career

If only he had not joined the Shah's government!

CHAPTER SEVEN

The Moving Finger writes, and having writ,
Moves on, Nor all thy piety not wit
Shall lure it back to cancel half a line,
Nor all thy tears wash out a word of it!
        Omar Khayyam (Rubaiyat/ Twelfth Century)

With the strikes continuing, my attempts to acquire gasoline to visit Shoja were futile. Just as things seemed hopeless, my sister's English tutor, Azad, volunteered to give me a ride to the prison on his motorcycle. This was my first time! Awkwardly, I wrapped my coat around me and got on the seat behind him, tying my scarf under my chin. I hesitated to grab ahold of Azad's coat. He was not exactly a friend. Azad roared the engine on his motorcycle. When he let go of the brake, a sudden jolt jerked me back and almost threw me off. Azad laughed as he adjusted his half-inch eyeglasses on his large fleshy nose. "*Khanom Vazir*—Minister's wife—hold on to me. You won't get yourself soiled by touching someone outside your class!" he mocked.

Azad was raised on the wrong side of the tracks, but through self-determination and hard work, he had become a teacher. Although he respected my family, his snide comments revealed his deep-rooted resentment for the upper-classes. He was a Leftist.

About 100 meters from the garrison, I climbed off the motorcycle, not wanting to be seen by anyone who knew me. Azad whined that he needed a refreshing beer to quench his thirst. While I visited Shoja, Azad would indulge himself in a liquor store.

"I doubt if you'd find one in the entire city. As you know, the government has recently shut down all liquor stores. Buying alcoholic beverages is strictly prohibited," I reminded him.

Azad persisted. "For someone seeking the juice of life, nothing's impossible," he laughed, smoothing down his thick mustache.

"Good luck. I'll see you in half an hour," I said smiling and walked away towards the prison.

Ellen Aram and her children were also at the prison's waiting room. Her husband had advised them to leave Iran without him, but of course, they needed permission from the new Martial Law Administrator, General Rahimi. Apparently, families of political prisoners now needed special permission to leave the country.

"In a way, I've become a prisoner like my husband!" Ellen complained. A few faint lines appeared on her slender face.

"Why don't you attempt to leave through the American Embassy, since you are a U.S. citizen?" I suggested.

"I wouldn't dare." Ellen blinked her blue eyes. "The editor of the Atash newspaper has already accused me of being a spy for Richard Helms, former American Ambassador in Iran! Could you believe that? Any contact with the embassy might jeopardize my husband's situation. The only person I could think of asking for help is Mrs. Rahimi, an old friend who happens to be the wife of the new Martial Law Administrator. What do you think?" Ellen asked.

"Go for it," I said.

I entered the visitors' room with 10,000 touman concealed inside a handkerchief in my pocket. Generously, Mother had loaned it to us. Pretending to stop a cough, I took out the handkerchief, held it close to my mouth and then, carefully, passed it on to Shoja. His hands encased the handkerchief with its hidden content. As the officer in charge turned his head to scan the other couples in the room, Shoja smoothly slid the bribe money into his trousers pocket. Now he had a small chance to get some cooperation from his guards!

"I know this money's not enough, sweetheart, but this is all I could get my hands on right now," I whispered.

"It'll do. Thanks, love. So, how are the kids?"

Talking abut family matters took our minds temporarily away from the unpleasant environment. We discussed our children together, and decided that Roxana and Ramin should remain in the States and continue with their education, and their part-time jobs. Iran was not a safe place for them to return now, even for summer holidays.

Outside the garrison, I was unable to find Azad and his motorcycle. Perhaps the determined man had found his forbidden beer and had completely forgotten about me. Ellen gave me a ride back home.

The same day, Dr. Razmara, Iran's newest Minister of Health, held a press conference in which he strongly condemned the former Secretary of Health and Social Welfare. He claimed that Shoja, while in office, spent billions of dollars to computerize Social Security. A blatant act of pure luxury! The new Minister further accused Shoja of filling the pockets of an American-based computer company, and of course his own bank accounts, enabling him to afford a private helicopter and a yacht!

Helicopter? Yacht? Sheer fabrications! The new Minister was merely voicing the Shah's government. It had become politically popular to defame previous government officials, and to express anti-American sentiments. With this Minister's statement, the scandalization of Shoja had reached its climax.

The truth was that Iran had a primitive social security system before Shoja held office. After careful study, the Ministry of Health and Social Welfare contracted with the American company EDS (Electronic Data Systems) to design a new, computerized system. The work, which began in 1976, proceeded on schedule until the unrest began. Almost three months after Shoja's arrest, two top EDS representatives in Iran, Paul Chiapparone and Bill Gaylord, were also detained as "material witnesses" in the investigation of my husband's alleged corruption. This was an attempt to prove that Shoja had taken kickbacks from EDS, while in office. The Americans were still in prison until the authorities conducted an investigation.

On January 16, 1979, the air was crisp and the sky overcast. Perhaps we would see our first snowfall of the year. From the army camp close to our home, the sound of trumpets led the draftees through their daily routines. In a harmonious voice, they listlessly chanted, "Long live the Shah!"

After having spent many hours of tossing and turning during the night, I joined Mother in the kitchen. She served me tea from an old Russian samovar.

"So much shooting last night, I couldn't sleep a wink," Mother complained. "Such limbo! Either the Shah should leave, or stay and give up his dictatorship. These last four months of fighting have been hard for all of us. We're running out of supplies as well as patience." Her small fragile frame moved wearily.

I turned on the news, fearing the possibility of a much rumored military coup. Nothing of any significance was reported.

"Mother, things will never be the same for us," I said sadly. "Even if Shoja is freed, he may not be able to live in Iran after all this character assassination. His name has become like a common target for people to hate. Nobody cares to know our version of the truth. Perhaps we'll have no choice but to leave Iran for good!"

Mother turned to me. Wrinkles deepened on her delicate, serene face. She flickered her kind eyes. "Why on earth would you even think of leaving your own country? People will forget just as fast as they accept rumors. Believe me. I didn't get all these gray hairs for nothing. I know how people are," Mother paused to cough. "Now, stop all this negative talk and help me clean these vegetables. I'm making a hearty soup for lunch."

Helping with daily chores was a good distraction.

At 2:00 p.m. a television broadcast from Mehr Abad Airport made a long expected announcement: "Ladies and Gentlemen! Here is an important message by *Shahanshah*."

We all held our breath.

Pale and tired, the Shah, Queen Farah by his side, announced that the time had come for him to leave the country "for a rest." In his absence, the Monarch expected the nation to support his newly appointed government and the Regency Council, and help restore the economy by ending the strikes and returning to work. Shah Mohammad Reza Pahlavi cried as he bid farewell to his subjects and boarded his private jet for exile.

Within seconds, as if synchronized, people poured into the streets in ecstasy. The city burst with explosive bliss. Shouts of *"Shah Raft, Shah Raft!"*—"The Shah fled"—filled the air. The nonstop honking of horns was deafening. Babak and I dashed out to see for ourselves. At the army camp, people were offering the guards flowers and sweets in exchange for a truce. "Your Commander-in-Chief is gone! Don't you see? *Shah Raft!* Put down your weapons and join the Revolutionaries," they shouted.

The soldiers accepted the gifts with smiles. The frenzied crowd started towards the main road to meet the outpouring masses from all over the city, dancing and chanting, *"Shah Raft."*

Babak and I moved with the flowing crowd. Every vehicle suddenly displayed a picture of Ayatollah Khomeini on the front window. On the bridge over Shemiran Road, a stone statue of the Shah hung from a rope, an act which repeated itself all across the country. No token of the Shah's existence could be tolerated by Iranians any longer.

What a disgraceful departure for a dictator who had always acted as if he were invincible!

Ayatollah Khomeini instantly published another manifesto declaring the Shah's appointed Regency Council and the government illegal. He once again asked the military to join the people in their final fight for freedom. Bakhtiar, the new Prime Minister, emphatically defied the Ayatollah's dictum. "I will not allow Iran to be governed by any force other than the legitimate authority."

The military commanders splintered in their loyalty to the Shah. More than before, people became obsessed with fear of a possible coup. While many anxiously awaited the Ayatollah's impending arrival from Paris, Bakhtiar threatened that his plane would not be allowed to land in Iran.

As if we needed more worries, a frightening letter arrived from Roxana:

"Mom, Ramin has lost interest in his studies and has even given up playing his favorite sport, football. He is withdrawn and reclusive. What should I do?"

Frantically, I phoned Ramin. He barely wanted to talk.

"You must stop worrying about your father, sweetheart. Things are going to improve. Your father's strong. He'll survive," I tried to assure him. "Please, concentrate on your health and your school. The rest is out of your control."

"It's not just my father. What about Iran? Am I losing everything?" he asked poignantly.

"No matter what happens to Iran, you'll always have your family. We love you, son. Do you hear? We all love you!"

Ramin listened quietly.

On February first, half of Tehran's population converged on the airport to witness Ayatollah Khomeini's triumphant return to Iran, after over fifteen years of exile. The country exploded with anticipation. Would Bakhtiar follow through on his threats to prevent Ayatollah's plane from landing? My family felt uneasy about Babak and I being on the streets that day, but we were determined to visit Shoja. The prison's waiting room was almost empty. Hardly any of the prisoners' families had remained in Iran. After the Shah's departure, the remaining elite had also run for their lives.

As if he never moved, Major Sharafat still sat under the icon of his hero, the Shah, but unlike earlier times, he seemed too preoccupied to talk. With his Commander gone, the officer's life had changed, and, possibly within hours, he could be arrested by the Revolutionaries. It was foolish for him just to sit there.

Shoja felt betrayed by the fact that the Shah had departed, leaving him in prison, but he was glad to be alive. Luckily, the rumor of his execution by the Shah had not materialized.

"If Bakhtiar leaves too, there's a good chance that the new regime will exonerate me of all charges," he remarked optimistically.

For the first time in months, we talked about the future. Shoja felt there would be no reason for us to leave Iran once he was free, and his name cleared. He would go back to his private practice and stay away from politics for the rest of his life!

At the end of the thirty-minute visit, Shoja showed more emotions than usual. He kissed my hands and held Babak close against his chest and waved until we were out of his sight. Did he have a presentiment of some sort?

In the evening, Ayatollah Khomeini's arrival was broadcast by the television. Surrounded by his followers, the victorious

Ayatollah vowed to replace the Shah's "satanic regime" with an Islamic Republic. While being escorted to a car, Ayatollah Khomeini waved to the thousands who had been climbing on one another for a glimpse of their new leader. From the airport, he went straight to the Behesht-e-Zahra Cemetery to pay respects to the martyrs of the Revolution.

Prime Minister Bakhtiar, unable to prevent the Ayatollah's return, warned: "I will not share the government with anyone. The Ayatollah should act as a religious figure in the holy city of Qom, and leave politics to me!"

I had seen Ayatollah Khomeini up close, about seven months ago. Shoja, then Secretary of Health and Social Welfare, and I were formally invited by the Iraqi Government to participate in the tenth anniversary celebration of the Ba'th Party. It was this party which had seized complete power in Iraq since 1968.

One day, with our beautiful hostess, the wife of the Minister of Health of Iraq, I went to the city of Najaf to visit the Shrine of Imam Ali, the son-in-law and cousin of the prophet Muhammad. It was an extremely hot evening and under the long veils, which we had to wear for the occasion, the sweat was pouring down our faces.

While circling the tomb, I saw a clergyman on the quiet periphery prostrating himself in prayer. Two men stood close behind him. The hostess brought her face near mine and whispered, "Do you know who that is? Ayatollah Khomeini, sent to Najaf by your Shah."

At that moment, the pious man raised his head, and I saw his ancient face and piercing eyes.

"Since his eldest son's recent mysterious death," my hostess continued, "the Ayatollah comes here to pray every evening with his bodyguards."

Suddenly, I remembered the events of 1963—the beginning of Ayatollah Khomeini's adamant opposition to the Shah which resulted in his exile to Iraq. I did not have the slightest clue that this spiritual leader's arrival in Iran and our fate would be inextricably intertwined.

Immediately after his arrival, Ayatollah Khomeini appointed Mehdi Bazargan as the head of the government. Still, Prime Minister Bakhtiar did not give up his post. Within the next ten days, with two governments, Iran was more chaotic than ever. A major event soon hastened the victory of Bazargan over Bakhtiar. At Dushan Tapeh Air Force Base, many officers defected and distributed government weapons and ammunition among the Ayatollah's supporters. More people gave up their lives in confrontations with the military to finalize the victory in an ongoing war.

For several nights in a row, the incessant gunfire had kept us from sleep. No one had left the house for fear of being shot, not even to buy daily bread. We lived off of hoarded food. Today we all gathered in a small, windowless room next to my sister's kitchen for breakfast. While I ironed Shoja's laundry from the prison, my sister snapped at me, "People are dying outside and you are ironing?"

"If I don't keep myself busy I'll go crazy. Besides, tomorrow's visiting day, and Shoja needs his clothes."

"What are you talking about? We may not even have a country tomorrow," Aryan protested.

"Please, I have to do this for Shoja."

The national radio and television broadcast no news of any kind. They were rerunning old documentaries. Their silence in regard to the street battles was ominous. Amir Hosain, whose house was across from the army camp, called. "The revolutionary forces have attacked the camp! Leave the neighborhood, if you can. Otherwise, stay indoors. It's going to be bloody!"

We discussed our options. Where could we go? Surely, the remaining military installations all across Tehran were being attacked too. We decided to stay. What was happening at Jamshidieh garrison? How would I know if Shoja was safe?

The morning passed slowly. After a simple lunch in the room off the kitchen, I preoccupied myself with sewing the unraveled hem of Shoja's woolen sweater. Babak was writing a letter to Roxana and Ramin. Outside, the war was continuing.

At 5:30 p.m., a sudden forceful explosion shook the house. Sounds of screaming and glass breaking resonated through the kitchen. The lights went off. Mother shouted: "*Ya Ali,* " calling on the son-in-law of the prophet Mohammad for help. Babak and I huddled together in a corner. Through the broken windows in the kitchen, a blistering cold rushed into the room, penetrating our bodies. My brother-in-law lit a few candles. Aryan cried.

"Now! Be quiet, nobody here's been hurt," her husband tried to calm her.

"What about the others? Who knows how many have been killed?" Aryan continued to cry.

"Trust me. The army will give up the fight soon. They have to. This can't go on for much longer!" her husband said again.

Phone lines were down, and we could not contact my brothers. On Babak's battery-operated radio, we heard a classical burial march. Which of the two governments' death was being mourned? My nephew, Armin, showed us a bullet that had fallen in the hallway. It could have killed anyone of us!

We started cleaning up the broken glass and hanging sheets on the open windows before another explosion shook the house forcefully.

"Everyone's dead! There's no one left!" Aryan wailed hysterically.

We fell to the floor. I thought of Shoja and my two children in America, and prayed. I feared I might never see them again.

We spent a long, cold night pressed close to each other on the linoleum floor of the windowless room. The blasting winter wind waved the hanging sheets in a ghostly dance. Gunfire and cannons reverberated throughout the night. The rumble of military helicopters added to the pandemonium. What was happening?

We had survived the night with no knowledge of the outside world. Aryan's husband decided to leave the house and find out what had happened. Before he crossed the threshold, a bullet passed over his head and lodged in the door frame. Quickly, he ducked back into the house.

At breakfast, we realized that Armin was missing. Aryan went berserk. "He must have joined the Revolutionaries. I'll never see my son alive again!"

She had hardly finished her sentence when another deafening explosion occurred. Breakfast was strewn everywhere. Holding our ears, we dropped to the floor. How much longer could this go on?

Within a few hours, the heavy fighting changed into sporadic shooting. We waited and prayed quietly.

At 3:00 p.m., forty-eight hours after living in a battle zone, the phone rang. We were connected to the outside world again.

"*Khanom* Sheikh? This is Dr. Aram's brother. I'm calling from the neighborhood of Jamshidieh garrison," a man said.

I remembered the man from my prison visits. "We've been cut off from everything for two days. What's going on out there?" I asked anxiously.

"An hour ago, the army announced its neutrality," the caller went on excitedly. "The Joint Chief of Staff disappeared; the Commander of the Ground Forces was killed; the Commander of the Air Force was arrested; Bakhtiar fled the country!"

"It all seems so unreal," I said, my spirits beginning to rise slowly. "So, why doesn't the fighting end? Our neighborhood is still a war zone!"

"I suppose the Imperial guards are resisting in some areas. They stand no chance, though," the man said with confidence.

"What news from inside the garrison?" I shouted in the phone. "Have you heard anything about the prisoners there? I'm so worried for my husband."

"The garrison's quiet. No one knows for sure what's going to happen later. Some people, expecting amnesty from the new regime, have managed their way here to get their prisoners. I've come for my brother. I called in case you want to meet Dr. Sheikh, here," he said with great optimism.

The man spoke so assuredly, as if the doors of the garrison had already been opened and all the prisoners pardoned! I put my hand over the mouthpiece and briefly told my anxious family what I had just heard. Everyone screamed and applauded with sheer joy. We all forgot that our neighborhood was still in the midst of a battle.

"What do you think? Should I go to the prison?" I asked my family.

"It's suicide! How can you go through the center of a besieged city?" everyone objected.

"But they say the army's given up, and the fighting's over."

"Maybe so, but not in our neighborhood. Anyway, Shoja doesn't need an escort home," my brother-in-law said strongly.

I returned to the phone. "Sorry, I can't come. It's too dangerous. But, thanks for the news. Good luck on your brother's release."

Shortly after the man's call, the shooting died down. The combat seemed to be over. We finally had a chance to have our first meal of the day.

At 4:00 p.m., February 11, 1979, an exuberant voice interrupted the radio broadcast of a death march: **"Attention please! Attention please! The Revolution is triumphant! Congratulations, heroic nation of Iran! Congratulation on your great victory!"**

Next, we heard an obviously prerecorded revolutionary song. It was an indescribably happy moment. We all stood up with spontaneous exultation and screamed. "It's over! It's over!"

The Revolution had ended! People had triumphed!

Just at that moment, Armin came home in one piece. His young round face showed a flush of excitement. My sister rushed to her son with mixed feelings. She was grateful to God for his safety. Yet, she was angry enough to kill him for worrying her. Armin had sneaked out to see the street fighting, but because of the gunfire he was forced to take refuge in a neighbor's house.

"Is it safe to drive?" I asked my nephew, wondering if I could go to the garrison to be with Shoja.

"Absolutely not," Armin answered. "Our neighborhood is barricaded with sandbags. Fighting's expected to continue in some parts of the city between the Revolutionaries and the Monarchists. It's too risky to be out." His slightly slanted brown eyes shone with foresight as he spoke.

"Heard anything about the prisons being opened?" I asked again.

"No—but it seems logical. I understand your concern for Uncle Shoja, but with all the changes, he'll be just fine," he consoled me.

We stopped our conversation to listen to the news on the radio. The newsman, without giving a full account of events, declared boastfully: **"The war is won! The treacherous Monarchists are defeated! The Iranian nation is now free!"**

We smiled at each other. A free nation, at last! The newsman, with a voice shrill with authority, went on, "Everyone's allegiance is required! Soldiers must give up their weapons! All previous prisoners will be free! Members of the former regime must turn themselves in! **Surrender guarantees amnesty!**"

Babak and I hugged each other and cried. Together, we had survived the worst nightmare of our life. Shoja's ordeal had come to an end! The new government had just promised to release all prisoners immediately!

Once more, the phone blasted. For a second, I could not believe the voice who called my name.

"My God! Where are you, Shoja?" I shouted with joy.

"Out in the street," he said, panting heavily. "The prison doors opened. We all ran! I escaped death by inches!"

"Are you all right?"

"Yes. No time to go into that now. Is our neighborhood safe?" he asked rapidly.

"No! The militants still control the street leading to the army camp. No one can pass through. Stay away tonight, sweetheart."

"Stay away?"

"Yes! Come home tomorrow, when the streets are safe. Call me! Okay?"

"Where am I supposed to go tonight? With no transportation, no money? I left everything behind when I ran!" He sounded so powerless.

"Well, the radio just announced that all former prisoners who surrender will be pardoned," I reported. "They're promising public amnesty!"

"Surrender? I don't know. What do you think, Azar?" Shoja asked after a short pause.

"If you're going to live in this country, I think you have no choice, sweetheart. Do you?"

Another pause, this time longer. "You may be right. I'll surrender!"

He abruptly hung up the phone. There were no good-byes. Shoja was running for his life.

My spirits sank. Doubts began to invade my thoughts. *What if I am wrong? What if there is no amnesty ? Why didn't it occur to me to suggest that he flee Tehran, and if need be, Iran?*

Around 8:00 p.m., Dr. Boomand, Shoja's colleague, called. "Congratulations! The Pahlavis are toppled, at last," he laughed. "Fifty years of Reza and Mohammad Reza's—

the father and son's—oppressive rule is over!"

The phone lines were disrupted by static. I had trouble hearing him.

"Listen, Shoja's out of prison, on his way to turn himself in," I shouted.

"I know! I know! As we speak, he's here with me at my office," Boomand reported. "Dr. Mola'i, another close friend, is here too. We have decided to go together to Ayatollah Khomeini's temporary headquarters. It just happens that our mutual friend Esmail Yazdi, the oral surgeon, has an older brother named Ebrahim who is one of the Ayatollah's top advisors. He'll help Shoja."

"Let me speak with my husband, please."

"We're in a hurry. He'll contact you later. Better yet, wait until tomorrow. He'll be home by then!"

Dr. Boomand's voice reached my ears even through the static. His happiness was catching. My doubts instantly disappeared.

"Wait! Tell Shoja that I am proud of him. And you, no matter how late tonight, please call to let me know what's happening. Oh, one more thing—tell Shoja I love him."

It seemed like an endless time before Dr. Boomand reported back, precisely at midnight.

"The authorities respectfully received Shoja at the temporary detention center within Ayatollah's headquarters," Boomand said. "They promised to tend to his case in less than three days. Isn't it wonderful?"

"Three days? Before, you said he'd be home tomorrow!"

"What's a couple more days after so many months?" Shoja's friend chuckled.

He is right, I thought. Shoja will be home soon, and, this time, I will not let him out of my sight!

After many sleepless nights, I had just closed my eyes when Roxana and Ramin called. They were anxious to know how we were holding up in the face of the Revolution.

"Mom! Is it true that the fighting is over? Are you all okay?"

"What about Dad? Is he still in jail? What will happen to him now?"

"Mom! Take Babak and leave Iran right away. Can you get out soon? Could Dad escape somehow?"

The children were throwing rapid questions at my exhausted mind.

"Stop! Listen! It's all over. Do you hear, sweethearts? It's all over, and your father's safe and almost free. He'll be home in a few days!" I said jubilantly. "Then, we'll decide about the future. Do you hear me?"

They cheered. They laughed. They believed as I did. My distant children's shouts of joy traveled across thousands of miles. Victory had brought us together!

CHAPTER EIGHT

The next morning, Babak and I ventured out to see what was left of our neighborhood, of our home. Quite a risky decision. The shops were closed. Neighbors were still in hiding, experiencing the aftershock of Revolution. Above the entrance gates to the army camp, now in the hands of the Revolutionaries, two white flags waved in the breeze. The militiamen, or *Pasdars*, wearing green fatigues, toted heavy artillery, seized from military arsenals last night. They appeared tired and unkempt, but proud. A few of them were loading the blanketed body of a martyr into a waiting ambulance as two dazed men took off their caps in respect of the dead. Someone hosed blood off the street and into the drains.

We moved on cautiously. Our small, insignificant Mosque bustled with activity. It had become the home of the local Revolutionary *Komiteh*—committee—which now controlled our neighborhood. Komitehs acted as local security forces until the resurrection of the army, police force, and gendarmerie. Zealot Revolutionaries had taken the place of the worshipers at the Mosque.

Two hundred feet away, alongside the bakery, a young boy

with hands cracked from the cold played with a gun. This was a trophy he had pillaged from the ransacked garrison. He seemed oblivious to the changes.

Most houses facing the camp, including Amir Hosain's, were marred where bullets impacted into the walls, as if they had been afflicted with smallpox. The walls surrounding a neighbor's house had given way from the detonating grenades.

Halfway from my brother's house, we were stopped by the teenage neighborhood bully, Hasan—his gun pointed at Babak's chest.

"Satan tells me to end the life of the *Vazir's* son with one shot," he shouted.

Fear charged through me like an electric current. My entire body went numb. Babak turned ashen. The gun had given a maddening sense of power to this poor boy, who harbored many resentments towards the upper class. He was ready to carry out his threat. My son was about to be killed, and I was totally helpless.

"Hey! Stop! What on earth do you think you're doing? Having a gun doesn't give you the right to kill. Put that down. Now!"

Hasan spun around to confront the face behind the imposing voice. It was Amir Hosain. His hands balled into fists, his strong jaw extending out. As if by divine intervention, my brother had come to our rescue. Their furious eyes met in silence. Horror clinged to the passing seconds. The ruffian yielded. He pulled back his gun and walked away, leaving behind a penetrating aura of contempt.

"Azar, you and Babak return home, immediately. The streets are not safe yet," Amir Hosain warned. "Go home!"

We ran back, panting and stumbling, knowing we were barely escaping with our lives, only to face another shock. Three armed men in green fatigues between the ages of eighteen and twenty were trying to break through the front gate of our own house. We froze.

"Ex...cuse me, gentlemen. Can I help you with... something?" I faltered.

A man sporting a Stalin-like mustache tossed me half a glance. "We don't need anyone's help to burn this house of corruption down!" the sour-faced *Pasdar* answered. He carried a can of kerosene.

These Revolutionaries were intoxicated with the new power of destruction. We were at their mercy.

"But... this is my home," I implored as I stepped forward, my voice still weak with fear.

"No! This is the house of that traitor Sheikh, who escaped from the prison last night," he sneered. "The *Komiteh* wants to even the score. C'mon, comrades, he's probably hiding inside!"

"Listen! My husband has turned himself in to the authorities."

"Out of my way," he ordered.

"If you don't believe me, call the Refah Alavi School, the temporary detention center, where he's being held. Please!"

A few neighbors, alerted by the presence of the *Pasdars*, gathered around not daring to interfere. Then, things began to happen fast. Pushing through the gate, the leader signaled to his fellow conspirators. One of them spilled the kerosene around the nearest tree—a solid poplar that had been standing firm for ages. Another held the lethal matches in plain view, poised to strike, wanting to start the conflagration. Soon, our beautiful home would be destroyed. Instantly, I threw myself in front of the leader.

"This is madness. Totally unfair—unjust! I told you my husband's not here. How else can I convince you?" I pleaded.

The man struck the match. Enraged and startled, Babak disregarded his own safety, and grabbed the man's arm. "Please, stop that! I swear my father gave himself up. You've got to believe us," he demanded.

The leader studied Babak's innocent face for a few seconds. The boy's boldness meant that he must be telling the truth. The leader commanded his comrades, "Hold on! Let's radio the headquarters to check it out."

The radio communication revealed the truth. Shoja was not an escapee. Our home received a temporary reprieve from being burned down. Babak and I resumed breathing. But our fear lingered on. We realized that the victory of the people was not our victory. Indeed, our real confrontation with the people had only begun!

The following day, the local *Komiteh* announced that all males, fourteen years and older, must register for patrolling and guarding neighborhood streets, until trained *Pasdars* took over. Babak and his nineteen-year-old cousin, Armin, were not excluded. Alarmed, I put a scarf on my head, and rushed to the Mosque to speak with the Mullah, Hadji Sharifi. The Mullah, who with his limited clerical training, previously served the neighborhood only concerning simple marital, burial, and religious matters, was now the Administrator of our *Komiteh*. In this new position, he handled secular problems, complaints, and grievances too. He had just finished his noon prayers, when I walked in.

Confidentially, I told him about the horrible incidents we had experienced and asked him to exclude Babak from patrol duty. "It is not wise to have my son on the street with a gun. Please, consider our circumstances."

The Mullah, a small, bearded man with a round belly and a kind face, disagreed.

"Now that, with God's help and Imam Khomeini's guidance, our Revolution has borne fruit, it is every Moslem's duty to pay his dues. Participating in community services is important—especially for your son, considering his father's situation. He *must* prove himself. Go home! Kind and merciful God will watch over you and your son, Sister!"

I returned home dispirited, but with a new title. The Mullah had addressed me as "Sister", a term used by religious men for any woman who was not related by blood. He also addressed Ayatollah Khomeini as *"Imam"*—the spiritual leader—a title usually reserved for the saints.

After a rather long lesson on the use of a gun, Babak and Armin were assigned tacky uniforms and two Uzis. They would begin their tour of duty the same evening.

At 10:00 p.m., our two young men set off to maintain the curfew in our neighborhood until 5:00 a.m., and if necessary, to use their guns. They both seemed proud. My son, especially since his recent experiences, felt powerful.

"Don't misuse your rifles, please," I implored while hugging them. "Be careful!"

Aryan gave them a thermos of hot chocolate. Mother ceremoniously lifted the Qur'an and passed it over the heads of both grandsons as they left.

We worried all night for their safe return. Just last night, the Monarchists, who still held hope for the Shah's return, had attacked and seized the National Radio and Television building for a few hours. Several lost their lives, before the Revolutionaries counter-attacked, bringing the siege to a close.

What if a gun went off by accident and killed my son, or worse, someone deliberately killed him because of who he was? Hopefully, Shoja would be home any day. He would protect us!

Three days after the Revolution, I was restlessly looking out the window, anticipating Shoja's arrival, when from the living room, Babak called, "Mom! Come immediately!"

On the evening news, Hoveyda was shown at the temporary detention center. He looked uncharacteristically disheveled. The television camera scanned to one side of Hoveyda, to reveal the former head of SAVAK, Nasiri, who had gauze bandages wrapped around his head and neck. Had he been tortured after his capture on the eve of the Revolution? The former Mayor of Tehran, Nikpay, also appeared to have been injured. On the other side of Hoveyda, a familiar dear face. Shoja! He was wearing an odd black-and-white checked shirt. Where did he get that? And what was he doing on television with Hoveyda and the notorious Nasiri?

"Meet a few of the filthiest traitors of the former regime, captured while trying to escape," the newscaster addressed the nation.

"Liar!" Babak screamed. "My father never tried to escape. He turned himself in!"

Shoving the microphone at the captives, the announcer badgered, "Do you have anything to say?"

Hoveyda refused to comment.

Nasiri's response was inaudible.

"I am innocent," Shoja declared in a shaky voice. "Truth will prevail at my trial!"

"The Iranian nation is anxiously waiting for that day," chided the announcer. "You criminals will get what you deserve!"

"How could they line Shoja up next to the head of the SAVAK?" I asked with alarm. "No other publicity could be more damaging than this. What will happen now?"

My brother, Amir Hosain, who happened to be visiting, tried to downplay the importance of the broadcast. "Shoja will be fine. Sooner or later, the truth will come out, and he'll be released. We must be more concerned with the power struggle which is apt to begin among ideologically opposing groups, the Leftists, the Islamic zealots, and others. The future of Iran will depend on who wins."

Mother patted Babak on the shoulder. "Your father seemed okay, dear. Really, he wasn't hurt or anything."

It felt as if a big hole grew in my heart. All hopes for Shoja's immediate freedom vanished.

Early the next morning, the bullet-ridden pictures of the top generals of the Shah appeared across the front page of all the newspapers. They were executed by firing squad, Nasiri among them. Nasiri's notorious assistant in the SAVAK, Sabeti—the most feared man in Iran—had fled the country, unscathed. Lucky him! Oddly, no mention of General Fardoust, the Shah's closest confidant. Had he managed to escape, or had he betrayed the Shah by joining the new regime as the rumor had it? What happened to Nasseri/Azodi—the

SAVAK's hideous torturer? And, what would become of other political prisoners?

Later in the day, I received an alarming call from Dr. Aram, Shoja's previous deputy at the Ministry. "I just called to say good-bye. I'm leaving the country," he announced informally.

"What? Where are you calling from?" I asked. "The last time we met, you were in the prison."

"Can't say! I can only tell you this: Shoja should do the same, escape!"

"Escape? Don't you know? He's already turned himself in."

"I heard. Big mistake!" Aram said. "From the recent executions, it's obvious that the new government will show nothing but vengeance towards members of the old one. I wish Shoja hadn't fallen into their trap."

"Well, it's a bit late for you to tell me this now! You should've warned him sooner!" My hand went to my head and stayed there in frustration.

"I tried, but it all happened so fast. The garrison was attacked, and the prison doors opened. I quickly blended into the crowd. I figured, before the Revolutionaries found out who I was, I should hide."

"You mean you and Shoja didn't leave the prison together?"

"In that chaos, no one could find anybody! Look, it's still not too late for him to find a way to escape. Money could buy his freedom. Iran is no longer safe for us."

Through my sister's window, I saw a group of *Pasdars* breaking into a neighbor's house, an influential former judge who lived with his wife and their three children. I caught my breath, knowing that we could be next.

"Hello? Are you there?" Aram asked.

"Yes! I just witnessed something scary. Tell me, will your family leave too?" I inquired nervously.

"Ellen and the children are already in the States," Aram said with excitement.

"Good! And Reza Neqabat?"

"He fled the country a few days ago."

"Fled? Already? With the two of you gone, Shoja's innocence will be harder to prove," I said with some bitterness.

"You don't expect us to stay and be killed? Wake up! You should leave, too. Fifty thousand touman would get you across the border!"

"I'll wait for Shoja to come back before making such plans."

Shoja's former deputies were running to save their lives. Shoja was left alone. It seemed unfair that he would have no witnesses to defend him.

I needed desperately to consult with Shoja's friends in regard to the recent events. There were only two persons that I could think of. Those were the ones who had turned Shoja in on the night of the Revolution. Dr. Boomand was nowhere to be found. Dr. Mola'i agreed to visit me at my sister's home. Despite a medical degree from the States, he remained a fanatically religious man. Mola'i had even converted his American wife to Islam. He had also been active in the Revolution. His record qualified him to have influential contacts within the new regime.

"Congratulations. *Alhamdollah*—Thank God—the Satanic regime has been ousted," Dr. Mola'i said as he entered my sister's living room. He made himself comfortable in a large armchair. With chubby cheeks, and a round protruding stomach, Mola'i showed himself as a man who enjoyed life. He also carried jade prayer beads in his hand to show that he was a faithful Moslem.

"Have you heard about Shoja?" I asked.

"Of course! I was there when he turned himself in," Mola'i gloated "I even lent him a shirt. He almost got killed that night, you know."

"No. I don't know anything. What happened to Shoja?"

Mola'i found an opportunity to exercise his oratorical skill. "Well, on February 11th, the Shah's army realized its defeat. All military personnel abandoned the garrisons and fled to save their lives. When the Jamshidieh garrison was attacked by the mob, the young private, guarding the entrance gates, was the only soldier remaining at his post. He would not open the steel gates until his commanders ordered him. The commanders had already saved their skins and fled. The Revolutionaries had to shoot the poor fool. In a floodlike motion, the mob rushed past the private's half-dead body. Soon the entire place was under their control. The weapons were seized. The prisoners were set free!"

"Is this when Shoja escaped?" I asked.

"Yes. He quickly made his way through the euphoric crowd and headed towards the gates. A few more steps, and he would have been out. But then he heard the private moaning on the ground. He pulled the body aside, took off his shirt, and pressed it on the injured man's chest to stop the bleeding. He also administered CPR, but the private was not meant to live. The naive soldier's loyalty to his post cost him his life."

"Hmph!" I interrupted. "If the Shah, self-appointed Chief

Commander, had only a grain of this soldier's courage, we wouldn't have had this bloody Revolution!"

"The Revolution was God's blessing on this nation!" Mola'i sternly corrected me.

"What did Shoja do next?"

"Well, the crusaders went on a rampage: breaking locks, shattering windows, destroying icons of the Shah, looting ammunition storage areas. Shoja left the body and turned to run, when he felt a gun against his forehead."

"What happened then?"

"A young man—perhaps a student—ordered, 'put up your hands and let's go.' Shoja obeyed," Mola'i continued. "The people swarmed past. When Shoja and his captor reached the street, the young man stopped. 'I know who you are, the traitorous former Minister of Health,' the Revolutionary student said. 'But you tried to save that dying man. I respect that. I'll let you go, before you're lynched by the mob. Run!' Shoja dashed off in the opposite direction."

"Oh, God! He might've got killed!"

"Before long, though," Mola'i added, "the freedom fighters recognized the true identities of the prisoners they had released. Someone yelled 'Don't let them get away! These are not ordinary prisoners! They're the Shah's criminals!' The chant 'Catch the *Savakis*! Catch the *Savakis*!' echoed through the night. The crowd ran everywhere in search of escapees. Nasiri, the former chief of SAVAK, was the first to be caught and brutally— but justly—beaten. His arrest fueled the passion to find the others. Hunting for the criminals continued late into the night."

"What happened to Shoja?" I asked impatiently.

"Well, shirtless in the bitter cold, he kept on running until he reached a safe place to phone you. In the distance, he could see smoke billowing across the sky, as if the whole city were ablaze, pronouncing the victory of our Revolution."

Mola'i seemed enchanted by the sound of his own words.

"Shoja's former deputies have fled Iran. Could this affect my husband's freedom?"

"It could. From what I hear, his trial is imminent. I have spoken to several prominent clerics on his behalf. Let's hope, with God's grace, his outcome will be favorable."

"But Boomand talked of immediate freedom, not a trial!"

"Be grateful for his life, and pray for him," my husband's colleague warned. "An influential hard-liner can order Shoja's execution at any time! Especially now that those two Americans from EDS escaped."

"When?"

"On the same night all prisons were seized."

"Would their escape change things for Shoja?" I cracked the knuckles on my hands nervously.

"One must expect some punitive measures by the government. After all, this is an international conspiracy!"

Dear God, have mercy on us!

The next day, Hushang and I drove to the Ayatollah's temporary headquarters, where Shoja was being detained. We hoped that the authorities would provide some information. The lack of news from Shoja was killing me.

This was my first travel to the city in weeks, and I was shocked by the changes. Both sides of the streets were lined with homeless villagers, waiting hopefully for their share of the victory. The Ayatollah had promised them that the new government would "take from the oppressors and distribute among the oppressed."

The peddlers were back in full force on Shah Reza Avenue, now named *Inqelab*—Revolution. The bookstalls were brimming with political and philosophical books. Documentaries on the Bolshevik Revolution and Mao's life were being sold, along with books on the Iranian Constitutional Revolution of 1905, and the recent Islamic Revolution. These "forbidden" publications would have been burnt by SAVAK, as would the people selling and buying them!

The most conspicuous change, however, was in the way the majority of people now dressed. Women were wearing either *chadors* or long-sleeved gray or black robes and thick head scarves. Men had put aside their ties and had donned open-necked white shirts, and plain dark jackets. Beards of any length identified men as pro-Islamists, while thick Stalin-like mustaches associated them with the Communists. Suddenly, Hushang and I became self-conscious about our Western clothes. We felt out of place among our fellow countrymen. We still belonged to the old regime.

Even as early as last year, I had noticed some of my students at the university had changed their attire in an attempt to make a political statement. *Chadors* and black or camouflage shirts and pants, and military boots had become popular among the students. At that time, it was the look of the impending revolution. Now, of course, this dress code had given the Revolutionaries a sense of national identity.

Revolutions have usually imposed new fashions and banned certain items of clothing. In Stalin's Communist Russia, silk stockings were considered a flaunting of luxury.

Mao's uniform style in China left no room for a Western look. This Iranian Revolution was no exception.

I looked up past the people and saw Iran's new flag displayed above every shop, waving in a silent celebration. The flag's three horizontal stripes of green, white and red had remained. The centerpiece, however, had been changed. The old symbols of a sun and a lion holding a sword were gone. Instead, an encircled religious motto in Arabic calligraphy—there is no God save Him—had become the new centerpiece. The theocratic regime left no doubts that *Allah* would be Iran's only protector.

Posters with verses exhorting the purpose of the Revolution were everywhere. Pictures of Ayatollah Khomeini were scattered everywhere too. Iranians had found a new icon.

Refah Alavi, an Islamic high school for girls, was now the temporary headquarters of the Ayatollah, and the new detention center for the top political prisoners. Located in a working-class district, the featureless three-story building was guarded like a fortress. Hundreds of pilgrims had gathered here today in hopes of catching a glimpse of their spiritual—and now their national—leader.

Some two hundred yards away, our car was stopped by the *Pasdars*. "Go back! No one without special I.D. may enter this area," one of them ordered.

"Could you perhaps tell us if the recent political prisoners are still kept here?" Hushang asked in a polite tone.

"Uh huh, at least till the prisons are fixed. They took a real beating during the takeover," the guard said overconfidently.

The *Pasdars* held the crowd back with their clubs as a black limousine Cadillac transporting several high-ranking officials of the new order entered the school. From behind that austere building, a handful of people were determining the future of a nation, and the future of my husband. There was no way to get in there. Hushang and I had to surrender to the situation and drive away in our Western clothes.

The evening television broadcast began with coverage of the ex-royal palaces. "Look how the royalty exploited the nation," the commentator announced, as the camera panned the palace of Princess Shams, the Shah's eldest sister.

"It's like a huge clamshell with a glass top. The garden with exquisite bushes and trees, water fountains and beautiful chirping birds is quite a picture out of a fairy tale. Some life! The Shah and his family were parasites living off the Iranian people," the announcer concluded.

Our house was attacked again by a band of thugs who tried unsuccessfully to break in the iron gate. These days attacking upper-class homes had become fashionable. I rushed to the Mosque to file a grievance against this criminal act. Several other plaintiffs waited before me to explain their problems openly.

A young man with a birthmark on his forehead complained to the Mullah, "We didn't fight a revolution so our children could die from hunger! My wife's breast milk has dried up. We can't get formula for our twins. For God's sake do something!"

"My son has vanished," a second plaintiff, a lean, disheveled, middle-aged father reported. "Three nights ago, he went to buy bread and never returned. He may be dead or arrested. God Almighty! My son was a Moslem blue-collar worker—not a *Savaki* or a *Vazir!*"

The word "*Vazir* " stung my ears. Until a few months ago, it was very prestigious to be a cabinet member. Now, "*Vazir*" was synonymous with "criminal."

"Brother, help me," a woman pleaded to the Mullah. "My husband kicked me out today. He just opened the door, threw me into the street, and said 'don't come back, or I'll kill you.'" As she cried, her white polka-dotted *chador*—a long scarf worn from head to toe—fell open to expose her battered arms and neck.

"Is this the result of his beating? Does he hurt you often?" the Mullah asked sympathetically.

"Every now and then. I'm not complaining about these little bruises. I just want him to take me back," the battered woman responded.

The Mullah invited everyone to be silent. "Patience is the key to open all doors! My brethren, it has been only a week since our victory, and we must exhibit patience and wait for things to stabilize and take their natural course. The word 'revolution' itself contains all the answers! It means 'change'. A corrupt system has been turned over and replaced by a virtuous one. By the grace of God, things will change for the better."

"But brother, I have no place to sleep tonight," the woman cried.

"Sister, you may stay here until we resolve things with your husband. Islam will not tolerate men beating their women! It's a sin."

I moved forward to voice my complaint quietly. The Mullah listened attentively.

"Sister, the undisciplined men who are attacking your home are not from this neighborhood. They come from the inner city, and we can do nothing to stop them. Take your grievance to the

Komiteh at the Youth Center, which oversees the region. *Inshallah*, they can help you," he advised.

Obviously *Komitehs* had grown overnight like wild mushrooms. How many of them existed?

Since I was afraid to go back to our own house for my car while the thugs were around, I decided to walk to the Youth Center *Komiteh*, some three miles away. It was not a pleasant walk in a cold drizzle with the wrong shoes, but I was determined. As its name implied, the Youth Center, up to a while ago, had been a recreational facility for the young people. Now, things were different for the new patrons of the *Komiteh*. Boys with shirts opened to the waist displaying gold chains, and girls in miniskirts and fancy hairdos, had been replaced by somber uniformed Revolutionary guards. Loud rock 'n roll music had given way to the soft chanting of the Qur'an. The tennis courts were filled with rows of confiscated Mercedes.

"Where is one to report a complaint?" I asked a guard.

He looked at my Western clothing disdainfully. "Until further notice, complaints must be directed to the Qoba Mosque. Ask for the Hojatolislam, Dr. Mofatteh."

I had heard of the name. It was rumored that Dr. Mofatteh was from the Ayatollah Khomeini's inner circle and a member of the secret Revolutionary Council. His two titles also revealed that this cleric was one rank below an Ayatollah, and held a Ph.D. too.

Despite blisters on my feet, I rushed to Qoba Mosque, ten blocks away. Crossing the street, a taxi hurtled by, spattering mud all over me. Wet and soiled, I continued on my search for justice.

When I arrived, the devout Moslem men were being summoned to evening prayer by the cries of the *Muezzin*. I was led into the Mosque's small library. The librarian, a young man with round black spectacles and a three-day beard, was conversing with a chap in impoverished clothing. "Brother, here's 350 touman to cover your overdue rent. *Inshallah*, you'll find a job soon and won't need our help," he said.

"God bless you," the needy man said. His bleary eyes flashed as he hid the money in his sheepskin cap and walked out.

This was a familiar scene. In Islam, the Mosque has always been a source of public provision for the relief of the poor.

"Is there something I can do for you, Sister?" The librarian addressed me. His rigid voice indicated that he did not approve of a woman visiting him alone in his workplace.

"Yes. I would like to have a few words with Dr. Mofatteh, if possible. I was told I could find him here."

"I'm afraid my father is at prayer now and can't see you."

So, he was Dr. Mofatteh's son. "May I wait until your father is finished?"

"What do you need to see him about?"

"To ask for help. People have been harassing my family." Then, I told him briefly about my husband's arrest and the incidents following.

"You're the ex-*Vazir*'s wife?" he asked with resentment.

"Does it matter whose wife I am? No one should be afraid to live in her own home. My son and I are not safe."

"Sister, I don't believe you'll be able to see my father this evening," the librarian said sternly. "We are having a Qur'an study class here for students tonight. Come back some other time."

The following day when I entered the library, the librarian glanced up from the pages of a book he was reading and frowned. It seemed hard to get rid of me. He used a lame excuse. "Sister, my father has a very busy schedule. Perhaps, you should return to the Youth Center *Komiteh* in regard to your problem," he suggested curtly, and resumed his reading. I did not budge. It was imperative for me to speak to his father.

Evidently, my married name had turned him off, and he was giving me a runaround. In an effort at friendliness, I leaned forward and pointed to his book. "I see that you are studying Plato's *Republic*. Do you like philosophy?"

"Guess so. It's part of my major," the unfriendly librarian answered. Reluctantly, the young man revealed that he was a student at the theological seminary and intended to follow in his father's footsteps.

"That's interesting!" I said. "My brother, a professor at the University of Tehran, also taught at the seminary for a while. You may know him. He is a sociologist."

"What's his name?" he asked.

"Dr. Amir Hosain Aryanpour."

He inclined his head in acknowledgment. "Really? Why didn't you tell me sooner? I have a lot of respect for him," the librarian said with a change of attitude. Then, from a shelf, he lifted one of my brother's books, *The Sociology of Art*. "I've read this. Not that I agree with all his views, but I do think he is a great teacher," he added.

The fact that a copy of my brother's book was stacked in this religious library seemed astounding. Now, the young man saw me in a different light. I was no longer the wife of the infamous *Vazir*, but the sister of the highly esteemed professor.

"Sister, come back Friday. My father will see you then, after the noon prayer," Mofatteh's son assured me.

Friday was five long days away.

Two days later, I was bedridden with a flu when Mother called from downstairs.

"Azar, someone wishes to speak with you on the phone. You up to it?"

I jumped out of the bed. It could be news from Shoja.

The voice belonged to an anonymous caller: "*Khanom*, I must see you for a confidential message. Come to No. 17 Fawzia Street, second floor, at seven o'clock—alone!" There was some urgency in his tone.

I looked at my watch. It showed a few minutes before 6:00 p.m. In a normal traffic day, it would take me forty-five minutes to get to Fawzia, located in the busy southeastern Tehran. I began to get dressed for the meeting instantly.

"You don't really mean to go all the way across the city tonight to see this stranger!" Mother protested. "You're not well. And how do you know his call was real? Haven't you heard the stories about women like you being attacked, their faces disfigured by acid? There are people out there waiting to take vengeance wherever they can get it."

"Mother, please! I must go. It could be important."

"Obviously, you've made up your mind. At least, have someone go with you. Okay?"

Amir Hosain volunteered to drive me, but promised to wait in the car. If I did not show up within fifteen minutes, he would look for me.

At seven o'clock sharp, I climbed the stairway of a dingy

tenement to the second floor, then walked into a poorly furnished room, partitioned into two sections by thick drapes. My body was stiff and tense, aware of unknown danger. This side appeared to be a waiting area. At the sound of my feet, a slight man with nondescript mien materialized from behind the drapes. He was wearing a badly cut suit and no tie. He glanced around to make sure I was alone. "In here," the stranger croaked. I walked to the other side. The man closed the drapes.

That side was an examination room: a bed, a basin, and a trolley cart filled with medications. Was the stranger a physician serving the overpopulated, poor community of Fawzia? If so, the doctor's hours were over. What would I do if this man took it into his head to attack me? How would I defend myself? Realizing my vulnerability in the presence of a total stranger, I took a quick, clumsy step backward. It was too late to escape. The man's hand searched for something in his pocket. A gun? I went cold all over. He took out a small crumpled-up piece of paper and held it before my eyes. I was bewildered.

"W...What's this? You said you had a message for me," I faltered.

"Please, no details," the man lowered his voice in a whisper. "By chance, yesterday, I saw your husband at the Refah Alavi School—the temporary detention center. He gave me this to pass on to you."

I recognized Shoja's handwriting on the note. It read:

"I have been here 12 days. Seems like 12 years. Save me!"

This was a definite message of an imminently life-threatening situation. It was a desperate cry for help. A surge of panic raced through me. I put my hand on my throbbing, feverish forehead. "Has he been tortured?"

The man peeked uneasily behind the drapes and turned to me. "He seemed all right—physically—but as I told you, no details."

"If I write a few lines, would you take them to him?"

"No. I've already taken too many risks."

"Then please, if you see my husband again, tell him I'll do everything in my power to help him."

The stranger nodded as he struck a match to burn the note.

I flew down the stairwell, skipping one or two steps at a time. Back in the car, I burst out with tears. "Amir, Shoja's finished! We won't see him alive again!"

"What happened?" Amir Hosain asked anxiously.

I breathlessly discussed the note with my brother.

"It's not over yet, Azar. We'll do something," he consoled in a fatherly manner.

"How? We don't know anyone in the new regime. It's all my fault. If I hadn't told Shoja to turn himself in, he would be free now. I'm to blame for his death!" I cried.

At night, my fever ran so high that I became incoherent.

CHAPTER NINE

Turned from all doors, I come at last to thee
If thy door is denied, where shall I be?

Baba Taher (Twelfth Century)

On Friday, still weak from the flu and depressed by the alarming note, I left for Qoba Mosque. The weather had turned mild and the earth was breathing again. I lingered outside the library waiting for the noon prayer to end. Mofatteh, escorted by two bodyguards, exited the Mosque. The high-ranking clergy was wearing a stylish camel *aba*—a long, loose cloak—and a white turban. I ran after him, and before he got into his car, called, "*Agha*! Please, may I speak with you for a moment?"

Everyone stopped. The guards pointed their guns at me.

"Sister, is there something that you want?" Mofatteh asked calmly. He was a stately man, with a medium build and a soft voice.

"Yes, if these men with the guns allow me!" I answered, tucking down my head scarf.

Mofatteh motioned for the guards to lower their rifles. I introduced myself. "My husband has been detained with no word of a trial or release. I have been granted no visits with him. People have been trying to break into my house, and my son and I are fearful for our lives. I am here to ask for your help, Agha," I pleaded rapidly.

"Sister, Imam Khomeini has given strict orders that no one should enter another's home without a search warrant," the preacher of God said calmly. "As to your husband's situation, he and the rest of the political prisoners will be sent to Qasr Prison and given a fair trial soon. The visitation will be up to the prison administration. Is there anything else?"

His question sparked an idea.

"Yes! I have another request. Is it possible to send my husband a change of clothes?"

"A prisoner has little need for clothes, Sister," he asserted.

"Then, tell me if it is right for a Moslem to do his prayers in soiled garments?"

I had hit the right nerve. The religious man's serious face relaxed into a smile. "Sister, this afternoon you may bring a small parcel to my office at the Youth Center *Komiteh*. I will see that your husband gets it," he offered.

"Thank you, sir!"

Back at home, I grabbed some food, rested for a while, and then jotted down a very short letter for Shoja. My letter lacked intimacy and real content, but even this small note might be rejected by the censors. I placed it between the set of pants and shirts in a plastic bag, and left for the Youth Center.

Mofatteh's guards searched me and my parcel thoroughly before I entered the room.

"*Khanom*," the cleric addressed me formally. "Have you brought the parcel?"

I handed him the bag. He left it on his desk. Then, his face took a puzzling expression and his voice a didactic tone. "My son told me about your brother. How strange that the sister of such a respectable man could become the wife of an agent of a dictator." His forehead wrinkled in distaste.

"*Agha,* as much as I am proud to be Amir Hosain's sister, I am even prouder to be Shoja's wife. My husband is a devoted physician and a unique person who simply served the previous government. He never sold himself to the system. If you remember, it was the Shah who ordered his arrest."

"So be it, *Khanom.* You may go now," he said. "By the grace of God, you will see your husband soon. If you have any more difficulties, contact me."

Despite Mofatteh's candid disapproval of my husband, he did not sound quite like an enemy. Or, perhaps, I needed to think I could trust him.

The Qasr Prison repairs were almost finished. The same people who only weeks ago had attempted to destroy this place, like the rest of the prisons, and free the prisoners, had now restored it to accommodate new "tenants." Qasr, a former palace for the Qajars—the previous dynasty which ruled Iran for over 130 years—was a fortress surrounded by high concrete walls topped with barbed wire and guard towers. The steel gate opened across a vast plaza, which had once been asphalted but was now a deteriorated mass of cement and dirt. To my surprise, hundreds of people, mostly women, had gathered to inquire about their imprisoned relatives. They were, more or less, in the same situation as I was.

"Excuse me," I addressed an insolent *Pasdar*, "have all the political prisoners been transferred to Qasr?"

"If you mean the criminals of the former regime, yes. They're all here," he taunted me.

I swallowed my anger. "When do we get to visit them?"

"Pray that they haven't been executed, let alone allowed visitors!"

I quickly distanced myself from that evil man and mingled among the crowd. Over the loudspeakers positioned on either side of the prison gate, we were ordered to disperse. Nobody moved. Two military jeeps, roaring and honking, crept their way through the startled crowd and stopped in front of the steel gate to unload prisoners. Handcuffed men were shoved out of the jeeps, kicked and handed over to the *Pasdars* who in turn pushed them into the prison to start an uncertain ordeal.

"What crimes have these poor people committed to get such beatings?" a woman asked a male bystander.

"What else but a show of brutality to intimidate us? These days one doesn't need a reason to arrest and punish anyone," the man explained with dismay.

"You are just as heartless as the SAVAK," the woman shouted, waving her fist towards the *Pasdars*.

Others began chanting slogans.

"We gave lives for freedom!"

"We want justice!"

"Death to *Pasdars*!"

From the guard towers, shots were fired into the air. Frightened people ran wildly in all directions, creating a chaos. Those trampled were hosed down with cold water. I ran to take refuge in a small vegetable shop, where two other women were also hiding. The owner rolled down the metal door and turned on a light. We heard more screams and shots before people were finally "dispersed."

Determined to get some information about Shoja, I dared myself to return to Qasr a couple days later. Two long lines of people had formed in the prison plaza.

"What are these lines for?" I asked a woman.

"This line's for those who've been granted visits today, like me. The other one is for those who yet have to find out, like you."

"Did anyone call you about your visit?"

"No, someone over there told me," she pointed at the guardhouse. "Get in that other line to find out."

After an hour and forty-five minutes of waiting in the second line, I reached the guardhouse.

"Prisoner's name?" the *Pasdar* asked.

I gave Shoja's full name.

"Former position?"

"Uh, Minister of Health and Social Welfare."

He gave me a haughty stare. His finger began to search down one list and then the other. "No such name! Try your luck next week!" Disappointed and confused, I left the plaza. Where could Shoja be? How come his name did not appear in the guard's list? Was he still held at the School?

Fifty feet away, two familiar faces took me by surprise. I had not seen Mrs. Asfia and Mrs. Khalatbari since that showy royal gala to honor Romania's dictator Ceausescu and his wife ten months ago. Ten long months ago.

I approached them cautiously. Their husbands, both members

of Hoveyda's Cabinet, were in jail. Like me, they had no news of their men.

In Iran, the executions of high-ranking military officers continued. Although few civilians had been executed so far, my frustrations and fears mounted. My brother-in-law, Doctor, who was more worried about Shoja than he admitted, managed to persuade Hadji Sharifi, the neighborhood Mullah, to accompany us to the holy city of Qom, 100 miles south of Tehran. There, we would appeal for Shoja's freedom before Ayatollah Golpaigani, who was influential with Ayatollah Khomeini. The Mullah would be our official intermediary.

Early on Friday morning, we set out for Qom. Half asleep and sluggish, I sat in the back seat of the car listening partially to the conversation between the two men. Since the Revolution, the Mullah had become an instant expert on politics. From administrative to economic policies, he had an opinion on everything.

Southbound traffic was bumper-to-bumper. Honking horns accosted us from every side.

"How many children do you have, *Khanom*?" the Mullah asked, without looking back.

From under a black *chador*, borrowed from my mother's housekeeper, I answered, "Three." Wearing the *chador* was required for all women entering the holy city.

"*Mashallah*—Praise God. I have met one of your sons. He patrolled for us a few times—a fine young man."

My brother-in-law interjected. "He's taken after his father. Consider what Dr. Sheikh has done for the neighborhood alone. The man who owns the stationery shop next to the Mosque owes his life to Dr. Sheikh. If it weren't for him, the shopkeeper would've died from bone cancer. Dr. Sheikh personally paid for the man's prostheses and his wheelchair. That's only one example of Dr. Sheikh's benevolence. He really didn't deserve jail."

"God would not allow a kind deed to go unnoticed," the Mullah sighed.

"Look! Another innovation of Dr. Sheikh's Ministry," my brother-in-law pointed to a passing ambulance. "From anywhere in the city one can make a phone call and an ambulance will be dispatched immediately."

"The ambulances were very helpful during the height of the Revolution," the Mullah yawned. "This service alone would give Dr. Sheikh a place in heaven."

The rest of the trip was through barren, dusty desert land, forcing the imagination to come alive.

On the distant horizon, the golden dome of the holy shrine of Ma'sumeh rose like a sun. We were approaching Qom, the most important center of Shi'ite theological studies in Iran. The city, with low brick houses and flat roofs, was as usual busy with pilgrims visiting Ma'sumeh's shrine. Ma'sumeh was the sister of Imam Reza—the eighth male descendant of prophet Mohammad. Through Imam Reza, buried in the holiest Iranian city, Mashhad, and his sister, Ma'sumeh, buried in Qom, Islam's Shi'ite community was perpetuated in Iran. The Shi'a were followers of Imam Ali, the Prophet's cousin who had also become his son-in-law by marrying his daughter, Fatima. Historically, the Shi'a believed that the caliph should descend through the Prophet's lineage. Therefore, Ali and his male children by Fatima should hold Moslem authority and pass it on. In contrast, the Sunnis, who constituted 85 percent of the world's estimated 900 million Moslems, advocated Islam's leadership or caliphate through selection of the Prophet's closest associates. Moslem Iranians, however, were the followers of the Shi'ite version of Islam, and idealized Ali, the fourth caliph.

The Mullah suggested that we visit the Ma'sumeh's shrine first. We accepted. Ma'sumeh's vast chamber was elaborately decorated with mirrored walls, luxurious chandeliers, and elegant Persian carpets. In the center, her casket stood surrounded by gilt bars with arabesque designs and Arabic calligraphy. Chanting pilgrims crowded around, touching the shrine or hanging votive cloths on the bars while making wishes.

After *Vozu*, the ritual ablution, I went to an adjacent room for women, and standing towards Mecca and thinking of Shoja, I started to pray. Although I believed that religion was a personal dialogue between an individual and God and could take place anywhere, here, today, I felt peace.

Our next and final destination was Ayatollah Golpaigani's residence, which like most traditional homes, was made up of two sections. The exterior—*biruni*—comprised the Ayatollah's public office, consisting of a reception area, prayer room, and pantry. Behind the courtyard was the interior—*andaruni*—or his family's private home. In the middle of a sunken courtyard, a few old fig trees and a fountain provided a staging area, where the faithful washed before prayers. There were no bodyguards.

This was my first experience of visiting a high-ranking clergyman in his residence, so I closely scrutinized and imitated the Mullah's gestures. Before entering the birouni, we removed our shoes. The Mullah loudly greeted everyone in the all-male crowded room. "*Salam Alaikom*—Greetings to you." My brother-in-law and I followed suit. Men sat along the circumference of the room, which was furnished only with a carpet. We sat near the door, waiting for our turn to be heard. Being the only female in this gathering, I felt like an outcast, and receded further behind my borrowed *chador*.

Tea was served in small glass cups. The Ayatollah, frail and old, yet serene, in a black *aba* and turban, sat cross-legged at the upper part of the room, listening to each visitor. Next to him was a large metal alms box. As donors handed in gifts, a clerk recorded them in a ledger before dropping them into the box.

A humble man kissed the hands of the Ayatollah and handed him a small package. "Your Eminence, this money is for the poor." The Ayatollah nodded with approval and gave the man his benediction. His voice was weak but his words were clear and rhythmic.

Another gave a check. "My yearly religious obligation to Islam."

A third offered a gold ring. "This is for the Ma'sumeh's shrine."

The donors were numerous. The donations were abundant. Were such generous Moslems the significant financiers of the Revolution?

The Mullah found a chance to speak. "Your Eminence, we apologize for any inconvenience our visit may have caused. I, your servant, am here with two charitable citizens from Tehran to ask for your blessings. This well-known doctor is a pious Moslem. And, that lady is a relative of the doctor who has come on pilgrimage to Qom and to appeal for your Eminence's help. Her husband, a former Minister, is in prison."

The Ayatollah glanced at me curiously, but kindly. From

under the chador, I took out a long letter that I had specifically prepared for this occasion and handed it to the Ayatollah.

"*Agha*, this letter explains my husband's situation. Please read it and draw your own conclusions. I plead for your help, and pray for your justice," I said timidly.

As the cleric took the letter with his shaking hand, I realized my mistake! How stupid of me to call him *Agha*! What must he think of me—a female—addressing him, an Ayatollah, in the common term of respect? I quickly returned to my place, and hid within the safety of my *chador*.

A messenger came. Imam Khomeini, now residing in Qom, had summoned Golpaigani. With great effort, the aging Ayatollah got slowly to his feet and left to visit his mentor. We returned to Tehran.

I had reached out to *Allah* and a few of his chosen people today. They would hear me.

On March 11, at the prison guard station, Shoja's existence was finally identified: "Sheikholeslamzadeh, cell 4/1, no visitors!"

Shoja was alive! My prayers were heard! He was here at Qasr, although ripped of his title 'Doctor' and allowed no visits.

"Could you take this letter for my husband, please?" I asked almost cheerfully.

"No!" The guard threw scornful looks at me. "Mail it to Qasr. Make it brief—two or three lines only—or he won't get it." He puffed at his cigarette, and added, "And next time bring a set of fresh clothes for your prisoner. We don't provide laundry services here at Qasr," he jeered.

My first letter to Shoja in Qasr was just a short greeting:

"Dearest husband, I thank God for your life. How are you? Hope to see you soon. Keep up your faith. Yours forever, Azar."
Babak added one sentence: *"Dad, I miss you very much."*

Would Shoja receive our brief message?

A week before *Now Ruz*—the Iranian New Year—Mother returned to her own apartment. The city was relatively calm and she wanted to get ready for the holidays. Despite the early spring and the upcoming *Now Ruz*, no one seemed very festive. The aftermath of the Revolution had sucked the last breath of joy from most people, from me.

Mother invited Babak and I to move in with her. After nearly four months, my sister needed a break. All my problems had become hers. We accepted Mother's invitation. Shoja changed prisons. We changed homes! Where would we be next?

Mother suggested that I take up our case with Ayatollah Taleqani, second in the present hierarchy only to Imam Khomeini himself. Taleqani was more moderate than the other Ayatollahs, and had publicly voiced his disapproval of the recent death sentences imposed with summary trials. He might be of some help to us.

Outside his home, pilgrims had congregated in search of justice. Unfortunately Ayatollah Taleqani, suffering from years of torture in the Shah's prisons, seldom accepted visitors. One might, however, submit his or her request in writing. As I placed my appeal in the appropriate box, a peasant woman grabbed my arm. "I don't know how to write!"

I volunteered to write for her. The woman dictated something to this effect:

Mr. Ayatollah, Salam,

I took three busses, and did a lot of walking to get here today to ask for money. If I don't pay the landlord 75 touman by next week, my two fatherless children and I will be thrown into the streets. Please help. After God, you are all we have got. Allah bless you.

I also wrote a second letter on behalf of Shoja to the Islamic Revolutionary Prosecutor-General and personally delivered it to his office before it closed for the holidays. He was nowhere to be found. The secretary tossed my letter on top of an overflowing "IN" basket. I wondered if any of these petitions for justice would ever come to the attention of the prosecutor.

On March 21, 1979, we all gathered in Mother's apartment to celebrate *Now Ruz*, the beginning of the Iranian calendar year. *Now Ruz*, which dates back to the time of Cyrus the Great, over 2500 years ago, symbolizes rebirth. It is the most joyous national holiday in Iran. During a two-week festivity period, family and friends visit to exchange gifts and offer good wishes for the upcoming year. On the thirteenth day of *Now Ruz*, the holiday festivities culminate in an outdoor picnic.

Mother would always go to great lengths in preparation for *Now Ruz*. She would clean the house thoroughly, shop for new clothes, and prepare special holiday dishes. Because Father was the eldest child, his family would visit and have lunch with us on the first day of *Now Ruz*. He would give everyone a small gold coin or new paper money. After my paternal family left, we would visit my maternal family, in a hierarchical order—an ongoing process for thirteen days.

This year, like previous years, on Mother's traditional *Haft Seen* table, seven items beginning with the Farsi letter "seen" (S) were displayed: *Sonbol* (hyacinth), *Seer* (garlic), *Sekeh* (coin), *Sib* (apple), *Sweet Sumac*, *Samanu* (wheat pudding), and *Sabzeh* (green shoots). There were also two goldfish in a bowl. According to several thousand years of tradition, these symbolic items brought happiness, fertility, and blessing to the family. At the head of the *Haft Seen* table, two candles sat along with a mirror displaying brightly colored eggs. Legend had it that the eggs resting on the mirror would sway at the exact moment of the Vernal Equinox. On the thirteenth day of *Now Ruz*, out in a park, people would throw away the green shoots they had grown for the occasion. With them they hoped to discard the troubles of the old year, and begin fresh.

Today, I felt none of the joys experienced on holidays past. As much as the table of *Haft Seen* (seven S's) represented a perfect *Now Ruz*, my most precious "S"—Shoja—was missing. His absence hurt.

I remembered our last *Now Ruz* together. Right after Mother's New Year ceremony, we left for the Royal Palace. All government dignitaries and representatives of different classes were invited—and were expected—to attend the *Now Ruz* audience, to wish the Shah a happy and prosperous year. The wives were given an audience by Queen Farah in an adjacent all-mirrored receiving hall.

I wore a two-piece, light green and ecru silk suit with a matching hat. Shoja looked handsome in his formal attire. The men bowed to the Shah and received a gold Pahlavi coin, His Majesty's likeness stamped on its face. The attending women received a similar gift embossed with a picture of the coronation event.

This year, I was not wearing new clothes in observance of *Now Ruz*. I did not even wear a smile.

As the Vernal Equinox began, the television broadcast Premier Bazargan's *Now Ruz* speech. As the representative of the new regime, he promised the Iranian nation a safe and rosy future. It was hard for me to imagine when the present seemed so bleak.

Although Father had passed away three years ago, his family continued the tradition of visiting Mother on the first day of *Now Ruz*. When they arrived, I sneaked out the back door. I did not want to spoil their fun with my depressed mood.

Driving aimlessly around the quiet city with all shops closed for the holiday, I found myself at the perimeter of Qasr Prison. Facing the tall austere walls that separated my husband from me, I shouted into the wind, *"Now Ruz Mubarak*—Happy New Year, Shoja! There will be better years to come!"

Early in April, following a public referendum, the majority of Iranians voted for an Islamic Republic. Bazargan was reinstated as the head of the government. He ordered the schools to reopen. However, the institutes of higher education remained closed until all "anti-Revolutionaries" were weeded out from the student body, faculty, and administrators. Obviously, I would not be allowed to teach again. My teaching career in Iran was ended.

Thousands of Iranian students had returned from abroad to

observe the changes in Iran. Roxana and Ramin also wanted to quit college, and return home. With things as they were, they thought, the school was meaningless.

"If you come here," I warned them, "you may never be able to leave. The government's tightening travel restrictions. Do you know what that means? You'll be sacrificing your future, your dreams. Your father and I can't allow that."

Unwillingly, Roxana and Ramin accepted to stay in America.

It had been two days since the start of Hoveyda's trial. Denied an attorney, he had to defend himself. Last night, we had seen the ex-Prime Minister briefly on television. He looked totally dejected and depressed. The accusations against him were grave, but his international reputation might save him from death. His defense thus far had been based solely on the fact that the Shah gave him orders, and he obediently carried them out.

Anxious to follow Hoveyda's trial, I searched for the daily newspaper. "It hasn't been delivered yet," Babak said, avoiding my eyes. My son never lied, and so his face easily betrayed him. He must be hiding the paper from me.

"Have they written something vicious about your father?" I asked.

"No, it's Hoveyda."

"Let me see the papers! Now!"

Babak retrieved the latest edition of Ettela'at newspaper. On the front page Hoveyda's bullet-ridden body was displayed. Sadeq Khalkhali, the Tribunal Judge, had convicted Hoveyda of being "corrupter on earth" and "warring against

God." His sentence—death by firing squad—had been carried out last night. Khalkhali had fired the first shot!

The grotesque photograph nauseated me. Shoja was now in immediate danger because he had served under Hoveyda. With the ex-Prime Minister's death, Shoja's probable execution seemed imminent. No! I must not think in those lines. Shoja was going to live. He had to.

Still, the shadow of death hovered like a vulture over my consciousness. I needed to be alone. I ran to our abandoned home to find something of the past. Among scattered items in my drawers, I pulled out an album full of pictures of Shoja attending State functions. One photo featured he and Hoveyda smiling in front of Niavaran Palace immediately after Shoja's appointment as a cabinet member. It triggered memories.

The time was 1971 in the summer. I had taken our three children to a camp in the London suburbs. The kids were enjoying their camp activities, while I was enjoying sight-seeing in the country. To my disappointment, Shoja phoned to inform me that I might have to return any day.

"Why?" I recalled asking him. "I can't leave until the kids' camp is over."

"Hoveyda has nominated me for Minister of Health. You must be here when my appointment is announced," Shoja explained.

"What? Who on earth would choose a physician for a political position?" I asked, unimpressed.

"You can be sure it is not because I am so-and-so's son-in-law or nephew!" Shoja reacted, revealing his hurt male ego.

"I'm sorry, sweetheart. I don't mean to undermine your hard work and your ability. I just can't believe that in a country which operates mostly on favoritism, a self-made person would be even considered."

"Don't criticize the system on the phone! Do you want to get us into trouble?" Shoja warned.

"Sorry again! I still don't understand why a successful orthopedic surgeon needs to run for political office. Isn't being the Director of the Rehabilitation Center enough for you, Shoja?"

"Let's not argue for something which hasn't happened yet, love," Shoja softened his stance. "I'll call and let you know when to come home. In the meantime, be careful. You're in a strange country."

"Please, Shoja! I'm not a child, and this isn't my first trip to England, you know!"

"I still don't feel good about you traveling alone. Anyhow, I'll be in touch."

Shoja's call had been premature. His nomination was not approved by the SAVAK on the first round. Hoveyda was persistent. It took two more years before Shoja was sworn in on this day in the picture—April 28, 1973—as Minister of Social Welfare. The Ministry of Health followed soon after.

The photo of Shoja and Hoveyda in front of the royal residence documented a single moment, but seemed to hold the seeds of future calamity. For some odd reason, I kept it, tearing up all the others, including several pictures of Shoja with the Shah. I placed the scraps in a tin trash can, carried them out to the yard, and set them ablaze. A symbolic catharsis, to destroy all connections with the detested regime!

A few days after Hoveyda's execution, Mrs. Rouhani, the wife of the former Minister of Agriculture, phoned.

"Azar! This afternoon I'm going to see my husband—my first visit at Qasr! I'm so happy, I don't know what to do!" she shouted with excitement.

"That's great! Hope it goes well. Odd, no one's contacted me about visiting Shoja, though."

"Yeah, it's strange! Even Mrs. Khalatbari and a few others have visits today. Maybe you should contact the prison in case you missed their calls," Mrs. Rouhani advised.

"Thanks for telling me. Good luck with your visit." I ended the conversation abruptly to leave for the prison at once.

Later, at Qasr, I inquired from the prison guard, "*Agha,* please look at your lists and tell me if Dr. Sheikh can have visitors today."

The guard turned the pages in his book. "No. Next!"

My mouth dropped open. "But why?" I insisted, sensing the restless breath of the person behind me. "Other political prisoners are allowed visitors. Why not my husband?"

"Did you ever think that perhaps their situation is different? Maybe as in life or death, if you know what I mean," the heartless guard jeered.

Shoja might be on death row! I shuddered at my own thought and left the prison area immediately. I drove off quickly to Hushang's office. He was in the middle of a business meeting.

"I need to talk to you, right now—please—alone!" I told him.

He adjourned the meeting. "What's the matter, Sis? You look awful!"

"Shoja's on death row! That's why I can't see him. Other prisoners' wives have had visits," I blurted out.

"Wait a minute. There are hundreds of prisoners—perhaps even thousands. The new administration can't possibly arrange visits for all of them at once," Hushang tried to calm me down. "But if it makes you feel better, I'll contact a friend who works for the new government. He may've heard something."

"Hushang, hurry. I'm very scared!"

"I'll do my best, Sis. Go home, now. I'll call you as soon as I find out something."

My brother could not provide the assurance I desperately needed. Shoja's life was still unclear. Perhaps Dr. Mofatteh could help. He was my only connection with the new regime. I petitioned to him a third time with a flowery letter beginning with Qur'anic verses, *"Lo! My protector is Allah who has revealed the scripture. He is Hearer, Knower...."* , and pleaded for Shoja's life.

Mofatteh was a high-ranking clergy and I had to appeal to him in a special style. My letter must have impressed him since he invited me to the College of Theology where, aside from his political position, he was the Dean. Unlike his office at the Youth Center *Komiteh*, this one was lavish and the atmosphere more formal. He half rose as I entered and offered me a seat.

"I was very taken with your letter, Sister. Did you write it yourself?"

"We have been accused of robbing the nation, not plagiarism," I answered resentfully.

Mofatteh grinned broadly, but immediately lowered his gaze as the religion did not allow a man to look a woman in the eyes. "I did not mean to offend, but was merely complimenting you," he said. "Where did you go to school?"

His compliment did not distract me. This meeting was about Shoja.

"My real teacher was my husband," I boasted. "He taught me about honor and justice. Please, *Agha*, don't let a decent man remain in prison, or get killed. It's against our religion. My husband is innocent!"

The smile left his face. "As I have said previously, in regard to a resolution to your husband's situation, it is out of my hands," Mofatteh said in a serious tone. "I can only try to get permission for you to visit your husband. The rest is up to the authorities. Have faith in God, *Khanom*."

Dr. Mofatteh's slight hint of help sounded encouraging, but I needed action.

On the long line to the prison, which took up the entire plaza, a young woman was informed that she could visit her husband for the first time that day. The wife was bouncing up and down with joy. A second lieutenant in the Air Force, her husband had been arrested two months ago. An older, plump woman put discretion aside and said, "Hmph! Maybe they're about to kill him, so they granted you this first—and last—visit!" Unfortunately, her sarcastic remark was not completely untrue. The young wife turned white.

"That's not always true," I tried to calm her, tossing a stern look behind at the other woman.

My nonverbal communication was ineffective. "Who are you here for?" the fat nosy woman asked.

I dropped my eyes to avoid looking at her. "My husband."

"What was his job?"

I was taken aback. "He was a *Vazir*."

The woman pinched her cheek. "I hope not the Minister of Health, the one who imported outdated American vaccines and infected our poor children with polio?"

I was speechless with repugnance. This was, undoubtedly, the most hideous accusation against Shoja, so far. It darkened my mood.

"I only repeated what I heard, *Khanom*," the fat woman tried to justify herself.

Even if Shoja was freed by the court of law, his honor might never be redeemed. SAVAK had succeeded in its lethal propaganda against him.

A windstorm rose. Dusty heavy spring showers swirled in the air. I covered my face with a newspaper. Some people left, fearing a tornado. Still, there were at least thirty people ahead of me.

Two hours later, at the guard station, I was disappointed again: "No visits!"

Low-spirited, I exchanged Shoja's clean clothes for his dirty ones. We had been allowed to include one kilo of oranges in the package. On one of the oranges, I wrote: "We are all fine." My many letters had remained unanswered. Had Shoja seen any of them?

Back in the car, I searched through Shoja's dirty laundry in hope of finding a note, a clue, something tangible to reassure me of his existence. Nothing!

From the prison, I went to my in-laws' who now occupied my parents' old home. Boxes of furnishings still lay unpacked on the living room carpet. A servant and his wife ran the household below an acceptable standard. Who could protest?

Agha Joon had given up his law practice and had not left

the house for days. He just sat, sulked, sobbed, and drank, wasting away life! For Shazdeh Joon, time and place had rapidly lost their significance. She did not even recognize me. The poor woman had been diagnosed with Alzheimer's.

Chapter Ten

Nadir Shahin's visit on May 8, 1979, was most unexpected. When I answered the door, the young man standing six feet tall lightly smiled

"Hello, Mrs. Sheikh." He then walked into the foyer. Nadir's father, a reconstructive surgeon, was Shoja's friend, and a prior Minister of Health. The rumors said that the Minister had fled the country in time to avoid being captured by either the Shah or his successors.

"Nadir! What brings you here?" I said with surprise. "I thought you were in the States, along with your family. Come in!" I smiled.

"No, thanks. I can't stay long." Nadir moved closer. "I need to speak to you, alone! I have an urgent message for you from my father!" There was a nervous edge to his voice.

My smile faded. I began to feel queasy in my stomach. "My mother and Babak are in the living room and can't hear us. Tell me! What is it?"

Nadir gently put his strong hand on my arm. "Between the two of us, my father's still in Tehran, in hiding," he said in an undertone. "I left college in the States to come here and help him escape. My father has sent me with bad news: Tonight, Dr.

Sheikh will be before the firing squad!" He shifted his hazel eyes away.

I looked at him with suspicion. What nonsense! How would his father know anything from hiding?

"Sorry to be the one to tell you this," Nadir warned. "Tonight, twenty-three former government dignitaries—including Dr. Sheikh—will be executed! Trust me! The information comes from someone who works for the new government. He's reliable," Nadir said, blinking.

My eyes lingered on him dubiously. "Impossible! Just can't be!"

"Hard to believe, but a fact. My father thinks you should immediately contact Dr. Esmail Yazdi. His brother, Ebrahim, is the right-hand man to Ayatollah Khomeini. If anyone can save your husband, it's him."

"But how could they execute my husband without a trial? He's not a threat to them, like some of the generals were." I breathed rapidly.

"Mrs. Sheikh, the Revolutionary Tribunal doesn't work that way. Even Hoveyda's trial was a show to appease foreign dignitaries petitioning for his freedom. The Court wanted everyone to believe that the trial proved Hoveyda guilty, rendering the conviction and death sentence just."

My hands moved close together in concentration. What he said made sense. The doubts began to thin. The Revolutionary Tribunal could kill Shoja without any trial! My husband might face the firing squad—tonight!

The gory thought erased all my hopes instantly. My heartbeat became faster, irregular. I held onto the door frame as a numbness spread through my face, tightening my jaw. Breathing became an agony. I looked at the young man, helplessly.

"Are you feeling all right?" Nadir raised his voice in alarm.

I pressed my back against the wall and pointed at my throat. "Can't—breathe!"

Nadir helped me into the living room. Mother rushed towards me. "What happened? You were fine a few minutes ago! Here, sit down. Babak! Open the windows and get a glass of water!"

I shut my eyes. I needed to get a grip on myself. A few minutes later, the muscles in my face started to relax. Breathing became normal.

I opened my eyes. "I'm okay. Really," I managed to say slowly. "Stop—fussing over me!" Mother and Babak stepped back.

"If you don't need me," Nadir said quietly, "I'll go now to check on my father. I usually have to change cars to be sure no one follows me. Please, stay strong. I'll pray for Dr. Sheikh!" His special mission had ended.

I nodded in response and got up. It was almost 6:00 p.m. when Nadir left. I dashed into the bedroom to get my purse and my car keys. If I was going to save Shoja, I must set off at once in order to contact Dr. Yazdi. Midnight was only six hours away. That was when executions customarily occurred.

"Azar, where're you going? You are not feeling well," Mother implored.

"There's no time to explain. I must go at once! Please don't ask questions."

"Mom! At least, let me go with you," Babak offered with extreme concern.

"No! You stay here. I'll be back soon." My harsh voice startled them.

I hurried out. My car was parked by the front door. I jumped in and started the engine. This was one time I wanted the car to fly. A quick push to the gas pedal, and the car responded readily. If needed, I would go through all red lights to arrive at Dr. Yazdi's home in time, about thirty minutes away.

It was still hard to believe that Shoja could be killed. No matter how chaotic the country, innocent people should not be executed. Shoja was neither a criminal nor a traitor. As Nadir pointed out, the Revolutionary Court did not follow rational rules. It was driven by a frenzy of revenge, and fueled by violently intense emotions.

I pressed the gas pedal to the floor. The wheels screeched, the car leapt. I drove on madly. On Saltanat Abad, the traffic slowed me from all directions. I honked repeatedly. Was it always this crazy? Where were all those people going?

"You jerk, what's the rush? Do you carry a body to the morgue?" the driver in front of me yelled.

That might be the case soon!

The traffic eased, and cars picked up some speed. I ran a red light. The car clock showed 6:31. Still, another 10 to 15 minutes to my destination. The distance never seemed this far before, when I used to visit Yazdi and his family under better circumstances.

It was dusk now. The dim streetlights were already lit. My throat was dry and my body limp from an inexplicable exhaustion. I could not waste one tiny second. Otherwise, Shoja's bloody picture might appear on the front page of tomorrow's newspaper. At the thought of his death, tears began to emerge in the corners of my eyes, clouding my vision. I wiped them with the back of my hand and drove on swiftly.

Finally, the affluent neighborhood of Niavaran! The tall wall surrounding the Shah's winter palace loomed in the distance. I felt anger rising inside me. It was only last spring that the Royal couple hosted a garden party for the foreign diplomatic corps. The rose garden and the guests looked magnificent. Despite the growing signs of crisis within Iran, the Shah and his Queen appeared misleadingly majestic. Now that the Shah and his family had safely escaped Iran, taking their dogs and their treasures with them, we were left behind to face the raging Revolutionaries!

I turned right, then left, and stopped in front of a modern ranch house. Yazdi's doorbell vibrated under my finger.

"Who is it?" a young girl's voice asked from the intercom.

I gave my name. "I'm here to see Dr. Yazdi."

"My father's at prayer," she said listlessly.

"I'll wait. It's urgent—very urgent!"

Following a sudden period of strong lightning and thunder, the sky got black and it began to pour. The rain fell hard and steady, washing away the smells of spring jasmines. Unprotected, I waited on the sidewalk, outside the front gate, impatiently.

The girl's voice returned: "My father wishes to be excused from seeing you. He's busy."

"This is a matter of life and death! I won't leave until I see him," I shouted. The girl was gone again.

I glanced at my wristwatch. It was now 7:05 p.m.—less than five hours until midnight! I rang the doorbell again. How could I keep a grip on my fear?

At last, Dr. Yazdi's disembodied voice boomed through the intercom: "*Khanom* Sheikh, what do you want from me?"

"Please—it's about Shoja—I need your help!"

"We are at dinner. Come back tomorrow."

"Tomorrow? They execute Shoja tonight!"

"I'm sorry, but I can do nothing for him," Yazdi said bluntly.

"I implore you. Speak to your brother on Shoja's behalf. Please! Don't allow an innocent man's blood to be spilled!"

"I can do nothing. May God help your husband!"

"I beg you to—" There was a click. The intercom had gone dead. Our brief conversation had ended. He had left me rejected and abandoned at his front door out on the street. I had failed to save my husband's life! In exasperation, I pounded on the gate, screaming and begging. No response. Never had I felt as helpless as that moment.

Empty of hopes, I dragged myself back to the car. The rain had soaked my light clothes wet. The sky was crying for me!

I returned home in a morbid state. My world had begun to collapse. Mother and Babak were right at the door, waiting for me.

"Where have you been all this time?" Mother asked. "I've been sick with worry."

"Mom!" Babak pleaded. "If you've heard some news on Dad, please tell me."

"You'll hear soon enough. Now, just leave me alone. Please!"

When they were out of sight, I tried to make a few desperate calls to Shoja's close friends, hoping somebody would help. No one was answering his phone. Where were they? Had they all left Iran? My last hope was Hushang. I quietly dialed his number, cupping my hand to my mouth to prevent Mother and Babak from hearing.

"Something terrible is about to happen. Please, come. Now!" I pleaded.

My trembling voice frightened him. "I'll be right there, Sis. Leave the door ajar."

My brother lived twenty minutes away. Until he showed up, I looked at the clock a hundred times. My damp clothes clung uncomfortably to me. I needed to change, perhaps take a shower. I couldn't do it right now. Not as long as Shoja's life hung in the balance. Mother's cough broke the silence once in a while, but from Babak's room there was no sound.

I paced the room. A photograph of Shoja on an end table stared at me. My nanny used to say that one could determine a person's fate by looking at his picture. How silly it seemed then. Now, I needed to believe in this old superstition. Shoja's photo revealed nothing.

Hushang arrived in less than fifteen minutes. "What's up, Sis? You really got me scared," he said, wiping his wet hair by hand.

I told him.

Hushang's face hardened. "It doesn't make sense that from hiding, Dr. Shahin would have access to such information. Besides, Shoja can't be executed without a trial," he asserted.

"Of course he could! What kinds of trials did the others have? Anyone who has served the Shah is considered guilty and deserving of death."

"No wonder Yazdi didn't want to help you," Hushang said. "The man was probably afraid that he and his brother would be accused of collaborating with the old regime. Have you considered contacting those two guys that turned Shoja over to the authorities? They might be able to help."

"I tried. Couldn't find either one of them. Believe me, I considered all the people who might be willing to help Shoja, but there's no one," my voice cracked with sobs.

With a nervous stride, Hushang started pacing back and forth. "Whatever's going to happen will happen after midnight. We'll not hear about it until the early morning news. I'll spend the night here," he concluded.

The hands of the clock showed ten. Time was ticking away precious moments hastily, with ruthless precision. At one time a little bird would peek out and "cuckoo" when the large hand struck the hour. As the clock got older, the bird stopped singing, but the clock retained its chime.

Hushang started rapping his long fingers on the table, staring into space. His usually radiant face seemed darkened. Perhaps, like me, he was imagining Shoja's execution. Would they blindfold him? Would they grant him a last request? Perhaps a few tiny minutes to say "good-bye" to his aging father? Agha Joon would not survive. He still had the newspaper clippings about Zia's car accident hung over his bed. Soon he would be adding the grotesque final photo of his second son. I envied my mother-in-law. Her present condition would save her from the awful reality.

What would happen to my children and I after Shoja's death? How would we spend tomorrow and all the other tomorrows without him?

Just a few years ago, Shoja had taken the children to Isfahan, a city some three hundred miles south, for the opening ceremony of a new hospital. Because of heavy snowfall, their return flight was canceled. Shoja needed to be in Tehran the next day for an official meeting, so he rented an old car and drove it over dangerous, icy roads. The car broke down near Qom. I was furious that he had risked his life and those of our children for a stupid meeting.

Another time, during the cholera epidemic, he was so preoccupied that he drove into a wall. I always thought that, like his brother, Shoja would die in a car accident. Never—in my wildest dreams—did I imagine he would die in front of a firing squad!

Hushang resumed his pacing. It was pure black outside. The drizzle continued with a dull, dreary sound, making shallow ditches in the pavements.

Who would help me with Shoja's funeral? I thought. Hardly any friends came around. What if they disposed of his body the same way they disposed of some others, buried in unmarked graves?

The clock chimed eleven, and then, in what seemed like a flash of light, twelve times! Midnight was here! Did I hear shots? Screams? With my hands over my ears, I began to cry quietly. Hushang turned his face to the wall.

Shoja was no longer alive! He was gone forever. Did he feel pain? What were his last thoughts? Was he resigned to his fate? Did he embrace death as freedom from so much agony, so much dehumanization? Was death the absolute end?

I stretched out on the carpet, no longer wanting to face the clock. The countdown was over. No precious moments left. Nothing mattered now! The future? Just a massive void.

Unbridled memories—so real—not a single strand of fantasy in them. As a child, I used to relieve my pain through mental escape. At my grandmother's funeral, I gazed for hours at the semi-circle patterns on the wooden ceiling beams of the funeral home, imagining them to be people holding hands and dancing. Tonight, I was deeply entrenched in reality. There was no room for fantasy. Shoja was dead! It was over! Gone! Destroyed! Except for the bits and pieces of the past engraved in my brain cells.

Shoja and I had danced our first waltz at the fancy Ritz. We were just engaged and so unusually happy. We turned round and round to the sound of the violins, my head leaning on his shoulder, our hands intertwined. Shoja whirled me away to the end of the ballroom and kissed me on the neck. The whole world danced before my eyes.

My wedding night! How awkward and inexperienced we both were! Mother knew nothing about her own sexuality and had not permitted me to learn much about mine. My main guides were curiosity and instincts. We spent the first few months of our marriage floundering, working through my inhibition and his frustration.

Shoja and I were contrasting personalities—different backgrounds, different tastes. Where Shoja would be attracted by the ornate and extravagant, I preferred the simple and subtle. Shoja, extroverted and social, needed people as much as he needed air or food. I, on the other hand, a private person, felt uncomfortable in public places. Shoja had much more faith in people than I did. We shared one basic similarity: a heightened sense of social consciousness with all its responsibilities. We both longed idealistically for justice and democracy. Above all, we loved each other unconditionally.

Now he, and twenty-two others—some friends, some colleagues—were dead. Were they lined up in a row before the firing squad, like we see in a movie?

Hushang was slouched over in a chair, his slightly graying hair grasped in his hands.

Once I had asked Shoja, "If I died before you, would you remarry?"

"No one could ever take your place, love!" he replied genuinely.

I laughed coquettishly. "But, I would marry again. I can't live alone!"

At this moment, the thought of remarriage made me sick. Our life together was not flawless. Once in a while, the spoiled child within me surfaced to claim my husband's attentions. Growing up in a patriarchal society where men ruled over women, and in a household with four authoritarian males—my father and three older brothers—I hardly knew ways other than coyness when interacting with men. Sometimes, it worked.

My husband and I had misunderstandings, disputes, even a few fights. Shoja's career became my rival, a mistress I could not defeat. His possessiveness, to the point of jealousy, threatened my freedom at times. Our relationship, even with his brooding jealousies, was solid. We grew up together, sharing many tender moments, sharing three children. Shoja loved his sons and idolized his daughter. Was he thinking of them during the last minutes of his life?

Outside, the darkness was yielding to a grayish, violet dawn. The rain had slowed. The sun was somewhere hidden behind the clouds. It was going to be a long day. Hushang got up to make tea. I thought of the horrible tasks ahead—preparing for Shoja's funeral.

Hushang came back with a tray and set it on the dining table. He looked at his wristwatch and said loudly, "The big clock's three minutes behind! It's almost six o'clock. The news will start any minute."

The radio was turned on the morning recitation of the Qur'an. The chanting, celestial and monotonous, somehow soothed me.

Mother and Babak hovered around the radio. Babak's short straight hair stood on end, and his eyes twitched. Mother held her Qur'an close to the breast, all the blood drained from her tormented face. Had Babak and her known the terrible secret all along? We would all now hear the official account of Shoja's execution together. Strangely, I was calm. Or, so I thought.

The newscaster's voice boomed across the airwaves:

"Dear listeners, last night, the righteous Islamic Revolutionary Court found twenty-two traitorous agents of the former regime guilty of being 'corrupt on earth' and 'warring against God'. They were rightfully condemned to death. The executions were carried out early this morning. The following criminals are now dead: Dr. . . former Minister of Agriculture; Dr. . . former Minister of Foreign Affairs; Dr. . . former Mayor of Tehran; General . . . Commander of. . .; General . . . Deputy Commander of. . ."

"Twenty-two traitorous agents?" I cried. "What happened to twenty-three? Where was Shoja on the list? What was Shoja's number? Did they omit his name? Did I miss it?"

Mother came towards me, tears rinsing her face. "They haven't killed Shoja! God took mercy on us," she said. Her fragile body seemed to have shrunk.

Hushang hugged Babak. "Your father's alive! He wasn't among those executed!"

Why were the windows shut? There was no air. My lungs were struggling for oxygen.

"I can't breathe. I—can't—breathe," I managed to utter before entering a long dark tunnel that led to unconsciousness.

Lying on my bed, I sensed total exhaustion. Mount Alborz rested on my chest. The blinds were completely closed. What time was it? No matter. Inside me, the perpetual night continued. Even if Shoja had not been killed, his destiny remained a blank slate.

Mother peeked her head through the door. "You awake? Should I get you something to eat? It's almost nine o'clock."

Had I slept all that time? How long had I been passed out? I slowly got up, moved to the window and opened the blinds. The sun blared with audacity. Nature proceeded undisturbed, in spite of human suffering. In the shower, I let the water run over my body, still numb from last night's trauma. My stomach burned. While getting dressed, I heard the hushed voices of my sister and three brothers in the living room, probably pitying me. How could they understand? They had normal lives. I did not. My future no longer belonged to me. It remained in the hands of the Tribunal.

Wearing a white terry-cloth bathrobe, I sneaked out of the shower into my bedroom to avoid facing anyone. Babak entered, looking pale, his eyes blinking rapidly. He sat close to me on the bed.

"What is it, honey? Is something wrong?"

There was a moment's pause. He diverted his glance. "Nadir called. They didn't get around to Dad last night. Tonight he, along with eight more, will—" Babak's voice trailed off. He flung his arms around me, shaking.

Bastards! How could they do this to us? They delayed

Shoja's death to make him suffer longer, to torture us. No! We could not go through another vigil.

I left Babak and ran into the living room. My siblings, still trying to make sense of last night's drama, grew silent.

"Tonight Shoja will be—" The words would not come. "Please, everyone go home. Whatever happens, happens. I need to be alone!"

There! I was able to express some control. I returned to the bedroom to take a sedative. Lately, I used tranquilizers as often as I put sugar in my tea. Babak stood by the window, motionless, as I slowly tried to escape into oblivion.

At midnight, Hushang phoned: "Ayatollah Khomeini just gave amnesty to those prisoners on death row! Only those whose hands have been stained with blood will be executed," his voice shook with excitement.

So, Shoja's time had not come yet!

CHAPTER ELEVEN

Sheriff's pious, though in debauchery was bold
My debaucheries now at street-corners are told

Hafez (Fourteenth Century)

"We must meet immediately, *Madame*. It's for your own good," a stranger told me on the phone. Like previous times, I took this mysterious caller seriously, and hastily put some clothes on and set off. Especially now that Shoja had a close call with death only four days ago, I could not ignore any urgent call.

At 120 Kakh Avenue, "Dr. Rasti, Specialist in Internal Medicine and Infectious Disease" appeared in Farsi and in French on a metal plaque.

The stranger, a slim man of indeterminate age, in a well-tailored suit, greeted me in grand European style. He took my hand close to his lips, without kissing. He identified himself with a delicate voice: "I'm Dr. Rasti. Pleased to meet you, *Madame*. Have a seat. Would you like some café?"

He made sure that I realized he had spent some time in France. Before I could answer, the servant put a cup of *café au lait* in front of me, and left the room.

"Doctor, what was it that you wanted to discuss? It sounded

urgent."

"*Madame*, quite confidentially, I am the physician at the clinic in the Qasr Prison. Your husband is hospitalized there," he muttered.

"What happened?" I moved forward in my chair.

"After the recent executions, his blood pressure rose very high and he complained of chest pains."

"Is it serious? Is he okay?"

"He is stable but, of course, his status could change," the doctor played with my emotions. "You know, there is always the possibility of a *syncope*."

"A heart attack? Would they give Shoja the right treatment in prison? How did this happen? He never seemed to have any heart problems in his life."

"*Mon Dieu!* Must've been awful to watch his colleagues and friends being executed, knowing that perhaps he would be next," Rasti said.

"Doctor, do you know why they didn't—I mean, why he wasn't among those—" I could not utter the word 'executed.'

"That I can't answer. Fate? Luck? Or connections, perhaps?"

"What can I do for my husband?"

"You can help him escape," he lowered his voice.

"Escape? From Qasr? With all those guards around? It's impossible!"

"Nothing's impossible. If you are generous enough, *Madame*, I can help."

I looked the man squarely in the eye. "How generous?"

He scribbled an amount on a notepad, and pushed it across the table to me.

"Five million touman?" I almost choked on the coffee. "We

don't have that!" Of course, like many others, he did not believe me. The ugly rumors had tarnished everyone's mind against us.

"This is nothing in comparison to your husband's life," the doctor tore the note as he spoke. "*Mon amie*, sometimes we must sacrifice for our loved ones."

"If showing love is limited to money, then I'm doomed to fail. We just don't have it," I snapped.

Rasti played his ace in the hole. "Your husband's life hangs on a thread. Don't you care, *Madame*? Contact your friend, Dr. Shahin, before he flees the country. He'll tell you what the going rate is for an ex-Minister. Most of it goes into the pockets of the smugglers. Usually, these terms are nonnegotiable."

I rose. "I understand, but unfortunately I can't get my hands on that kind of money. Please, if you see my husband again, give him my love. And, *merci* for the coffee. Good-bye."

"*Au revoir, Madame.*"

Out in the street, the reality hit me. What else should I expect? In these times of tumult, opportunistic people would attempt to strike it rich. They're not in the business of helping anyone for the sake of doing a good deed. Yet, was Rasti who he claimed to be? A full-time physician, occasionally moon-lighting as a human smuggler? Dr. Shahin, the ex-Minister, was the only one who could verify Rasti's identity. Shahin knew about the executions, too. I had to see him and find out more about Rasti and Shahin's 'reliable' source as his son Nadir had once mentioned.

Nadir, the young handsome student, kindly volunteered to take me to his father's hiding place. The two of us changed taxis twice to avoid being followed. We walked the rest of the way through alleys and side streets to an abandoned house in Elahieh, a northern suburb. Shahin seemed to be the only tenant in that remote villa. I entered a room in the back of the house. Nadir waited inside, guarding the front door.

The ex-Minister of Health was not his usual composed self. Deep, dark shadows under his eyes revealed that the recent executions had shaken him. His respectable grayish hair had been distastefully dyed to jet black, and his wide face wore a short, rough beard, obviously as a disguise. Shahin had also become a chain smoker. His name appeared near the top of the Ayatollah's "Black List", and, naturally, he was afraid for his life. Why didn't he escape when everybody else did?

After months of seclusion, Dr. Shahin's restive face brightened to see a friend. There was so much news to exchange about those who had fled, as well as those who had been executed.

"Do you know a Dr. Rasti?" I finally found an opportunity to ask him.

Shahin lit a cigarette. "He was the same man who called to inform me of the twenty-three executions," he admitted reluctantly.

So, Rasti was Shahin's 'reliable' source!

"But part of his prediction did not come true, did it? Shoja's still alive," I said.

"Thanks to God," Shahin fingered his beard.

"Please, it's not easy for me to discuss this, but perhaps you can explain what happened. How was Shoja spared? Did Rasti tell you?"

Shahin took a nervous puff from his cigarette. "No, and I

don't think he knows. It's a mystery. No one knows why Shoja was not killed."

There was a moment of contemplation. Shoja had magically defeated death.

"One more thing, this Dr. Rasti said that Shoja's blood pressure shot up, that he's been hospitalized," I broke the silence.

"Hypertension could be dangerous, but Shoja is an energetic young man. Besides, with today's medication, it's easily controlled," Shahin explained professionally.

"Can Rasti be trusted? Are you sure he's not a government agent?" I asked.

The prudent politician waited a second to choose his words carefully. "These days, no one can be fully trusted. Yet, I know of one person he has helped to escape."

"He wants 5 million touman for Shoja's rescue! Too high! It's impossible for me to raise that much. If I could sell the house, then I would have the money, but as you know, the law forbids me."

"The fee is pretty reasonable, actually," Shahin said after another puff of gray smokes. "If Shoja were out and wanted to flee, it would cost only 200 to 300 thousand touman. To arrange a prison escape is extremely risky, almost impossible. Anyhow, the decision is entirely up to you. I only suggest that you and Babak get your passports ready immediately. Even if you have to break a few rules. You might need them on short notice," Shahin advised genuinely. He made no reference to his own imminent escape.

Within a few weeks, Shahin and his son fled Iran. Two less victims to the bloodthirsty Revolution!

Following Shahin's advice, I discreetly went to file for passports. Babak and I could not stay behind if Shoja escaped.

The passport agent at the local branch office was known to handle cases quickly—if given a bribe. He assessed my net worth by looking me up and down several times before asking, "Do you need only one passport?"

"No, two. For my son and I," I lowered my voice to a murmur.

"How old is he?"

"Under eighteen; no restrictions for his departure."

"What about you? Any restrictions?" the government agent asked with a smirk on his thin lips.

"I don't think so," I retorted apprehensively.

The dubious passport agent gazed at me again, making me even more uncomfortable. "Ever had a passport before?"

"No!"

Although I had a diplomatic passport under my married name, the chance of him finding out was slim. The man had no computers and I was asking for a passport under my maiden name.

"Where are you two going?"

"To visit relatives in America. We won't stay long." I presented my birth certificate to him.

The man tilted back his head. "Are you single?"

I blushed. "*Agha*, what difference does it make? I just told you, there are no restrictions for my departure."

He requested Babak's birth certificate. I quietly put it on his counter.

"Why didn't your son come?" the man wondered.

"He is at school. I'll fill out the form for him."

The passport agent stared at Babak's last name. He leaned across the counter, looked straight into my eyes, and mumbled guilefully, "*Khanom*, you realize that this name can cause a serious problem?"

My heart missed a beat. What if he called the *Komiteh*?

"You won't let that happen, *Agha*," I said quickly, and slipped a 1000-touman bill under Babak's birth certificate.

This was the first time I had ever bribed a government official, and I had a bad feeling about it.

The man's hand hastily removed the bill and stuffed it in his jacket pocket. "Fill these out and return in three weeks for the passports," he said in a formal tone.

"Three weeks?"

In those three weeks, things might change to our disadvantage. The Republic might publish more lists, and order more restrictions for travel. We might lose our chance to get a passport forever.

"Could you possibly have them ready sooner, *Agha*?" I pleaded as I slipped another 500 touman to him.

The man's eyes half-closed in a silent agreement. In three days, the passports were ready.

"A guy's at the front door, Mom!" Babak called out the back door to me. "Says he has something from Dad."

It was a beautiful day in late May, and Mother's sweet-scented roses were in full bloom. I left the unfinished letter I was writing to Shoja on the deck, and ran back into the house.

"What're you waiting for? Let him in," I hollered.

Our guest limped into the living room on a crutch. His leg and one arm were in casts. With difficulty, he managed to sit.

He was a balding man with strong features who appeared to be in his late thirties.

Our guest's name, we soon discovered, was Hariri.

"I'm just on my way home from Qasr, where I served time for a while," he volunteered frankly. "As a journalist, I was accused of collaborating with the SAVAK." Hariri looked up at us with a knowing smirk and continued, "That was more than enough reason to be jailed, or killed. Even if it wasn't true, as in my case."

Babak and I sat and listened in silence.

"Like Dr. Sheikh, in the beginning, I was kept in solitary, where I developed pneumonia. Khalkhali, the Tribunal Judge, or, as the inmates called him, the 'Hanging Judge', did not allow a '*Savaki*' proper medical attention. As far as he was concerned, I was better off dead. He sent me to Dr. Sheikh's cell— a dim, dirty dungeon. 'Let the two criminals look after each other,' the Judge decreed. That's how I got to know your husband, *Khanom*," Hariri said, turning to face me.

He moved his injured leg slightly in an effort to ease the pain. "Anyhow, Dr. Sheikh convinced the guards to get me medicine. He also set my broken arm and leg in casts. If it weren't for him, I wouldn't be alive!"

"How did your arm and leg get broken?" I asked sympathetically.

Hariri looked down. "While I was arrested. You know, the *Pasdars* can get pretty rough sometimes."

"Was—my father also injured?" Babak asked the words that I was afraid to ask.

"Everyone in Qasr has been injured one way or another," Hariri retorted in reflection.

For a few seconds, my mind was heavy with speculations.

How did this man get his freedom? Who bailed him out? Could we do the same for Shoja? Was he really who he claimed to be?

Were it not for my keen curiosity, this stranger might quickly be put out of the house. There was no place in our home for the spies of the regime.

"Anyhow, until that damned night, Dr. Sheikh's morale was okay," Hariri went on. "But the long waking hours of uncertainty started to get to him. Several times, he volunteered to work in the clinic, but Khalkhali didn't want any prisoner's public image to improve."

Babak entertained his father's ex-cellmate with a cup of tea. Hariri drank in short, quick sips. His hands shook and tea spilled over the sides of the cup. The man seemed to be on the threshold of a nervous breakdown. We waited for him to collect his thoughts. "They eventually allowed Dr. Sheikh to perform some low tasks like cleaning the bathrooms and the cells. Flies and lice ran rampant! At night, huge rats kept us awake. With Dr. Sheikh's help conditions improved."

How very much like Shoja to roll up his sleeves and help.

"One morning, two guards entered abruptly," Hariri continued. "We were having our meager breakfast—a tiny dot of cheese, stale bread, a colorless cup of tea, a couple of sugar lumps. One of the guards taunted, 'Finish your breakfast. It's your last meal, Sheikh!'"

"The Hanging Judge, Khalkhali, had summoned him. Ahem," our guest from Qasr cleared his throat. "Dr. Sheikh rose from his breakfast. He took a 10-touman bill from his pocket, jotted something on it, and along with his watch, handed them to me. He said, 'If you don't see me again, take these to my wife.' The guards then led him away."

Babak and I braced ourselves. Our visitor was going to talk about that horrible night of executions.

Hariri held a handkerchief to his mouth and coughed. The deep-chested cough sounded like a trace of pneumonia. He measured his words as he breathed. "Some fourteen to fifteen hours later, perhaps around midnight, Dr. Sheikh was returned to the cell. Alive! I could not believe my eyes. Twenty-two others died before the firing squad. Dr. Sheikh lived! Khalkhali had ordered the twenty-third prisoner back to his cell with the instructions, 'We'll do this one tomorrow!' Why? No one knows!"

"That was my father!" Babak snapped. "He's the only one who survived that night!"

"Yes," Hariri began. "He was a mess—pale as a corpse, hands on his chest, breathing fast, eyes half shut. Later, the guards took him to the clinic. I heard that on the following night, your father cheated death again." Hariri gave a slight smile. "At the last minute Ayatollah Khomeini ordered a stay of execution!"

Babak gave a stronger smile, something that held pride.

"How's my father now?" he asked.

"Well, since your father was put in the clinic ten days ago, I haven't seen him. He may still be there," Hariri explained. "Luckily, Khalkhali has been replaced by Gilani, a less radical Tribunal Judge, and executions have stopped—at least for the time being. God must be watching over your father!" Hariri fell silent. Slowly, he took out Shoja's Omega watch and the ten-touman bill from his jacket pocket and gave them to me.

"These belong to you, *Khanom*. Please consider me your brother if you need anything. I must go now."

Babak and I helped Hariri to the door where a taxi was waiting for him out front.

"Thank you, and good luck," I said to Shoja's loyal ex-cellmate. All my doubts about him had suddenly disappeared. Then, I turned to my son. "Here, sweetheart. You should keep this watch. I'll keep the money."

Babak proudly put the watch on his wrist. The penciled note on the 10-touman bill read: "My end is near!"

The next day, the man at the prison guard scanned his long list and said: "Sheikholeslamzadeh? Cell 4/1. Visits today!"

"Excuse me? Could you repeat that again?" I asked in a quandary.

"I just said you can visit your prisoner today. Just go to the visitation line, over there. If you don't have proper I.D., you won't get in."

My heart burst with joy. I had my birth certificate in my purse. I could see Shoja! Had Dr. Mofatteh's influence brought this visit about?

I dashed to the other long line at the entrance to the prison. Most of the visitors were women whose men had been arrested. In front of me was the classy wife of the ex-governor of Hamadan, who prepped me: "The visit will last only five minutes, behind bars. Speak very loud, otherwise you won't be heard. Your long-sleeved dress and scarf are okay, but these might be a problem," she pointed to my nylon stockings.

"Where would I purchase opaque stockings around here? If

I go home to change, I'll lose my place in line and miss my turn," I expressed with concern.

From behind, an elderly *chadori*—a woman covered by a *chador*—tugged at my sleeve. "I'm wearing two pairs of heavy black stockings for my rheumatism. Take one," she suggested generously, in a thick provincial accent.

This was no time to be finicky. I accepted her noble offer. Her stockings were stretched out and loose, but they would do. As a token of gratitude, I bought two cans of Pepsi from a street vendor and gave one to the *chadori* woman who pushed it away. "Thank you. I don't drink this kind of *najess*—unclean—stuff."

"There's no liquor in it," I explained. "It's just soda."

"Still, it's *najess*. The company owner is an atheist, a Baha'i.

I presented the soda to the ex-governors' wife. She also declined my offer. "No, thanks. I'm having a diet."

I passed it on to a pregnant woman in line. Her husband had been accused of assisting in Prime Minister Bakhtiar's escape.

"My husband's an opium junkie. He'll die without it," she confided in me.

The line moved slowly. There were still fifteen people in front of me. The ex-governor's wife continued to fill me in: "The prisoners can't shave. Radio is forbidden. And, of course, news of any kind!"

A fight broke out at the front gate. The guard ejected someone from the line and shouted, "No one except the immediate family can visit!"

By now the sun had turned to the west. Empty cans and food wrappings were strewn around. A little boy urinated on a wall. How could adults relieve themselves with no public bathrooms in sight? People, impatient from waiting, started to push from behind. The *chadori* woman yelled, "Hey, you Moslems! There is a pregnant woman here. Have pity!"

The lamps above the prison gate clicked on, flooding the plaza with a silvery glow. By now, I was second in line. Would I get a chance to visit Shoja today after all this waiting? Mother and Babak must be worried for me.

One visitor exited. The ex-governor's wife was admitted. I would be next! In my mind, I reviewed all the things I wanted to tell Shoja in the five minutes allotted. Would we be allowed any private conversation?

Someone exited and the guard lifted his gun: "Enter!"

I stepped into a drab lobby with a cobblestone floor. A man scanned my I.D., and asked: "Prisoner?"

I gave the full name. He checked the list and my I.D. and motioned for me to go to the adjacent room to be searched. Two young women in Islamic attire frisked my body thoroughly. They retained my handbag, and sent me through a second pair of doors to a courtyard where a crowd of people waited for a minibus.

"Why do we have to go on a minibus?" I asked someone curiously.

"It's a big compound, and they don't want anyone wandering around. When the minibus brings twenty people back, then twenty of us will go in. Here it comes now."

We drove through an area lined with old pine trees for approximately a mile, then the bus stopped before a guarded fence. The driver poked his head out. He and the guards exchanged nods, and the bus moved on through the fence into a large compound and stopped again. This time, we were unloaded. "Wait here until you are summoned," the driver ordered.

In front of us were a stretch of tall, dull, brick buildings with tiny windows near the top of each story. Prison cells! The prisoners could not see even the treetops or sunlight from those cells.

Even though I had already waited seven hours in the heat for a five-minute visit, these last few minutes seemed like time in purgatory. I was fatigued and nervous. I looked around. What was holding us up? A door in the building opened. There was a loud commotion of twenty exhausted visitors being rushed out and loaded onto the minibus. Our group was called in.

The visiting room, a rather large rectangular area, was divided into three sections by two sets of iron bars. Twenty prisoners stood on the far end, facing twenty guards in the middle, who in turn had their backs towards twenty visitors—us. The visitors scuttled to find a place before their loved ones. I claimed my place before Shoja who was back to the world of the living! We were separated by two yards, two sets of iron bars, and a husky armed guard. My heart was pounding recklessly in anticipation. From what I could see, Shoja's beard was thick. He wore a faded shirt with rolled up sleeves, and seemed to have lost considerable weight. Thank God, there were no signs of injuries, at least not on his face and arms.

A guard blew a whistle. The visitation had officially begun. Simultaneously, forty mouths opened to speak and generated an uproarious din which was indescribable. Shoja said something that did not reach my ears. I moved from side to side and even stood on my toes.

"How are you? Are you okay?" I yelled.

He nodded.

"Sure?"

He nodded again.

"Any news of your trial?"

He cupped his hands around his ears. "What?"

"I said, any news of your trial? Have you been interrogated?"

"No! Not yet," he yelled back. "What's up with you?"

"Not much. Your parents have moved into Mother's old house."

"What?"

Frustrated, I repeated myself.

"Why?'

Without referring to the landlord incident, I answered, "Closer to us."

"And you and Babak?"

"Moved to Mother's apartment."

The noise level reached so high that our voices were lost. Shoja's sad eyes stared through me, and I stared back. Just as we attempted to resume conversation, the damned whistle blew. The uproar changed into deep sighs, unfinished sentences, untold stories, and unexpressed feelings. Time to go. We were quickly evacuated. My eyes were still interlocked with Shoja's. What if this was our first and last visit?

"All charges against Shoja Sheikholeslamzadeh, son of Hosain, and former Minister of Health and Social Welfare, should be reported to the Prosecutor's Office within three days," the radio newscaster broadcasted the same day.

I rushed to Agha Joon's home. "Did you hear the news? Does it mean that Shoja's trial is near?"

"Perhaps, but in the enemy's court, the verdict is already decided," the old attorney remarked cynically.

"Agha Joon , is there anything we can do to help Shoja?"

"No! They will kill him anyway," he said without any reservation. He did not know that his son had miraculously escaped death twice. I had never been able to discuss the account of Shoja's near execution with him.

Shazdeh Joon looked into the room. Like an innocent gazelle in danger, her large eyes expressed terror. She mumbled, "Bobloboch!"

"Her famous '*Ya Bab Al Havaej*'—Oh, Lord, Gates to all needs—has been reduced to this! The poor woman's gone totally mad," Agha Joon conceded.

CHAPTER TWELVE

I visited Babak's school one day in June. The American president of the Iran Zamin School had left Iran on the warnings of the American Embassy, and the female Iranian principal was concerned about the future.

"*Khanom*, the changes make it difficult to operate. Every day, we receive a notice from the new Ministry of Education to separate boys and girls. They don't realize that this will incur more expenses for teachers, equipment, classrooms. Soon we may have to shut down," Babak's grim principal complained.

"I'm sorry to hear that. I was hopeful that you'd be able to help me with my son's emotional problems—you know, in regard to his father—but now I see that you have your own," I said.

"Unfortunately, *Khanom*, there are many like Babak, whose close relatives have been incarcerated, even executed. Just a few days ago, a student whose father had been killed slashed his wrists in the bathroom. Luckily, we got to him in time," the principal confided in me.

I realized Babak had to think of another school soon, perhaps in America. When I left, the school yard was empty of happy, carefree youngsters. Like the rest of the country, it had become permeated with the austerity of the times.

For my second visit with Shoja, I arrived two hours early to be first in the prison line. Not early enough. Forty-two people were ahead of me. I spread a ripped newspaper on the ground, sat, and had a mock picnic lunch with a pastry and a soda. Having a second visitation with Shoja was significant. It meant he was still alive. In front of me, a grayish man had fixed his eyes on a young woman's ample bosom, which flowed out of her rather tight, open-necked dress.

"At your age, *Agha*, it's shameful to ogle," the young woman protested.

"If you don't like it, why do you dress like that? You ought to know that they won't let you in the prison like this!"

"Not that it's any of your business, but I'm wearing this to spite the dress code of the Mullahs! I don't care if they turn me away," the young woman said belligerently.

The prison gates opened at one o'clock. Twenty people were admitted. I expected to be in the third group.

As the line moved, I rose and picked up the ripped newspaper. My eye caught bold type on the second page, third column: "*Charges Accepted Against the Following Criminals.*" Our name was on top of the list! I crumpled the newspaper. Everywhere I went, our name showed up among a list of criminals. It was disgusting.

Today, the guard between Shoja and I was shorter, so I could see better. Shoja was wearing the same faded shirt.

"How are you?" Shoja managed to get across to me.

"Fine."

"Then why so gloomy?"

"Nothing serious. Are your living quarters and food okay?"

"Never mind. Any news in the papers about me?"

Obviously, he had read and heard nothing.

"The Prosecutor—"

"What?"

"They're collecting charges," I yelled. "Your trial seems near."

He shrugged, trying to give me the impression that he didn't care, but his expression betrayed him. Minutes went by quickly and the uproar continued.

"How's Babak?

"Okay, but he misses you. Hopefully, they'll let him come to see you soon. He—"

"Listen, you'd better consult the dentist about my bad tooth. Do you understand?" Shoja interrupted.

It took me a second to realize that he was referring to Dr. Esmail Yazdi who was an oral surgeon. Of course, Shoja had no idea that I had already gone to him for help, and was rejected. There would be no sense in trying again.

We had no more time for reflection. The guard blew his whistle hard. Five minutes were up. Damn it!

Outside, Mrs. Asfia waited to enter with the next group. We nodded hello. Mrs. Khalatbari, the wife of the ex-Minister of Foreign Affairs, no longer came. Like Mrs. Rouhani and many other unfortunate women, she had only a first—and last—visit. Her husband was executed.

Traditionally, the family dined with Mother on Fridays, the Iranian Sabbath. Today was no exception. We had *chelo kabob*—white rice and lamb. Mother's cooking was unrivaled. After we ate, Amir Ashraf and Hushang played backgammon. Others watched.

"You're losing, brother! You don't know how to play

backgammon. Go play with marbles!" Amir Ashraf ranted.

The telephone in the hallway rang. I was delighted to hear Roxana on the line.

"Hi, sweetheart. What's the matter? Why are you crying?"

"Is Dad okay? An Iranian student here told us today that Dad had been killed. Is it true? Dad's dead?" Roxana sobbed.

"No! It's a lie. He's alive! I saw him a couple of days ago."

"But—we heard—"

"Listen! He's alive! Calm down, now! Put Ramin on the phone."

"Mom?"

"Son, don't pay attention to vicious gossip. Your father's alive and doing as well as he can. Really! How are you holding up?"

"Never mind about me. When will Dad be released?"

"Soon. Be patient."

"You always say that just to make me happy. They're going to kill Dad, and you know it too! So, why lie to me? I'm no fool, Mom?" Ramin said angrily and hung up the phone.

I slipped into the bedroom to take a sedative. It hurt to see my children in anguish.

Babak, waving a white envelope in the air, came in. "Mom! Here is a letter for you. I found it under the front door." He handed it to me and went back to watch the backgammon game.

There was no return address on the letter. Who could have sent it? I tore it open and read:

My beloved wife,

I almost lost hope of seeing you and the children. If I must die without farewell, remember that I love all of you dearly. I have tried to remain strong. You always asked me to. It's hard.

I want the children to stay where they are and look for jobs over the summer holiday. They must learn to be financially independent. I also expect them to continue their education and make careers for themselves. Babak must join them. I would feel more at ease if they were all together, and safe.

In regard to you, Azar, I can give no advice. Trust your own judgment. Yours forever, Shoja

Was this the final will and testament of a doomed man? The date—two days after the executions—decoded its content. Shoja must have written it while his life was pending. I had seen Shoja twice since the date of this letter. Was it held up to be delivered after his destiny was sealed?

I clung to the letter tightly, as if holding my husband.

In our next visit, Shoja looked tidier. He had shaven his beard. The guard between us permitted a better view by standing slightly off to the side.

"Some of these men are really nice, but some—" Shoja slid his hand across his neck, suggesting that other guards would happily slit his throat.

"Has your blood pressure come down?"

His face contracted. "How do you know about that? I never mentioned it."

"Just heard."

"Forget about it. Everything's back to normal. No need to worry. " He put on a forced smile.

"Did you receive any of the letters I mailed you?"

"No! Not even one. Could you send some books? Days're very long here!"

"Things will change soon—for the better."

He nodded. "I want to believe that."

The belligerent sound of the whistle frayed our nerves. Did they take away one valuable minute from us?

On the way home, I stopped to see my in-laws. Shazdeh Joon was sleeping and Agha Joon looked abnormally pale and worn out. They had found a tumor in his liver. It could be a cancer.

"Did you see him?" the old man asked as he poured himself a glass of *araq*.

"Do you mean Shoja, Agha Joon?"

"Who else? Don't expect me to speak a name that has been stained by those bastards."

"Shoja looked good. No news of his trial, though. Now, you must do something about your own health and listen to your doctor. We all need you."

He shook his round, bald head in despair. "I'm not going to check into a hospital. Why prolong a miserable life? I only wish to see Shoja's freedom before I die!"

Summer had arrived early. Tehran had no rain for over a month, and a drought seemed inevitable.

As the number of prisoners grew, so did the crowds that thronged at Qasr Plaza. I wondered if any adult male who had held a significant position would be spared.

Scattered, isolated rioting had been reported in the city by the pro-Shah activists. Their hopes for the Shah's return were declining. In exile, General Oveissi who had been leading the

'Free Army' against 'the usurpers' was assassinated by the Iranian government mercenaries. In Iran, many more men and women had been arrested. Dr. Razmara, the Shah's last Minister of Health who had wrongfully spoken against Shoja, was now in the same predicament as him—a prisoner at Qasr. A relative, a former Iranian military attaché to America, had recently been sentenced to twelve years. What would become of his family?

"Is the line always this long?" Babak asked, as we waited outside the prison, wiping the sweat from our faces.

"Yes—but it's worth it, right?"

"I suppose so, if it makes Dad happy to see us."

Starting today, children under sixteen were allowed to visit their fathers. This was Babak's first visit at Qasr.

"Babak, I've been meaning to tell you something. Your father and I would like you to leave for the States, sooner than we planned. He was concerned for your future in his recent letter."

"No way! I'm not going anywhere. I want to be close to you and Dad. No more changes! I want things to be the way they were."

"Sweetheart, things may never be the same. Even your school is closing down for good."

"Please, Mom! Drop this conversation. Don't spoil my visit with Dad. Okay?"

"Sure. We'll discuss this some other time, soon." My son was not ready to make a commitment to leave, yet.

Six and a half hours later, we entered the lobby, exhausted. One guard took the books we had brought along and said, "If not forbidden, the prisoner will get them."

Selecting books for someone in a Revolutionary prison was

not easy, especially when the recipient could be on death row. Babak had chosen The *Count of Monte Cristo*, which he had recently read and liked. Mother had picked *Desireé*, a novel set during the French Revolution. I had contributed Nehru's auto-biography—which Shoja had left unfinished, on the night before he was abducted.

"Show me your I.D.s" the grumpy guard asked.

I handed him our papers.

"Weren't you told children over sixteen are not allowed in?"

"My son's only fifteen. Look at his birth certificate."

He pushed away the document. "I don't need to look at this! He's tall enough to be sixteen."

Babak was not particularly tall for his age. The guard was being obstinate.

"Even if you were right, which you're not, is it a sin to be tall?" I made the mistake of questioning the guard's judgment.

"Yeah, it is, when you have sucked the blood of the poor!" he taunted.

Babak turned white with rage. "Watch your tongue, jerk!" he shrieked.

The guard instinctively grabbed his source of power—his machine gun. "You bastard! I'll show you who's a jerk."

Instantly, I threw myself in front of my son. "Go ahead! Shoot me!"

The guard stared, spat and pulled back his gun. We passed through, but our moods were badly spoiled.

In the visiting room, father and son, who had not seen each other in four months, could barely talk over the noise.

I watched from the sidelines as tender eye glances and hand gestures took the place of words between the father and son.

Their love was stronger than a thousand iron bars.

Back from prison, a letter from Roxana with a shocking photograph of Ramin on his nineteenth birthday was awaiting me. Ramin appeared very thin, almost anorexic: a pair of sunken eyes, hollow cheeks, and a long protruding chin. Her letter was more frightening:

Ramin has lost interest in everything. Mom, if you don't come to help, we will lose him!

Dear kind God, from several thousand miles away, what can I do for my son? Until Shoja's situation is cleared, I cannot leave Iran. But what if something awful happens to my son? I must write to Mr. Samadi—an old friend and a diplomat in Washington D.C.—and ask him to check on Ramin. As the children's guardian, he has an obligation to them. I must also share my concerns with Shoja. Ramin needs immediate attention.

The following week, our conversation in the Qasr visiting room seemed impossible. The constant chattering of forty people became too loud. The guard between us was reluctant to budge. Putting my hand through the first row of bars, I poked the guard in the back.

"What?" he asked in a nonthreatening way.

I pointed at my throat and lowered my voice. "Sorry to startle you. I have laryngitis and can't shout. Could you move just a little bit?"

To my surprise, the guard offered a better solution. "Come

through these bars and stand next to me. That way, you will be closer to the prisoner and won't have to shout."

I bent down and squeezed through the first iron bars. Now, there was only the second set of bars between Shoja and I. I could actually reach out and touch him. Of course, I refrained.

Shoja was beaming. "What excuse did you use?"

"Never mind. Fill me in—quick."

"I'm in a regular cell. Compared to the 'School', it's okay. There, we were eighteen in one room. Here, I can at least stretch out at night. No country club, but some of the guards are friendly and sometimes invite me to play volleyball with them in the yard."

"Heard anything about your trial?"

"No! Of course, if I'm to be eliminated, as the others were, there won't be a trial."

"Shoja, don't even joke about that."

"Can you believe it's already nine months since my arrest? I miss my parents. What's keeping them away?"

"Emotionally, they're just not ready yet."

"How are the kids?"

I began to tell him about Ramin, but changed my mind. Shoja had enough worries of his own.

"The kids are fine and send you their love. I'm sure they would like to hear from you," I replied, trying hard to hide the anxiety in my voice.

"I still can't get myself to write to them," Shoja sighed.

The darned whistle blew. He reached out for my arm, only to be pulled back and led away.

An unshaven young man was waiting for me inside Mother's apartment, a revolver exposed in his holster.

"Who are you? What do you want?" I asked automatically.

"No need to be alarmed, *Khanom* Sheikh," the man said softly. "I just need a few minutes alone with you."

"What's your business here?"

"My name is Sa'id. I'm the special assistant to Ayatollah Mohammadi Gilani."

"Who?"

"The new Tribunal Judge. I'm also a former student of your brother, Dr. Aryanpour. A very dedicated and respectful instructor."

"Has the Judge sent you here?"

"No! I'm here on God's mission. If this boy will leave," Sa'id pointed to Babak who was standing by me, "I'll discuss it with you."

"I am not a boy, and I won't leave my mother alone!"

"Anything you have to say can be relayed in front of my son," I told the man. Babak's determination had given me new confidence.

"*Khanom*, what I have to tell you might be inappropriate for the boy's ears, but if you insist." The young *Pasdar* cleared his throat. "All of the accusations against your husband have been severe. But not as severe as the sex offenses. If you can't do something to defend him, your husband is finished."

"What sex offenses? What do you mean by that?" My voice took on a fierceness.

The messenger removed a typed letter from his pocket. "Secretly, I managed to get a copy of this for you. Read it."

The unsigned, poorly written letter was addressed to the Islamic Revolutionary Prosecutor:

Your Honor, Sir,

You know about the grave sins of the former Minister of Health and Social Welfare. Yes! He stole from the poor. Yes! He sold our country to foreigners. Above all sins, Dr. Sheikh did not esteem the chastity of our women. He actually turned the Ministry into a whorehouse. Now, under the leadership of Imam Khomeini, this corrupt and sinful animal must be punished, perhaps publicly castrated. Let others learn a lesson from this.

At the bottom of the letter, the names of twelve women, supposedly victims of Shoja's lust, appeared, all one-time employees at the Ministry. I recognized two. One was the happily married wife of a well-known physician and mother of two children. The other, a grandmother! This letter seemed to be a vile attempt by some fundamentalist against working women. I threw it on the floor.

"This is ridiculous," I shrieked. "What's your purpose in showing me this totally outrageous, slanderous letter? It is nothing but vicious gossip. These women are innocent and so is my husband!"

"Perhaps. But, the Prosecutor would waste no time in using it as evidence, *Khanom*. I thought if you could prove these accusations untrue, you might save your husband's life. Trust me. I'm on your side," the young man said.

"I can't react to hearsay. If this anonymous letter can be admitted as evidence in a Revolutionary court, then my husband is already condemned! I should give up all hope for justice."

"Believe me, I understand your situation."

"No, you don't understand anything," I yelled again. "My

husband is a decent, moral man and has not touched any woman but me. Please, leave us alone!"

"*Khanom!*"

"You heard my mother, go!" Babak shouted.

The *Komiteh* was outdoing the SAVAK in making dossiers. Or, was this dossier a souvenir from the Shah's time? Would evidence such as this be valid in the Islamic court? If so, Shoja was ruined.

Soqra, my childhood nanny, who was visiting us from the holy city of Mashhad, tried to comfort me. "Child, I hung votive cloth at the shrine of Imam Reza before coming. You know about his miracles. He will save your man."

I threw my arms around my old nanny, and sobbed.

"Cry, child! Empty your sorrows on me," she said and stroked me on the back.

Soqra had married a servant while both were working for my parents. At the time, Father was the president of a combined plant in Mashhad that generated electricity as well as produced cloth.

We lived in a large house with an orchard—apricots, cherries, and plums in the summer; pomegranates, quinces, and persimmons in the fall. I was told not to ever venture too far into the overgrown wilderness of the orchard alone. Soqra claimed that a jinni lived there, one who ate little children for snacks. She had told me about all kinds of jinnis; they seemed to be everywhere—in chimneys, beneath rocks, above clouds— some good, some bad. Curiosity drove me to investigate these jinnis for myself.

One afternoon, I slipped out cautiously to the farthest part of the orchard and waited by the creek for the mysterious creature to show himself. Out of the quiet, something started to waddle near me, on the ground. The odd animal had a long snout and was covered with sharp bristles—a porcupine, as I later found out. But at four years old, I thought that this jinni was the strangest thing imaginable, especially since it passed by me without even a glance.

When I confronted Soqra with my experience, she confirmed my assumption that in fact it was the good jinni. "Next time, child, you might not be so lucky!"

Sweet childhood memories!

My father moved his family to Tehran, when I was seven, but Soqra and her husband stayed behind. Now, it felt good to be embraced in my old nanny's familiar soft, fleshy body and to be assured that Imam Reza would save my man. How much I needed to believe in his miracles.

Today, on our way home from a short visit with Shoja, Babak and I were stopped dead by the shouts of a newspaper boy: "*Ettela'at! Ettela'at!* Sheikholeslamzadeh trial coming soon!"

The Revolutionaries had taken to referring to Shoja by his long formal last name.

"Impossible! Dad said nothing about his trial," Babak argued.

The headline in *Ettela'at* read: "New Unspeakable Crimes of the ex-Minister of Health Revealed! He Could Face Death!"

An unusually frightening photograph of Shoja created a demonic image to support the print. Passersby rushed to throw down coins, pick up copies, and read, devouring each word. I

A young Azar Aryanpour.

Left to right: Azar's mother, Fakhri Maryam Sepehri (Aryanpour), Azar at 15, Amir Mehdi Aryanpour, Azar's sister, Aryan.

A wedding picture of Shoja and Azar in 1957.

A happy moment! Azar and Shoja in 1976.

Left to right: Ramin, Shoja, Babak, Azar and Roxana in 1977.

Now Ruz (The Iranian New Year) audience at Niavaran Palace. Shoja is the third from left. Primier Hoveyda is seen next to the Shah. Hoveyda was later executed.

The Shah of Iran gives an audience at Sa'd Abad Palace. Shoja is second from right.

Now Ruz audience at Niavaran Palace with Queen Farah. Azar, first from left. The Queen is handing out gold coins.

An official visit with the Sadats in 1975.

Shoja's trail: The Revolutionary Court, summer 1979.

Evin Prison's clinic where Shoja worked as a general physician and surgeon for several years, taking care of over 200 patients a day.

An unofficial
picture:
Shoja and
his guard
at Evin Prison

Reunion after eight years at JFK Airport in New York! Left to right:
Ramin, Shoja, Roxana and Babak.

A historical picture of four generations of women in Azar's family, including her grandmother, aunt and cousins. Left to Right: Hamideh Kalantar Zarrabi (Sepehri), Mahin Banoo Sepehri (Hayatghaib), Mahin Francis Hayatghaib (Fallah) and Lilly Fallah (Lawrence).

Azar with grandchildren. Left to right: Kamron, Kayvan, Kimya and Azar.

waited for the curious crowd to disappear before stepping forward, fearing to be recognized.

"How many copies do you have left?" I inquired with some reservation.

"I dunno. Maybe sixty, sixty-five," the newspaper boy answered.

"I'll take them all. How much?" I asked in a hurried voice.

"Mom, what are you doing?" Babak pulled my sleeve.

"Never mind," I said sternly.

The newspaper boy eyed me suspiciously, until he saw the money in my hand. I paid, picked up the remaining bundle of papers, handed half of them to Babak and, together, we walked away hastily.

"Now, sixty-five people aren't going to read this trash. Some consolation!"

Back in the car, Babak and I read the article word by word. To our surprise, no trial date was mentioned in *Ettela'at*. Yet, Shoja had been charged with every conceivable offense, including one we never heard before: drug smuggling! Shoja had become the Revolutionaries' newest Satan!

Infuriated by the accusations, I crumpled and tore the paper apart.

Thirty minutes later, in Mother's courtyard, I set the entire libelous papers on fire. Babak looked on with an unreadable expression.

Late in the evening, a sharp knock on the front door alerted me. It was our new acquaintance, Sa'id.

"*Khanom*, please listen to me for only a few seconds. I know you are angry at me, but I just dropped by to tell you that Dr. Sheikh's trial begins tomorrow at 5:00 p.m.," he reported.

"Tomorrow? There's no mention of it in today's papers."

"I know. I suppose the Court wanted to keep it a secret as long as possible."

"Will I be allowed to sit in?" I asked with a visible note of tension in my voice.

"No! Only the complaining parties and the press will be permitted in the courtroom. If you want, I can tape-record the sessions for you, but no one must know. Eh?"

The young man seemed sincere. I accepted his offer. There was no one else to turn to for help.

CHAPTER THIRTEEN

If Allah should punish men
According to what they deserve,
He would not leave so much as a beast!
                    Qur'an (Surah 35)

Half-disguised in a large scarf and dark glasses, I
arrived outside the courthouse, on the east wing of
Qasr Prison. I was too restless to stay home on such a
decisive day. Quietly, I mingled with a group of reporters,
plaintiffs, and curiosity seekers. It was 4:00 p.m., July, 1979.

A short mousy-looking man in poor clothing rushed up to
the guard. "Let me in, Brother. I'm a plaintiff, and this is my
proof." He pointed to a brown folder in his right hand.

"Court does not convene until five o'clock. You have to
wait," the guard explained curtly.

"I've already waited three long years to avenge my son's
death. I will no longer be silent!" the man shouted in protest.

A nearby reporter's attention was aroused by the man's agi-
tated voice. He stepped forward. "*Agha*, I'm from *Kayhan* newspaper. Tell us your story. We'll print it in tomorrow's paper,
with your picture, of course."

Others, including me, pressed closer. The plaintiff suddenly found himself the center of media attention. He put his hands on his sides and cleared his throat. "Ahem! You see, it all started three years ago, in a remote village near Damqan," he related. "My little boy—hardly six—was bitten by a rattlesnake. You know, one of those killers. My pregnant wife and I panicked. Our poor little boy was going to die. We had to save his life. The dirt road to the nearest clinic was not passable by car. So much for the Shah's great modernization! I carried the delirious child on the back of a donkey. It took two hours to get to the clinic. When we got there, it was closed and the doctor was gone for the day. By the time I found him, it was too late. To make the story short, my son, my innocent little boy, died in my arms!" The man paused to wipe his eyes with the edge of his sleeve.

The audience had tightened around the grief-stricken father, yearning to hear more. The plaintiff composed himself and continued with his story.

"All in all, from that day on, I have lived a dog's life. If our village had a clinic, or at least a decent road, my poor son would be alive today. I sold my small farm—my only livelihood—and traveled to Tehran, going from court to court and writing many letters. I even took my complaint to the Minister of Health, this evil person now on trial. He was too busy to see me. Now that, with God's help, the reign of the ruthless is over, I've come to seek justice," the plaintiff declared.

Random cheers broke out.

"We are behind you!"

"An eye for an eye!"

"The Minister should be hung!"

The storyteller, with an artificial sad look, posed for the camera. He was guaranteed to have his picture in the front page of the newspaper. I listened with horror, not being able to make sense of the whole thing.

By now, the line of plaintiffs had grown. What other horrendous stories were concealed within those brown folders they carried?

Two women in black *chadors* swaggered up to the guard. "Sweetie, let us in. We've got an even juicier story to tell about this '*Vazir*'." As they giggled, their prominent gold caps sparkled in the sun.

My head began to spin. What were those women up to? I had never seen their like in Tehran by daylight.

"Hey, you can't just walk into the courtroom. You must have documentation," the guard asserted.

One of the whores seductively pulled aside her *chador* to reveal a garish purple dress, cut low to expose ample cleavage. From a face caked with makeup, bright red lips crooned, "To document the offense, we'd have to expose ourselves immodestly! The guy raped us!"

The guard's face reddened. This was even too much for him to digest. "Get lost, you two! Or I'll arrest you for prostitution!"

The women left the scene, shaking with laughter. The crowd's cheers amplified in my ears, driving me mad with rage. How low would these plaintiffs go in their lies?

At five o'clock, the court opened its doors. The plaintiffs and the reporters entered. The rest remained. Without weighing the consequences, I walked to the guard and quietly introduced myself. "I'm the defendant's wife. Could you please let me in?"

"You are the *Vazir's* wife?" he said loud enough for everyone to hear. "No! A defendant's wife can only attend the trial with special permission from the Prosecutor-General or a higher authority," the guard said with a scowl.

"The *Vazir's* wife!" someone called out. Instantly, a camera flashed before me. I quickly covered my face, and turned to run away.

"Hey, *Khanom Vazir*, just one picture to complete my story! How do you feel about your husband cheating on you? Did you know about his affairs?" a reporter, emerging from behind, yelled after me.

I threw myself into the car and locked the door. My whole body was trembling with violent sobs. "Oh, God, take me!" I screamed with repulsion. "I don't want to live among such people!"

"They've convicted Dad!" Babak tossed the morning newspaper to me. His eyes started to twitch.

The headline read: "Sheikholeslamzadeh Is Guilty!"

According to the newspaper, the Prosecutor had charged Shoja with a new offense: impregnating a woman and then forcing her to undergo an abortion, paid for by the Ministry. If proved, each one of these charges would justify a death sentence in an Islamic Court.

I slapped the palm of my hand against my forehead to make sure this was not a nightmare.

When we had lost all hopes in mankind, Reza Shayan, an old friend of Shoja, bravely came to our rescue. He knew Shoja from medical school years.

"Listen carefully, Azar. I know the real story behind the alleged abortion case," Reza disclosed on the phone. "The woman, Belqais Ebrahimpour, had uterine cancer. Her son, a poor worker, pleaded to Shoja for help. He, in turn, referred the patient to Pars Hospital. The gynecologist charged her nothing. Other expenses were covered by the Ministry. And get this, at the time of the operation, the woman was sixty years old!"

"This is unbelievable. They have turned daylight into darkness. Do you have proof of this, Reza?" I asked frantically.

"Yes. But please keep my name out of it."

"I promise. Just get the documents to me fast, so I can have them printed in tomorrow's newspapers. Please, hurry! Shoja's life's on the line."

"Meet me in my office in an hour," Reza said.

This could be a turning of events for Shoja. I jumped into my car and drove recklessly to Reza's office. The humane doctor provided the lifesaving documents. I enclosed a short cover letter addressed to the Prosecutor, and dashed across the city, fighting the traffic, to meet the newspapers deadlines.

The two national newspapers, *Ettela'at* and *Kayhan*, refused to publish anything in Shoja's defense. Only *Bamdad*, a more liberal publication, agreed to print a copy of the letter and the evidence. Of course, I paid their 23,000-touman advertisement fee, on the spot.

In the afternoon, having been granted a special permission letter by Dr. Mofatteh, I hoped to attend the court session and get a copy of the new evidence to the judge. Fearful of the people's reactions toward me, Aryan had come along.

"New orders. The defendant's wife is strictly forbidden, no matter who writes on her behalf," the guard bullied me.

"Could you at least take these documents to the Judge?" I pleaded.

"No! Not my duty. Mail them."

I returned to Aryan, helplessly. "What now?"

"Give me the stuff. I'll try to enter as a plaintiff," she said.

Before I could say no, my impulsive sister was speaking to the guard, waving the documents in the air. Soon she disappeared inside the building, leaving me behind. I quickly retreated to the safety of my car and waited.

Half an hour later, Aryan walked out of the courthouse. Her disheveled look indicated that something had gone wrong.

"What happened? You are back early," I asked with concern.

"They threw me out!"

"Why?"

"Because I dared to speak briefly on Shoja's defense. Go thank God you weren't there. It was a real kangaroo court! All defiance and no defense. The Prosecutor? A regular executioner! Your poor husband was not even permitted legal counsel."

I clasped my hands. "Not more charges, I hope?"

"Oh! New charges, old charges. Nothing but charges! They claimed that Shoja's responsible for the death of hundreds of people in Rezaiyeh during the cholera epidemic. Can you believe it, Azar?"

"How did Shoja respond?"

"They wouldn't give him a chance! A gutsy woman, who got in under the guise of a plaintiff, dared to speak on his behalf. You should've heard her address the Prosecutor! 'I am a journalist from Rezaiyeh,' she said. 'Contrary to your account, two years ago when there was an epidemic of cholera, not one death was reported there. The Ministry of Health worked hard to contain the disease. Dr. Sheikh himself came to assess the situation.'" Aryan paused to take a breath. "The Prosecutor ordered the woman to state her relationship to the defendant.

'No relation. I am only here because of my conscience. As a Christian, I swear on the Bible to tell the truth,' the woman from Rezaiyeh said. The Prosecutor announced, 'This witness has no credibility in a Moslem Court.' All hell broke loose."

I shook my sister's arm gently. "What happened then?"

"Shoja found a chance to say that in villages without city water or proper hygiene facilities, cholera is bound to be a problem. 'I did everything possible to prevent the spread of this endemic disease,' he said. The Prosecutor quickly switched gears, trying to link Shoja to the F.B.I.," Aryan blurted out.

"F.B.I.?" I asked with surprise.

"Yeah! His so-called proof was a copy of a letter Shoja had once written to the F.D.A.! As if the Prosecutor couldn't tell the difference? Then, he jumped to the alleged sexual offenses. I couldn't stand it any more, so I shouted, 'This is an Islamic Court! Stick to the truth.' Before I realize what's happening, they kicked me out. Sorry, Azar, I didn't get to deliver the documents."

"Never mind. I'll mail them. How many people were there?"

"Let's see. There was the Presiding Judge, the Tribunal Judge, the Prosecutor, about thirty armed guards, a few reporters, and four plaintiffs. Plenty of enemies against one person! Poor Shoja won't survive!" Aryan concluded.

Nothing in the next morning's papers about the woman defending Shoja or his defense. The newspapers had, however, quoted the Prosecutor: "The defendant wasted the nation's money on foreign-built ambulances, not even bothering to have the name written correctly. The word 'ambulance' appeared backwards on the front of each vehicle!"

At least the *Bamdad* had printed my letter along with the hospital record under the headline "The ex-Minister's Wife Addresses the Islamic Revolutionary Court":

"The honorable and righteous Islamic Court must not be defamed by false testimony. The Iranian people have the right to know the truth. I am convinced that to maintain the public's trust in the new legal system, the Court would enter the enclosed documents in evidence of my husband's innocence. May God and the people be on your side."

In the evening, again, we heard a knock on the outside door. Sa'id was waiting for us in the dark. He delivered a tape. "Doctor did a good job defending himself, today. Let's hope that tomorrow goes as well. *Khanom*, your letter to the Prosecutor was very compelling. It might save your husband's life. Anyhow, I've got to run now. I'll be in touch."

Babak was anxious to hear the tape, but I was dubious. After the unspeakable scenes outside the court, I could only imagine what went on inside.

On the fourth day of the trial, Robab, Shoja's sister who had come from Tabriz, gained admittance into the courtroom as a plaintiff. Strangely, the guard did not ask her to present any documents. Considering this was Robab's first visit with Shoja since he was in prison, I was surprised. She never liked me. Whatever her motives, I was glad that someone from his family finally represented him in the trial.

Robab was five years younger than Shoja, married, and the mother of two children.

She returned to the car drenched with sweat. Her large

chest was heaving. "No air in that awful room! Hot as Hell!"

"Yes, I can imagine. Here, drink some water," I said.

Robab took the bottle and drank incessantly, then wiped her mouth with the back of her hand.

"Tell me about the court. Did something unusual happen?" I asked tensely.

"How is this for unusual? They claimed that Shoja and his deputies embezzled millions of toumans through that computer contract. Of course, they had no evidence—just talk," she paused to fan herself with a handkerchief.

"Go on, please!"

"Shoja found a minute to defend himself. He said the computer contract began after a thorough study. No crime was committed, and EDS, the American computer company, was paid only for completed portions of the job. The Prosecutor cut him short and turned to the spectators. He said, 'You be the jury. EDS comes to Iran, promises to automate our Social Security System in return for several hundred million dollars, takes the money, and leaves the job unfinished. Then two representatives of that company, jailed on charges of bribery, escape from prison. Now the defendant says no crime was committed?'"

"That's not true," I protested. "EDS representatives in Iran had been jailed as 'material witnesses' in the case, not for charges of bribery! Now, go on please. What happened then?" I asked Robab restlessly.

"I'll tell you what happened," she continued, moving her heavy body. "Shoja insisted that there was no bribery committed by EDS. Everything was above the board. The Prosecutor jumped to another allegation. He brought up the alleged 48 million touman transfer of money—you know, the infamous 'List'.

He held up a bank statement, claiming that Shoja owned 170 million touman in one account! 'Look for yourself,' he said to the audience. 'Isn't this large amount of money proof enough that the defendant took bribes? That he could afford to transfer 48 million touman out of that account to a foreign bank?'"

"What did Shoja say to that?"

Robab gulped down the last drop of water. "Well, Shoja looked at the statement for a second, and calmly said, '*Agha*, this paper shows 170 thousand touman, not 170 million. Perhaps your eyeglasses failed! Also, this is not my personal account, but rather the Ministry's. I quit over a year ago as a Minister. At that time, I gave up my power of attorney to co-sign checks from this account. This document is outdated. You should check with the new Minister, if these funds are unaccounted for.'"

"Good! What was the court's reaction?"

"You should've seen the whole bunch! They all stood there with their big mouths hung open like zombies! There was only one high-ranking clergyman who seemed impressed by the way my brother defended himself."

"Who was he?"

"Let me think. Oh, yeah, his name was Ayatollah Gilani," Robab said and leaned back in the car seat. "Now, take me for a short visit with my parents before I go back to Tabriz tonight."

"Can't you stay a few days? Your parents need you. They are seriously ill and may not live long," I tugged on her sleeve.

"I can't! My husband would have a fit if I'm not back tonight. Besides, I hate this weather. Tehran's too hot for me," she said bluntly.

We had a surprise guest at dinner. "Admiral Ahmad

Madani is waiting outside in the car," Hushang said with a smile as he entered Mother's apartment. "Is the coast clear for him to come in?"

Mother nervously started to clean the table. "Why didn't you tell us earlier? The house is a mess!"

"Mother, Madani is not here for a social call. He is now Ayatollah Khomeini's Defense Minister, so it is risky for him to be seen with us," my brother explained. "Madani is only here for moral support. He can't stay more than a few minutes."

Since twenty-two years ago, when I broke our unofficial engagement, I had not seen Madani. I had heard that he left the Navy because of his anti-Shah sentiments, and was exiled to a small island in Bandar Abbas Province on the Persian Gulf, where the weather was extremely hot and the living conditions poor. What irony! As the man I married was rising in the political arena, the man I didn't marry fell from favor. Now things were completely reversed.

Madani entered through the back door. His appearance had not changed noticeably over the years, except for a receding hairline. He still had the same calm, graceful manner. Madani hugged Mother and shook hands with Babak and I. "You're too young to have a son this age," he politely commented. The Admiral was happily married now, and had two children.

Mother congratulated him on his new post and expressed her wish that he become the first President of Iran.

Madani smiled, but Hushang spoke for him: "That day is very near!"

"I am following your husband's trial," Madani said with concern. "He seems to be an innocent victim of recent changes. Unfortunately, the Revolution has sparked some extreme reactions. The quick executions were an example. I hope that the radicalism will mellow with time and the country will achieve its goals of democracy and freedom."

"Admiral, what if they execute my husband in the meantime?" I asked anxiously.

"We must keep faith. Hopefully your fears will be over soon," he wished.

The Islamic Republic's Defense Minister gave me no false promises to help Shoja. He couldn't. The Revolutionary Tribunal worked independently.

The next day, Sa'id called from the court. "One of the plaintiffs accused your husband of negligence in the death of his twenty-eight-year-old son during an operation," Sa'id rapidly disclosed. "Dr. Sheikh didn't remember such a patient at Pars Hospital. *Khanom*, if you can locate the medical records, you may be able to save your husband's life. But act fast. Remember, the Court may order a death sentence based on murder!"

I decided to contact the hospital, immediately. Confronting Shoja's old colleagues would not be easy, but there was no other way to get the information. I would face them for Shoja. I would even meet with Satan, if needed.

Akbar, the hospital's security guard, turned his face away as I entered. He had spoken against Shoja, here and there. How fashionably revolutionary these days!

At the medical records department, my request was flatly rejected. "Without written permission from the hospital administrator or the surgeon, you could not gain access to such records," the hospital clerk informed me.

"Who is the administrator now?" I asked with disappointment.

"Dr. Yazdi!"

He was the one who had unkindly rejected me at his door over two months ago. Obviously, he would offer no help now.

"Give me the name of the surgeon, please," I said desperately.

Looking in the file the woman said, "Miri, a neurosurgeon."

A gleam of hope lightened my heart. Neurosurgeon? So, Shoja definitely could not have been involved in a brain surgery. Besides, I knew Dr. Miri from older and happier times. He had done his residency at the same hospital in Ohio as Shoja. He would cooperate with me.

In his office, I quickly explained my urgent request. Dr. Miri, standing behind his desk in a white uniform, slid his hands into his pockets and said in an unfriendly manner, "I can't possibly provide that kind of information. It will jeopardize my position." He raised his voice and shifted his carefully-brushed head to one side. "They will think that I killed the man. That patient had a brain tumor even God could not have cured!"

"Believe me, I'm not trying to get you into trouble, Doctor. I'm only trying to save my husband's life," I reasoned with him. "At the court, Shoja had been wrongly named as the surgeon, and the death declared murder. If there was no negligence on your part, you should have no fears. Please, time is crucial."

Miri stubbornly refused to obtain the document for me.

"You know, I could report you to the Court and the media for obstructing justice. Your medical license may be revoked, " I bluffed.

The doctor rested his hand pensively on his forehead and weighed his options for a while. The bluff worked. He, reluctantly, went to the records room and retrieved a copy of the patient's file. I thanked him hastily and headed for the newspaper's office to submit the document in time for tomorrow's edition.

This time *Bamdad's* editor had received a court order: "Nothing may be printed in support of the jailed Minister!"

There was no sense pleading to the editor. I ran to the nearest post office and express mailed a copy of the patient's records to the Court. I knew that the authorities might not acknowledge the document, but I was not going to give up the slightest chance for justice.

On the sixth day of Shoja's trial, around noon, a bearded representative from the *Bonyad-e-Mostaz'afin*—Foundation for the Disinherited—arrived at Mother's door.

"I have been sent to take an inventory of your own possessions. Do not be concerned, *Khanom*. The intention is not to confiscate your property. It is just a *formalité*," the emissary explained, trying to substantiate his statement by using a French word.

Babak and I escorted him across the street to our home. Shahri had obviously lost interest in our garden. The lawn had grown tall and brown. The rose bushes were wilted. Long, overgrown branches of the weeping willow swept the ground, and leaves floated decadently on the surface of the pool. The water was green with moss.

The man from the 'Foundation' went from room to room, and scrupulously recorded everything—from artwork to kitchenware. We followed him patiently. He also obtained a copy of the house deed as well as the titles to our cars.

"What do you need those for?" I asked him.

"Just a *formalité*," he said without looking at me. "Since your husband has been accused of embezzlement, our organization, appointed by the Court, is authorized to investigate your assets."

Good! Finally someone had decided to look beyond accusations for proof. Soon it would be disclosed to everyone that our rumored excessive wealth had been nothing but a myth.

Later in the day, Hushang called. "A businessman named Jamshid, who claims to have top connections, says he can help Shoja. He could have the influential director of the 'Foundation for the Disinherited' talk to Ayatollah Khomeini's son, Ahmad, on Shoja's behalf. Of course, this favor would cost us four hundred fifty thousand touman in the form of a 'donation' to the Foundation! What do you say?"

"Forget it! Where are we going to get that much money? Besides, the guy may be an impostor," I warned Hushang.

Shoja's trial and the mudslinging continued. The Prosecutor's office was still requesting plaintiffs to add to the bulk of an existing huge volume of defamatory evidence. Hadn't Shoja already been viciously accused enough—embezzling, drug smuggling, spying for the C.I.A., corresponding with the F.B.I., running houses of prostitution, ruining the nation's health care system, causing hundreds of deaths during the cholera epidemic? What could be left?

According to our God-sent friend, Sa'id, a worker named Danesh, who had entered the court today as a plaintiff, actually turned out to be a defense witness for Shoja. While in office, Shoja had performed an operation on the young man's debilitating congenital hip problem, gratis. Judge Gilani had been moved by the account.

Unfortunately, Sa'id was not able to tape the session, and the press had deliberately omitted this important testimony in their daily reports.

On Sunday, July 22, after eight days, the radio announced: "The trial of the ex-Minister of Health and Social Welfare is over. The Court is deliberating its verdict."

The whole family spent the day in a frenzy.

"Whatever the verdict, you must accept it gracefully and with dignity," Amir Hosain advised.

"Shoja has to be freed! He's innocent," I insisted.

By nightfall Sa'id showed up at the front door, and we all rushed at him. This time he came in.

"What happened?" I asked hoarsely.

"Well, I heard some rumor that could be good," Sa'id said. "Dr. Sheikh might be exiled for a few years in Bandar Abbas, on the Persian Gulf."

"Exile? How could they? He's not guilty!"

"*Khanom*, your husband is not totally innocent! He served the Shah!" Sa'id said coolly.

Would Shoja survive the disgrace of exile? The scorching climate of Bandar Abbas? The isolation? What would become of us?

At night, my dreams were nightmares filled with the hell-like heat, scorpions, and snakes of Bandar Abbas.

I turned the pages of the morning papers frantically, scanning every column. For the first time, after months of notoriety, our name did not appear in print. This sudden silence was not comforting. The mood pendulum swung. What did this silence mean?

Our life, however, was far from quiet. My sister rushed to Mother's apartment, crying and screaming, "My husband was just handcuffed and taken away by the *Komiteh* for interrogation. His crime? He protested to the *Pasdars* searching our home, looking for 'hidden documents' that supposedly belonged to Shoja. I'm going out of my mind. What if they put my husband in jail?"

I felt guilty. Guilty and angry. My existence was becoming more of a burden to everyone. We had already lost friends—now family too.

While Aryan had hopes that her husband would return, I hoped for mine to live.

Waiting for the verdict had become excruciating.

CHAPTER FOURTEEN

On Wednesday, July 25, at 12:05 p.m., there was a sharp, demanding bang at the front door to my mother's apartment. We were having lunch. As Babak hurriedly opened the door, two heavy-heeled *Pasdars* with pointed machine guns forced their way in. They ordered me to go with them. I sprang to me feet. My heart thumped in terror. Mother turned as white as a ghost. Babak's eyes began to twitch. Fear froze deep in his young face. The menacing men shoved me out. There was no chance to utter a word, to protest. What were they going to do with me?

Outside, the armed men turned right and pulled me with them. Their grips on my wrists were painful. Running and stumbling, I followed my executioners all the way to our house. The house, only a block away, was surrounded by jeeps full of Revolutionary military guards. I froze in panic.

"Move," one of the *Pasdars* shouted.

I did not move. He grabbed my arm and dragged me forward, his fingers cutting into my flesh. We reached the front gate.

"Your house has been confiscated. Open the gate!" a voice commanded from behind a Stalinesque mustache.

I refused. "No! My husband's verdict hasn't been announced yet."

"Open the gate before I break it down on your neck!"

My hands began to tremble as I took the key out of my dress pocket. The guard grabbed the key from my hand and opened the front gate. Ten to fifteen *Pasdars* rushed in, pulling me along with them. We passed through the garden and reached the terrace. Spray-painted slogans screamed from the interior garden walls: "Death to the great enemy of God and the people!" Had they invaded our house before?

The men in green fatigues swarmed past me into the house.

"Who authorized you to take our home? Aren't you listening to me? Stop!"

The intruders were already moving from room to room, and tearing the furniture.

"Listen! You can't touch my house. There's been no verdict yet!" I pleaded again.

"Oh yes there has—and a sentence too," the leader taunted me. "You just don't know it."

"What did my husband get? Please! Tell me!"

"Out of the way, you hussy."

I ran after him begging, "What was it? For God's sake, tell me. What was my husband's sentence?"

The leader stopped and turned to me, his dark eyes burning with hatred. "You really want to know, hussy? Your traitorous husband got the sentence he deserved: DEATH! And it was carried out instantly!"

At once, a tremor passed through me. The word 'DEATH' struck my throbbing head with the speed of lightning. The room with everything in it began to feel wobbly—rocking unsteadily back and forth. My knees buckled and I leaned against the wall for support. My eyes lost focus. The enemy watched me triumphantly as a sharp pain seized my chest, right above the heart, and spread to my left arm. I might as well die.

The cold metal of a machine gun pressed against my right temple. "Move it! C'mon! Let's go! Upstairs now!"

With one hand clasped on my heart, I forced myself to move. My aching body swayed from side to side, legs slipped, arm frantically grasped for the banister. The man and his machine gun climbed behind, prodding his victim up the steps.

At the landing, Roxana's room appeared. A vile stranger in fatigues was ransacking her dresser drawers. I shut my eyes! The armed man shoved me from behind. "C'mon, move it!"

We entered the storage room.

"Open the safe!" the man ordered, pointing to the steel-gray box on the floor. "Quick!"

On my knees, I began to turn the dial desperately, but my mind was fuzzy, as if a storm had just raided my brain. It was hard to concentrate, not knowing if the enemy would shoot me once the safe was opened.

What was the combination? Was it 5...26...8...10...? The fifth number? Six? Sixteen?

"Damn it! C'mon, open it! Don't waste time!"

My shaking fingers worked on the lock, turning left, then right and then left again. The safe did not open. The Angel of Death looked down at me. I tried the numbers again—this time using sixteen instead of six. The damned lock still did not open!

The dark shadow over me became alarmingly impatient.

"What the hell's the matter? We don't have all day!" He rammed the butt of his gun deep into my stomach.

The pain was excruciating! Tears spontaneously ran down my face. I took a breath and tried the lock again. My hands trembled uncontrollably. The ramming of the gun had only made matters worse. The numbers were all gone! I looked up at my captor pathetically.

"Do it! Or else—"

I rubbed my temples. The numbers were not there. My memory was as bare as the desert. Let him kill me, I thought.

He kicked me aside. He aimed his machine gun at the lock. One shot. A second shot. A third. Bang! A jangling sound. Our treasures spilled out onto the floor: the diamond earrings that Mother passed on to me on my wedding day; a few gold coins; Roxana's graduation present—a gold-plated bracelet; the kids' report cards; our marriage certificate.

"Get up! Back to the first floor."

I obeyed like a robot. My existence simply depended on his mercy.

Downstairs, vultures rifled through every drawer, emptied every closet, and moved each piece of furniture. Objects were pulled out, thrown around. Men in fatigues had their arms laden with booty.

A piercing voice blasted in my ears. "Go to the bedroom and pack your underwear. Do you hear? Your other clothes have been confiscated for the poor!"

In the bedroom, I took one last look at the family picture on the dresser. The children's faces beamed, full of life. But Shoja's eyes appeared lifeless—like those of a dead person. Of course! What else? He was dead!

"Done? C'mon out here, damn it!" the same voice shouted.

I left the bedroom empty-handed. Who needed things?

Through the thick, black mustache, the vampire took one last deep drag on a cigarette and tossed it on the parquet floor, crushing it out with his heel.

Compulsively, I bent over to wipe the floor.

"Don't touch that, you idiot! This ain't your home! Not any more." The man gathered saliva in his mouth and spat on my hand, his bloodshot eyes teeming with disgust. The spit stung my flesh—and my heart. I felt lower than the dirt.

"Go on. Get lost, hussy!"

Wobbling, I exited the building. Someone tossed out the family portrait behind me. The children smiled, even through the broken glass. Two men pushed past, carting off a trophy, a large oil portrait of what used to be me. A third man opened his zipper and urinated on a rosebush.

I left what was once our home. I was reduced to nothing.

My heavy feet slowly took me back to Mother's apartment. Though always so close, it now seemed miles away. The *Pasdars* had the entire block surrounded. A tingling sensation crept across my skin. My teeth chattered.

I entered the apartment which was swarmed with wailing relatives. Everyone hushed out of respect for the recent widow. A funeral? Even Shoja's unkind younger brother, who was hardly ever around, was present. "Did you see what they did to my beloved brother?"

At the sound of his voice, the volcano boiling inside me erupted. I pushed him aside, screaming with full force, "Go away, you hypocrite. Go away!"

Shoja's sick mother, barely comprehending what was going

on, started to cry. The old man, Agha Joon, placed his handkerchief over his eyes and sniffled. Shoja's brother, balding and
sporting dark glasses, scolded, "Don't be like that! We're all
here to console you."

I picked up the first thing that came to my reach and flung
it across the room against the wall. "Yeah? Don't lie! You're here
for the reading of Shoja's will! But guess what? There's nothing
left! It's all been confiscated. Understand? Nothing—zilch!
Everything's gone! So you can all go home. Now!"

Losing balance, I collapsed on the floor.

"Somebody help. The poor girl's gone mad!" a female voice
said.

"Azar, dear, just drink this. It'll make you feel better,"
another soothing voice reassured.

"Let me die and join Shoja."

"Listen to me, Azar. Shoja is no—"

"I don't want to hear Shoja's name again. It's over. All o-
ver!"

"But, Azar, Shoja's alive! He's not dead!"

Another voice confirmed the statement: "Shoja is alive!"

I gave them all a confused look and moaned, "How cruel to
appease me in this way."

"Here, look for yourself!" Mother said as she held up a
newspaper for me to read.

The headline read in bold type. "Sheikholeslamzadeh
Condemned To Life Imprisonment!"

"Life imprisonment? No! God, no! Death would've been
more honorable." My strained voice cracked into a hysteric sob.

Aryan's husband, after twenty-four hours of gruesome
detention, returned to Mother's apartment. "Azar, I know

whatever I say can't take your pain away, but you must be happy for Shoja's life. We were certain he would be shot. The life sentence doesn't mean anything. Before you know it, the publicity will cease, people will forget, and he'll be paroled or pardoned," he said in an exhausted voice.

So, I should be grateful that Shoja's life had been spared. How could I? The humiliation of Life Imprisonment weighed like tons on my chest. The burden would kill me.

At four o'clock the verdict was announced over the radio: "*Besmellah, Arrahman, Arrahim — In the name of God, the Merciful, the Compassionate. After nine days of trial and deliberations, the Islamic Revolutionary Tribunal found Dr. Shoja Sheikholeslamzadeh guilty of working with the detested former regime, being a cabinet member of the illegal governments under Hoveyda and Amuzgar, destroying the health system of the country, embezzling from the poor, and allocating the budget of the Ministry for personal use. He has been acquitted of the murder and sexual offense charges, due to lack of evidence. After special consideration, the defendant received a life sentence. All of his property and that of his immediate family have been confiscated for the poor. Justice has been rightly served!*"

I wailed and pounded the wall. "You spiteful bastards! Shoja's been tormented enough at the prison in the past several months. Why should he be tormented more with a life sentence? Why? Why?"

Babak appeared, his complexion gray, his eyes twitching. He sat alongside of me silently. I took his hands. We both needed the assuring touch of someone we trusted. Tomorrow was his sixteenth birthday. What did the Revolution care? It had claimed his father from him.

Hushang tapped him on the shoulder. "Babak, what do you

want for your birthday? Just name it, and I'll get it for you."

"Nothing!"

"Could you arrange for him to leave Iran? Please! Babak has no reason to stay any longer," I implored.

"Okay. I'll do my best, Sis. Don't you want to call Ramin and Roxana with the news?"

My two other children! What could I tell them about their father's sentence? How would they react? If only I had not encouraged Shoja to turn himself in.

"I'll call them tomorrow. Let them have a few more hours of hope," I answered.

Later, Shoja's sentencing was televised. His sad face turned dumbstruck as the decision was read: "...The defendant was given one degree of pardon for acquittal of murder and adultery charges, as well as for his superb medical skills. His death sentence was reduced to life imprisonment. He will serve his time in prison, working as a physician without compensation, for the rest of his life."

Mother hugged me. "You saved your husband's life. Without the evidence you provided, he would be dead."

"Our Revolution is victorious/It is just—" From the television, a chorus of Revolutionaries chanted their celebration at our destruction.

My stomach turned. I ran to the sink and splashed cold water on my face and hands. Not even the fountain of Paradise could remove the stinging spit. I had been soiled forever. The bathroom mirror reflected the face of a stranger, hollow and void of life. All that I had were the hellish gory details of the day. From Shoja's death, to his life imprisonment, to being banished from our home like trash! Would the ransacking continue?

Would they spare anything? Who would sleep tonight on the bed that belonged to Shoja and me?

Back in the bedroom, Babak was asleep. Even in repose his face looked pained. How would Shoja spend his first night of a lifetime in prison? At least, I had my family. Shoja had no one. Today we both began a life sentence, he within the prison walls and I outside.

Through the window, I saw shadows in the backyard. Shadows followed by strange noises—trash cans clattered, metal chairs clanking together. Was my tired mind playing tricks? A sharp shattering sound was heard, and glass crashed into our bedroom.

Mother shouted, *"Ya Ali!"*

Babak jumped up. "The mob is attacking us!"

We managed to grab Mother quickly, carry her to the bathroom, and lock the door, just as the window over her bed broke into a hundred pieces.

The three of us huddled each other in the dark, in fear, in silence until this well-staged spectacle of power and intimidation concluded with a few gunshots.

We began the second day of our sentence. By order of the *Komiteh*, Mother's phone was disconnected, so we had limited contact with the outside world.

Because our street was under surveillance, Amir Hosain entered through the back door. "Roxana's on the phone," he said.

Together, we sneaked out through the backyard to his house. When I picked up the phone, I still did not know how to tell the children of their father's life sentence.

"Roxana, I don't have good news for you and Ramin. Your father has been sentenced to life, and all our property was confiscated," I said bluntly.

She started crying. "No! Why? Dad's no criminal! How could they do that to him?"

Tears were choking me. My heart was empty of hope, so I could not find any consoling words for my daughter. Ramin was emotionally unable to speak.

"Sweetheart, try to break the news to your brother gently. I'll talk to both of you soon," I said through tears.

Roxana continued to cry as I hung up.

In the afternoon, two armed *Pasdars* pushed their way into Mother's apartment and, without a search warrant, started ransacking her belongings. Mother's hand reached for her heart. Babak swiftly put his arm around her. I burst with uncontrolled anger.

"What do you want now?" I shrieked. "Have you no decency? Didn't you take everything we ever owned?"

"We want the real valuable things. You know, a *Vazir's* house usually has a whole lot more fancier stuff than what you left behind," one of the two thieves stated.

"Oh, so you didn't like my interior decorating?" I asked sarcastically. "I hope you find adequate compensation at the next *Vazir's* house!"

His insolent comrade started waving a piece of paper in my face. "Where'd you hide these treasures?"

"What treasures?" I shouted.

"The ones buried in the garden."

"Buried?"

"These are what we're after. This list."

I glanced at the paper: Lavendula, Juniper, Rhododendron—

Ignorant boobs! That was a list of the Latin names of trees and shrub seedlings with their precise location in our garden that the landscaper had left us. He wanted us to identify the plants when they started growing. I tried to explain but, of course, the *Pasdars* did not believe me. They took the list as a secret code.

"We'll look for the treasures ourselves!"

"By all means!" I said with profound contempt.

"And where's your car? The *Paykan*? It wasn't in the garage or the driveway. Where did you hide it?" the other *Pasdar* demanded, exposing his Kalashnikov assault rifle more openly.

"Ha! So you've come here to look under my mother's bed for it?"

"We'll find it. Everything you ever had now belongs to us," he gloated.

"Fine! Go ahead! Take everything you want. Only remember, I am not your prisoner!" I said insolently.

The search went on for some time. The only item they seized was Shoja's photo in Mother's living room. We watched with disgust as the disappointed thieves vengefully tore the picture into pieces, and stomped out of the apartment. The intimidation was over for now.

Half an hour later my nephew, Armin, came by. "Auntie Azar, I needed a car yesterday so I borrowed the *Paykan* with Babak's knowledge. When I returned, the house was surrounded. I decided to park the car a couple streets away—just a hunch. Here is the key. I hope I didn't get you into trouble," he said apologetically.

"It's okay. Just don't mention this to anyone, please."

That explained the *Pasdars'* search. Before long, they would find the car and would come back to haunt us. My words would not be accepted. There would be more harassment, maybe more arrests. I could not expose my son and my mother to further pain. I had to get rid of the car. But, how?

I waited until dark. Then, from the back door, unrecognized in a black *chador*, I ventured out into the quiet street, and slipped past the *Pasdars* guarding the front of Mother's apartment. It was a hot evening with no breeze in the air. A crescent moon brightened the cloudless sky. Quickly, I walked three blocks, then made a right turn into a narrow street and stopped. There it was! The *Paykan* was parked in front of a vacant house, just as Armin had described. With quick glances to each side, I slowly moved towards it. A miserable looking creature—a scrawny street dog— crawled out from under the car, barked feebly, and limped across the street. I slipped into the car, scared like a thief caught in the act. As I drove the car to Hushang's office, I began to grin at my own ingenuity. I had stolen my own car!

"Hushang, help me sell my car. I could use the money for the children in America. They're desperate," I told him, entering his office. He was working late on some project.

"What car? Didn't they take both your cars?" he asked, baffled.

"Not mine! Armin had borrowed it."

"I prefer not to get involved in this matter, Sis."

"Please, you've got to help me! If the *Komiteh* finds out that I have the car, I'll go to prison!"

Weighing the risks, my brother softened. "Well, let's talk to my driver. He mentioned he was looking for a car. He's right here."

Nationwide, all auto assembly plants remained shut down, resulting in a black market for cars. The model I had went for 120,000 touman—$12,000. I struck a deal with my brother's driver immediately that night. He felt that he had lucked out to buy my car for 30,000 touman—$3,000. But, I was the lucky one. It was one less thing that the *Komiteh* would rob from me!

At night, Mother, Babak and I took our bedding to the living room, where it seemed safer. The bedroom windows were still broken. The Mullah had assured us that the events of last night would not be repeated. Still, we were hesitant to fall asleep.

Babak, who had been strangely quiet since yesterday, suddenly felt like talking. "Mom, I'll take revenge someday for Dad."

I never wanted my son to grow up with vengeance.

"Let me tell you a true story," I told him. "Years ago, both my paternal grandfather and great-grandfather, natives of Kashan, were hung from gallows. 'Outlaws,' they were labeled. Indeed, they had rebelled against a ruthless government. My father, only sixteen, was sentenced to two years in jail. What was he charged with? Being the eldest son of a convicted rebel. Everything his family owned was confiscated. Their reputation and their name was unjustly defamed. Once released from prison, Father found himself responsible for a mother, grandmother, two younger brothers, and a sister who was born blind. How did he do it against all odds? He gave up his own dreams for the future and went to work to support his family as best as he could. And he did a fine job, working his way up to become the chief accountant of the National Oil Company. Vengeance would've gotten him nowhere."

"Mom, if need be, I would do the same for my family," he stated like a man.

His candor warmed my heart. In the darkness, I squeezed his hand. "Happy birthday, son!"

Although it was almost noon, I was still in bed with depression—severe fatigue, complete loss of interest, a feeling of helplessness, worthlessness. As the shock of the verdict settled, its implications grew more grim. They had confiscated not only the assets of Shoja, my children and I, but of Shoja's parents as well. The old couple had been living off their savings. How would they survive? Without access to their accounts, they would not be able to pay rent to Mother. She would not be able to support us. The conviction had a domino effect. We were almost destitute.

Mother was busy in the kitchen, and Babak? He must be somewhere sketching—his only outlet these days. Amir Hosain dropped by to check on us.

"Get up and do something, Azar. It's not like you to give in to despair. Don't dwell on the past," he scolded. "Here. I've got something for you, a poem by Rudyard Kipling. Translate it. This one is quite appropriate," my brother suggested.

"A poem? I don't know how to find a source of income for my children," I said with frustration. "And you bring me a poem? The damned government won't let me work to support my children. If only the house—"

"Forget about the house. In a time when lives don't count for much, mourning for the material things is vain. Shoja is alive. That's all that matters."

"But we lost more than a house. The invasion, the violation of one's privacy, the injustice—on top of everything else."

"That's all behind you. Focus on your children! Now you're totally responsible for them. Be sensible. Look to the future," my old mentor advised.

The illusive future again!

CHAPTER FIFTEEN

There was a Door to which I found no key
There was a veil past which I might not see
Some little talk of Me and Thee
There seem'd-and then no more of Thee and Me
*   Omar Khayyam (Rubaiyat/Twelfth Century)*

My inheritance from the pre-Revolution time included six photo albums, some memorabilia, and a few pieces of clothing, all of which could fit into one suitcase. Items from the past to justify the cause for a future!

Numerous photos of the children were heartwarming. Roxana's famous smile. Candid shots of Ramin—he always hated having his picture taken. My favorite photo of him was the one in his football outfit, muddied from head to toe. In another, he chased our dog, a brown dachshund dog, named Tootsie, right before her fatal collision with a passing car. Babak's pictures expressed neither the gaiety of Roxana nor the carefree mood of Ramin, but the seriousness of a boy rather too mature for his age.

The few photographs of Shoja were among my most tangible connection to his past. In the oldest, he wore a gray uniform and sported a close crew cut upon entering first grade. Not at all enthusiastic about going to school! In another photo, Shoja was thirteen or fourteen, his left hand under his chin displaying a watch—a *Now Ruz* present from his uncle. Later pictures attested to Shoja's outgoing and sociable personality, always lots of friends gathered around. Most precious, though, were the photos of Shoja and I together.

I also owned a folder containing valuable mementos from my children. A drawing from Roxana's childhood, under which was scrawled "Happy Family," depicted a pretty girl with her parents. Babak's early drawings revealed his interest in cars and planes. No artwork from Ramin, but a few humorous poems. At the age of eight and a half, being angry with me for some silly reason, he gave me this poem on my birthday, written on a postcard:

> *To my old Mother,*
> *Who punished me today,*
> *Should I still bother,*
> *To say happy birthday?*

In a separate folder, I had saved all Shoja's letters, including his short messages from prison. Priceless items! I was not truly poor!

The next morning, Mother's phone was reconnected. We were no longer considered a threat to the Islamic Republic. Our first call came from Evin Prison, around nine o'clock. Shoja had been transferred from Qasr to here and had started working in the prison clinic. The caller said, "You can visit your husband today. Be there at 2:00. Expect a long line."

My excitement for the visit was short-lived. "Mother, I don't know what to say to Shoja when I see him. The last time we talked we still had hopes of his freedom."

"Act naturally. There's nothing wrong with expressing your true feelings. Just don't add to his misery," Mother offered with wisdom.

In preparation for the first visit with my husband at Evin, I took a mild tranquilizer. The long-sleeved, high-necked brown dress that I had borrowed from Aryan was two sizes too big for me, and looked tacky. All my own clothes had been confiscated. I had nothing proper to wear. Altogether, I looked unattractive. My skin was rough and had lost its vitality. My eyes were red and puffy from crying. My hair was unmanageable and falling out in clumps with each brush. It was useless to try to look nice and cheerful.

Babak and I drove off for Evin, borrowing my sister's car. Our street was clear of all surveillance. Apparently, the government's wrath against my family had receded.

Evin, the maximum security prison in the northern suburb of Tehran, took its name from a village at the foothills of Alborz. Not long ago, this area was considered countryside, with fruit and vegetable farms and prolific gardens. Now it had become a much developed part of the greater city itself. However, the immediate area around the prison had retained its rural, isolated atmosphere.

We parked the car by a cliff overlooking a deep ravine. In the scorchingly hot sun, through masses of men, women and children we found our way to the window in the tall guard tower where numbers were distributed. Ours was 108. The loudspeaker had just announced 43. We would be waiting for several hours.

A *chadori* woman, standing close to us, had started a conversation with an old man whose son, a cabdriver, had hit and killed a pedestrian. The father—as I overheard—had sold his home for 200,000 touman to pay the family of the dead person in return for his son, a practice allowed under the Islamic law. His son was being released today. I looked at the man with envy. He had lost his home, but at least he was able to purchase his loved one's freedom.

"I thought only political prisoners were kept in Evin," the woman remarked.

"Oh no, *Khanom*," the old man said. "At the rate they're arresting people, they'll have to build new prisons soon! You'll find all kinds here—rich and poor, *vazir* and *faqir* alike."

So, prison was indeed a great leveler.

I looked around. Huge hungry flies were feasting on a pile of trash. No trees provided refuge from the blistering sun. My thick scarf was sticking to my sweaty skin. I felt limp and languid from too much heat, anticipation and sedation. Babak offered me a thermos of cold water that he had brought along.

"Hey, don't drink! It's the holy month of Ramadan. Our heavenly book Qur'an was revealed in this month," the *chadori* woman reminded me. "Drinking in public's forbidden! You could get punished."

Of course! Ramadan—the thirty days of fasting from dawn to dusk! Since Shoja's verdict, I had completely lost track of time.

Although my throat hurt from the thirst, I turned down Babak's offer. Hiding from the sun, I slouched against his back, my eyes fixed on the morbid fortress. Shoja would remain behind those tall walls until his death. A life sentence was real, immutable!

Babak was lost in his own thoughts. Together, we waited a long time.

"Number 108," the loudspeaker blared. We ran to the prison gate to show our I.D.s to the guard. He examined them and asked, "Are you the family of Dr. Sheikh?" His voice showed no trace of condescension.

"Yes!"

He eyed us curiously, wrote our names on a pink pad, and handed it to me. We entered Evin, Shoja's permanent home. Half a dozen armed *Pasdars* in green fatigues guarded the entrance gate. Babak's hand and mine clasped for support. Despite the tall, deciduous trees, the inside compound looked parched and wilted from drought. We walked a short distance before being led into a featureless building close to the entrance gate. There, our pink slip was collected, and we were sent to a rather large, raunchy waiting room. Two dozen people from all walks of life sat around the room silently. A poster on the wall read: "Woman! Do not seduce men with your nakedness. Keep yourself veiled!"

Involuntarily, I obeyed the poster's message and pulled down my scarf. Since there were no chairs left, Babak and I stood in the corner, near a restroom. The stench was nauseating. I crossed the room and walked towards the open window. A guard, a village boy no older than fourteen, wielding a machine gun taller than himself, ordered me to return to my place. I quietly complained of the odor.

"Just listen to this woman," he called to his friend loudly. "The stench from our bathroom bothers her! She and her kind've been shoving us around and shitting on us for years. Did they listen when we complained?" His mocking grin was replaced by contempt.

Embarrassed and defeated, I returned to my place thinking that no Marxist ideologue could have settled the issue more deftly.

"Attention! Numbers 100 to 110. Line up down the hall for a physical search," we heard on the loudspeaker and rushed out to the hall, along with other visitors. In a large area divided by a curtain, the men and women were searched separately. No parts of our bodies were spared from intense scrutiny. Then, Babak and I were handed a white sheet of paper, on which was written: "Cabin 4." From that point, our ten-minute visit had officially begun.

After searching frantically up and down the corridor, we located our cabin. It was a space twice the size of a telephone booth. On the other side of a thick glass divider, Shoja stood motionless like the initial casting of a statue. His coloring was yellow—almost green. His eyes were lifeless. He had his old shirt on. Through cracked lips, Shoja forced a weary smile at Babak. His eyes met my gaze. He gestured for me to speak into the intercom. Obviously, our conversation was being monitored. I refrained my tears. I could not allow myself to cry in front of Shoja. His torment was greater than mine.

"Hello, Shoja," I slowly spoke.

He shook his head slightly in response.

"Are you sick? You look rather—"

"Nothing wrong. Just fasting."

Fasting! Of course, he should be giving thanks to a God who did this to him!

A few seconds passed in silence. Over sixty thousand words and phrases in Farsi, and yet not a single one seemed appropriate to express what I felt.

"What news from the kids?" he asked finally.

"They're fine and very happy that you're alive. Me, too," I managed to answer.

Another pause.

"Many hands were working to destroy me. They used the same dossier that SAVAK had fabricated." Shoja's voice rang with pain.

"You're working in the clinic, then?" I asked, choking with emotions.

"Day and night. My only salvation. I heard our property was confiscated. The house, too?"

"Yeah, and everything else. Even your father's bank account is frozen."

"Why? How will my parents survive? How are you and the children going to live?" he asked ruefully.

At last, I found an opportunity to articulate my genuine feelings.

"Shoja, remember many years ago when we started our life together with just one suitcase? Well, we can do that again. After all, we have each other, right?" I tried on a smile.

He gave me a faint nod. "Tell my father to..." He could not finish his conversation. The phone went dead. A guard tapped firmly on Shoja's shoulder and led him away, without giving him a chance to wave at us. I looked at my watch. Our visit had lasted only seven minutes. They had stolen the other three precious minutes from us.

Babak's face and hands were still pressed against the bare

glass. He had not spoken even a word to his father. I put my handkerchief to my eyes and cried softly.

A 1974 Plymouth pulled up across the street from Tehran's Blood Bank on Vila Avenue. I got in. It was exactly ten days after Shoja's sentencing.

One look at the driver, and I regretted accepting to meet him alone. He had a bold stare and a malicious smile.

Without cordial greetings, the stranger drove on, shooting back quick glances through his front mirror to make sure we were not followed. He stopped the car in a side street, then turned around in his seat and assessed me. I looked away.

"What did you want to see me for, *Agha*?" I asked cautiously.

"I work at Evin. See the Doc almost every day," he answered. "Nice chap. Too bad he's gotta waste his talent treating criminals, hundreds of 'em."

"Who are you?" I inquired.

"Never mind my name."

"What do you exactly do at Evin?" I wondered if he was reliable.

"Well, I'm what you'd call a jack-of-all-trades. Bad pay. Bad conditions. Still, a job. But the Doc, he won't survive. I've seen people of his kind before. They just rot in prison," he warned. His eyes were now glued to my purse.

"On the phone, you said you had a message?"

"Yeah, strictly between us. In a couple of days, we're taking the Doc for a medical visit to a VIP's home near the Parliament Building. Top clergy. Broken hip or something," the man paused to see my reaction. "We could arrange for you and the

Doc to have a private visit, on the way. Or even better—" he laughed nervously.

I listened without reacting. However, it intrigued me to know why he was so concerned.

The man lowered his voice. "Certainly a rare opportunity to disappear. Catch my drift? Things like that happen. But, of course—" His eyes were on my purse again. Was he a spy? An extortionist? I could not trust him.

"I really can't think about such plans when we are hardly managing our day-to-day living," I said.

His expression changed at once. Eyes narrowed into a threatening look. Lips curled with disappointment. "If I were you, I would think twice! Your own dossier is still open." He sounded just like SAVAK. He must be bluffing.

"What dossier? I have nothing to hide," I objected.

"Let's not get into that now, *Khanom*. Where were we? Ah, yes! Your husband's visit with the VIP—"

"Never mind. I'm not interested," I said as I opened the car door and jumped out.

"You'll be sorry," he called after me.

I walked away without looking back.

Shoja's first letter from Evin Prison was agonizing:

Dear Azar,

It's been a month since I wrote to you. I didn't know what to write. How could I ask for forgiveness from you and the children? Am I in prison because I wanted to help our people, or because of my political ambitions? I still don't know. All I know is that I'm innocent. I cannot console you. Our home and everything else are gone. In comparison to what you've lost, I have fared worse. I have lost my integrity! They have publicly defamed my two most cherished moral values: chastity and honesty. I only hope to live long enough to redeem my name.

At least, I am still useful as a doctor in the clinic here. Give the children my unending love. Sorry, but I have no prescription for their grief, or yours. Perhaps God can help!"

"I will redeem your name, Shoja!" I vowed. "I promise!"

After the life sentence and the confiscation of our property, we were still in debt to many people. The Mullah insisted that his prayers had saved my husband. Jamshid, a man I had never met, claimed to Hushang that his special recommendations to the director of the 'Foundation for the Disinherited' had been influential in reducing Shoja's sentence. The rumor mill fabricated other stories. Some people thought that Dr. Yazdi was my husband's savior. Others simply said, "What money can't do!"

A week after the sentence, I went to thank Mofatteh for his services. The kind clergyman took no credit for the commuting of Shoja's sentence. "You owe your husband's life to God's justice."

"Is this God's justice? Life imprisonment?" I protested.

"Blasphemy! A grave sin, *Khanom*," he cautioned.

"Someday the truth will come out," I said.

"In time, your soul will be consoled. Turn your mind from your own concerns to God. Employ your writing talent to serve God and His people," he advised.

I never met Mofatteh again. Before long, a fundamentalist

hard-liner assassinated him for being a "moderate." He was considered dangerous to the Islamic Republic.

My in-laws, who were fatally ill and heartbroken, were out on the terrace as Babak and I walked in for a short visit. Shazdeh Joon stared at us for a second, then resumed spinning in circles and repeating her now-incoherent famous phrase: "Bobloboch!"

Agha Joon, enervated and sulky, faced our deserted former house while snacking on cheese and bread. He held a shot glass of *araq* in his hand, probably bought on the black market. Even his grandson's presence did not excite him. It was obvious he had drunk a little too much.

"Agha Joon, I'm sorry about that doomed day when our house was confiscated. I was not myself, as you probably realized. Forgive me?"

The old man shook his head in acceptance.

"I saw Shoja. He seemed okay," I said. "He's working in the prison clinic. Why don't you visit him? He always asks for you."

Still no verbal response from him.

"Mother says you needn't worry about paying the rent. Stay here—like it's your own home."

Unannounced, two men from the *Komiteh* showed up to search the premises. Babak turned quickly to his grandfather. "Agha Joon! Perhaps you should hide the bottle before they see it. That will get you into trouble."

The old man's lips quivered, but he held onto the bottle.

"Please listen to Babak. This is no joke! The *Pasdars* will arrest you, flog your feet, and send you to jail for drinking!" I added.

"Good, then I'll be with my son," Agha Joon mumbled.

At the sight of the *Pasdars* , my mother-in-law, fear frozen in her eyes, started to bang her head on the wall. Babak tried to hold her back. The sick woman resisted. The *Pasdars* watched her in amazement. Agha Joon, half drunk and yellow with jaundice, raised his glass to the uninvited guests. "Welcome! Join me!"

Muscle spasms cramped my legs as Agha Joon gulped the last of the vodka and wiped his lips with his sleeve. "You see that house over there? Dark and abandoned? Used to be a bright, happy place. My son and his family lived there," he ranted. "Then you vultures came and took everything away, even my son," he stopped to take a quick breath. "Have you come for my old mad wife and me now? What the hell, take us! We're one step away from the grave, anyway!"

"*Agha*, we're not here to arrest anyone. Just carrying out orders to search for a *Paykan*."

"Oh! That car's gone. You won't find it here," I said fearfully. "These old people have no need for a car. Please don't disturb them. They are both very sick."

To our great surprise, the *Pasdars* left as quietly as they had come. Perhaps, like the jinnis of my childhood, there were two types of *Pasdars*: Some of them had hearts!

Summer was at its peak: 101 degrees! At Evin, we were allowed to purchase 20-touman worth of mixed fruit or one watermelon at the new prison shop. Items would be delivered directly to the prisoners.

"Sister, I'll pick out the very best watermelon for the Doctor. He will get it in the evening," the grocer remarked casually. "Around here, he's everyone's favorite prisoner!"

Months of hostile propaganda had depicted Shoja as a public enemy—a living symbol of a detested regime. He had served their purpose grandly. Now he was just a prisoner, "everyone's favorite!"

In cabin 4, beyond the thick glass, Shoja seemed slightly better than last week, at least in appearance. We spoke briefly through the telephone while the *Pasdars* monitored us. Then I handed the phone to Babak. I watched as the father and son spoke on the two sides of the glass wall.

"Okay, Dad," was all I heard Babak say. The phone line had gone dead.

"Technical problems," the loudspeaker announced. Babak and I were rushed out. We were given only three minutes visit instead of ten.

On the way home, I was curious. "What did Dad say to you? He seemed very serious," I asked.

"He wanted me to accept whatever plans you have for my future. Mom! What exactly did Dad mean by that?"

"Sweetheart, if you remember, we discussed this once before. With everything that's happened, we haven't had time to talk about it again. You know, there's really no future for you here. You must get ready to leave for the States."

"I'm not going," he said automatically.

"Please, for your own safety, and for your father and me. Hushang has checked. There seems to be no restrictions for your departure, yet. Go before things change. Soon the government will enforce new restrictive travel laws and it will be too late," I warned him.

"I'll think about it. Okay?"

Babak and I were summoned to appear before the Revolutionary Tribunal. What else could they possibly want from us? How could I protect my son against them? I wondered.

The Court was moved from Qasr Prison to a modest building inside the Evin compound, not too far from the entrance. We entered a room full of *Pasdars*. Their dark and hostile eyes stared at us. From behind a huge desk, a rather young man in a flashy suit, bold floral silk Leonard tie, and gold Rolex watch, invited us to sit in the two vacant seats closest to him. He contrasted with the guards in their fatigues as well as clashed with the image one normally would expect of a Revolutionary Court.

"I am Naraqi," the official identified himself in a grandiose tone. "I participated in your husband's trial as the only secular legal advisor. I also know of your paternal ancestors, *Khanom*. In fact, our families were at one time mortal enemies. Yours actually routed mine in Kashan!" He stopped to assess my reaction with a slight shake of his head and a supercilious smile. The official had subtly given me the message that he was the one with power.

Something clicked in my head. I remembered hearing stories from my father in regard to the alleged animosity between the two families. Had an old vendetta affected this legal advisor's judgment in condemning my husband?

"*Agha*, I've heard the story differently. However, I don't think that you've called me here to settle an old family feud," I said in a nonconfrontational tone.

"Of course not," Naraqi replied. "Soon enough, you'll find out why we've summoned you and your son here. I expect you appreciate the fact that your husband was not executed. He was only one step away from death, but at the last minute God and Imam Khomeini saved him."

"Appreciate? How can I appreciate having my innocent husband condemned to a life in prison?"

As if conducting a cross-examination, the court official swiveled his chair around and faced his jury of *Pasdars*. "Brothers, you were there in court with me. You heard the voluminous charges. The defendant deserved death. Did he not?" he interrogated shrewdly.

His *Pasdars* all nodded their heads in agreement. Naraqi put his thumbs into the armholes of his vest, looking cockily at me and resting his case. Babak and I nervously squirmed around in our seats.

"Now, why was your husband's life spared?" the court official played. "Because, *Khanom*, from the notorious computer scam, Dr. Sheikh personally gained nothing. Do you follow? Nothing! His deputies divided the millions among themselves and ran off, along with those Americans from EDS. It is possible that the defendant was not aware of the crime. Still, as a Minister, he was in charge of the computer deal. He should have known. Thus, he must be punished."

"First of all, *Agha*, there was no proof of embezzlement," I interrupted him. "Second, you put my husband on trial not in place of his two deputies, but in place of all the ex-government officials who escaped the country—the Shah and his family included. In fact, in him, you attempted to condemn the entire former ruling class of Iran!" My voice rose.

"Ah, *Khanom*, you are every bit as guilty as your husband," Naraqi said, waving his forefinger at me. "While you were indulging yourself in luxury, driving in your Mercedes Benz to cabarets and discotheques every night, people were dying from hunger in the streets of Tehran. Did you ever even bother to roll down your window and look at those poor individuals?"

"You must be mistaking me for someone else, *Agha*. I never owned a Mercedes. And I'm not the cabaret type. As for the poor and hungry, our family did what it could. But poverty is still an issue, isn't it, even after the Revolution?"

"A souvenir left to us by that corrupt regime," Naraqi shouted. He watched as his entourage of *Pasdars* nodded. "Now, in regard to our summoning you here today," he continued, "with the confiscation decree, the Court has granted you and your minor child a minimal monthly allowance. This will help you to get by—barely. For the first time, you aristocrats will get a taste of how the poor live." He smiled ostentatiously.

"Very generous of you, but we don't need your welfare!"

He squinted his eyes. "Did I hear correctly? You refused our charity? Do you still hold assets of which we are not aware?"

"Yes! One that can't be confiscated." I pointed to my head. "Don't forget we are educated people. We will use our intelligence to live comfortably again," I asserted calmly.

Naraqi's eyes rolled in fury. He looked from his *Pasdars* to me in frustration.

"*Khanom*, if you don't change your attitude, I'll have your dossier activated. Believe me, it could be quite incriminating," the court official threatened.

Babak fisted his hands in anger. My heart pounded wildly under my cool facade.

"I've done nothing to be afraid of," I said in my defense.

"We have been told that you met privately with Prime

Minster Hoveyda on several occasions," Naraqi confronted me with a wicked smirk.

His implications appalled me. My feelings were ready to explode, but my reasoning told me to calm down. *This could be a trap. Don't say the wrong thing.*

I sat back in my chair and presented a ridiculing smile to him.

"*Agha*, have you also heard about my personal visits with many Ayatollahs? I turned to anyone who could help my husband," I spoke with sheer confidence.

Naraqi was taken off guard. "Go thank God that you're not on trial here. Just know that we are well informed. According to the SAVAK's own dossier, now in our possession, Dr. Sheikh got his cabinet position through your—uh—special favors, so to speak? But, lucky for you, we believe that Hoveyda was a homosexual. Otherwise, *Khanom*, the dossier could have cost you your life," he stated with malicious authority.

Fear dawned on me. SAVAK had deliberately built up a case against me—just as it had done against Shoja. The Islamic Revolutionary Court had conveniently used SAVAK's elaborately plotted dossiers to condemn us. In this case, however, the Court differed from SAVAK in its belief about Hoveyda's sexual preference. Lucky me, indeed! If the ex-Prime Minister was not perceived as a homosexual by the Revolutionaries, I would have definitely faced a terrible death!

I could no longer tolerate such a shameless court and the presence of its evil official. I loathed Naraqi for what he was doing to me in front of my son.

"Since there's nothing else to discuss, with your permission, my son and I will leave." I stood up.

"You may go! God be with you," Naraqi said, discernibly unhappy about the way his show had ended.

Outside, Babak and I exhaled with relief. We had both walked out of the enemy's court safely, and with dignity.

"What a creep! You really handled him well, Mom."

"Forget about him. Let's plot a scheme to see your father today. We'll never have another opportunity like this to walk freely inside Evin."

"What do you mean? We can't visit Dad. The *Pasdars* are everywhere."

"Trust me. If you don't panic, we'll go straight to your father's clinic. Just follow me, sweetheart."

Instead of walking to the exit gate, I took the opposite course into the inner compound of the prison. Babak walked closely behind me. We passed patches of grass, a few shrubs, and some wilted trees.

"Halt!" A young *Pasdar* jumped out from behind a tree with his gun. "Where you think you're going?" he demanded.

Babak grabbed my arm. I pulled my scarf over my face and put on an innocent look.

"Brother, we are returning from the Court, looking for the clinic. I feel sick. Could be from fasting for Ramadan," I ad-libbed. "Perhaps the doctor could advise me whether or not to break my fast. I don't want to be a sinner." My instincts for self-preservation worked quickly.

God almighty, please forgive me for this lie! It's for a good cause!

"That way, Sister," the guard pointed to the east side of the compound.

Within three hundred meters, we encountered another *Pasdar*. I repeated the same story, this time with more details.

"Straight ahead to the checkpoint. Clinic's to the left." The second guard raised his rifle to show the way.

At the checkpoint, two bigger, more menacing *Pasdars* gave us a complete body search. No words were exchanged. One of them led Babak and I through a gravel courtyard into a plain three-story structure: Building Number 9. Another *Pasdar*, equally stern, escorted us along a narrow corridor and stopped by a door. The small sign read: Infirmary / Clinic.

"Doc, someone's here for you," he called to a man in a white uniform, standing with his back to us. Shoja turned his head. Our eyes met. He turned white. Perhaps, he feared Babak and I had been arrested.

"Are you the doctor?" I asked quickly. "I need to see you. I'm feeling very dizzy. Maybe you can help."

For a tiny moment, Shoja's eyes reflected confusion but he quickly composed himself and played along. He invited me into a rather large examination room. Babak remained at the door mutely. His presence conveniently distracted the guard who watched him without blinking.

"Sister, please lie down. I must take your blood pressure," Shoja spoke loudly.

I stretched out on the bed. He bent over me. This was the first time we had been alone in eleven months. I could feel his rapid breathing.

"What're you doing here?" Shoja whispered while he gently wrapped the blood pressure pad on my upper arm.

I briefed him on my visit with Naraqi.

"You should've accepted the aid. It was better than nothing."

"No! It would've obligated us to them. Then we'd always be

their subordinates. We'll manage without their help."

Why worry my husband about things beyond his control? I thought.

"Sister, your blood pressure is elevated, and your pulse is too fast. Let me see if you have a fever," Shoja said in a loud voice for the benefit of the guard.

"You know, from what Naraqi said," I mumbled, "I could tell he thought you're innocent. Perhaps they'll change your sentence."

"Perhaps." A wry smile curled at the corner of his mouth. "Sister, your temperature is normal. Continue your fast, but get plenty of rest. You may go now," Shoja instructed me. Then, he added in an undertone, "I miss you terribly!"

He had guarded his hands from touching my skin. But, his eyes were caressing me. My heart was torn by his words and his eyes. Why couldn't these few fleeting moments with the man I loved, this instant, stretch on forever? I had an irresistible urge to fly into the safety of my husband's great arms and bury myself in his warm strong chest and cry. I longed to touch and kiss his familiar dear face. I needed to feel his love. This was forbidden! A strange law had separated us from each other. We were not allowed to share anything together, not even a simple touch. Shoja and I were no longer husband and wife in the conventional sense!

I rose to my feet and left the room feeling miserable. At the door, Shoja suddenly took Babak by both arms and kissed him tenderly on the forehead. The guard looked on curiously.

"The boy reminds me of my own son," Shoja sighed heavily.

Three weeks after Shoja's transfer to Evin, Agha Joon finally consented to visit his son with Babak and I. He had come to realize that he would never see his son free again in his lifetime. The stubborn old man warned me in advance not to mention anything about his cancer to Shoja. He tried to put on a facade of strength, although his debilitating weakness and his sickly discoloration indicated that the terminal disease was nearing its final stage.

We were told by a phone call that today's visit would be conducted without a glass barrier, and the time increased to half an hour. They also advised us to take some decent clothes for the practicing doctor/prisoner.

A bus took the three of us on a short trip through a narrow dirt road in the prison compound, lined by a few trees, and dropped us in front of a low, flat-roofed modular building. The Alborz Mountains loomed to our left. We were led to one of several visiting rooms inside the building. There were no windows. The only things in this small room were a worn-out rug and a hanging dim light.

At the sight of his father, Shoja's eyes brightened. He rushed into Agha Joon's arms. The old man pressed him close to his chest and sobbed. "I never thought I would see you again, son."

Shoja stepped back and studied his father with alarm. The medical professional in him detected some health problems instantly.

"Is something wrong with you, Agha Joon? Your color is not good, and you have lost tremendous weight. Have you seen a doctor?"

My father-in-law threw a quick glance at me before he answered, "I'm fine, son. Just getting old. Please! Let's not talk about me."

"But, you—"

"Stop asking about my health, please," the unyielding old man demanded. "My life's finished one way or the other. I want to hear all about yours."

Shoja turned to me. I nodded my head and smiled faintly. He realized he had no choice but to respect his father's wish. We all squatted on the rug. Despite the poor accommodations, and the possibility of the hot stuffy room being bugged, we felt good. For the first time in months, we were going to talk without barriers, without watchful eyes. We needed this relatively intimate time to share our emotions.

"Tell me, son. I must know," Agha Joon asked with difficulty. He still held his son's hand. "How did you escape execution? They showed mercy to no one else."

Shoja looked down at his feet and shrugged. "I honestly don't know why I'm alive! One day at breakfast, long before the trial, they blindfolded me and led me to another part of the prison. There, they tied me to a chair. I could not see, but I could feel other people in the room," he reflected woefully. "Every thirty minutes or so, I would hear a prisoner's name called. Mostly cabinet members and generals. Somebody would shuffle them to an adjacent room, read their charges loudly and sentence them to death. Waiting was torturous."

He stopped without altering his sad facial expression. Babak and I watched him wordlessly. Agha Joon flinched his hand slightly. His feeble shoulders were hunched closer to his ears.

"It must have been awful. What were you thinking, Son?" Agha Joon asked hoarsely.

Shoja looked up and sighed. "Well, I began to think of you and the kids, but soon my memories wandered. Then, they called my name! They led me to the adjacent room. The blind-fold was removed. I blinked and saw a young, well-groomed, non-clergyman sitting at one side of a table. They sat me on the other side. I faced my interrogator. By the sunlight on the wall, I could tell it was late afternoon. I thought I would never see another sunset."

Babak moved closer to his father. "Dad! You had no food all day?"

A sad grimace crept over Shoja's face and deepened the lines at the corners of his eyes. He bent over to his left and hugged Babak. "When you are only one step away form death, you don't need food, my son!"

"What happened after they removed your blindfold?" I asked with edginess.

Shoja shifted upright. "Well, the interrogator questioned me about my services to the government. I didn't detect any hostil-ity. I found it difficult to concentrate, but I answered frankly and truthfully. Almost with indifference. The man listened intently. He seemed to be well-informed about the health care system."

"Who was this man?" My father-in-law interrupted, not lifting his eyes from his son. He moved his limp legs uncom-fortably on the rug.

Shoja stared past us. "To this day, I don't know. In any event, I was blindfolded again, taken back to the former room, and tied to the chair. Strangely, they hadn't read my sentence yet. Still, I thought that was my end." He stopped, lost in time and distance.

"Dad, if it makes you uncomfortable, don't talk about it," Babak said gently.

"It's okay, Babak. Sometimes it helps to talk. Where was I? Oh, yes. I waited for I don't know how long. I remember hearing loud shots. My ears were ripped by the sound. Bang! Bang! Bang! Then, helpless, desperate screams. More screams. Twenty-two men! All were executed! Suddenly, my guts felt like they were coming out of my mouth. I threw up all over the place. Someone, cursing at me, untied my hands and took me to the washroom. I passed out on the floor. When I came to, I knew it was my turn. I was the last one. I started praying," Shoja said with a low voice.

Agha Joon listened with his eyes closed, shaking his head slowly in disbelief.

"The bathroom door opened," Shoja reflected. "'Come on out, you lucky traitor! Your death's been postponed till tomorrow. Don't think for a minute you've been spared!' The guard taunted me. When they took me back to my cell, my blood pressure shot up. I collapsed. Sometime later, I woke up in the prison clinic. The next night, Ayatollah Khomeini gave amnesty to those in death row. Anyone who had not committed a murder, would live. . . You know the rest of the story," Shoja finished in an almost inaudible voice. His eyes had the confused look of someone who did not quite know how he had survived death. The other twenty-two administrators had been executed.

The dim windowless room fell silent. Shoja had relived his entire nightmare. I could envision my husband, soiled and half-wasted, on the cold filthy floor of a bathroom. No matter how hard I tried, I could never feel his deepest fears, his pain, and his loneliness. Shoja would never be the same after that night. A part of him had been ruined, destroyed.

I looked at my father-in-law. He sat speechless. His vexed

profile had shrunk. His jaundice had deepened. He rested his right hand on his heart. The shock of his son's near execution had paralyzed his brain temporarily. Babak's mouth hung open. Sweat began to drip down my hairline. The room felt extremely hot and airless. I took off my scarf. None of us knew what to say.

Shoja broke the silence. He put his arm around his father. "You'd wonder why they made such a monster of me. Believe me, Agha Joon, it was sheer political propaganda. I hope you never doubted my honesty," he said. Agha Joon squeezed his son's hand in reassurance.

"With Khalkhali as the Tribunal Judge in my first trial, I stood no chance. He acted as judge, jury and executioner, all in one," Shoja continued. "In my second trial, the new judge, Gilani, was less hostile. He intended to exile me away from my home and family, rather than imprison me in Evin. But Khalkhali, still a forceful presence, sent radical Mullahs to Qom to speak against me to Ayatollah Khomeini. Fearful that the Ayatollah would be pressured to order my death, Gilani quickly gave me the next highest sentence—life!"

My father-in-law fidgeted and took in a deep breath.

"Shoja, Where's General Fardoust? You know, he arranged our visits at the SAVAK prison. Now, people talk of him as being an accomplice of the new regime. Is this true?" I asked inquisitively.

Shoja shrugged. "I've heard the rumor too. I wouldn't know."

All the time we had hoped for a just legal system, Shoja's life had hung in the balance, between individuals engaged in a power play. There were so many unanswered questions. Would we ever find out what made them spare Shoja's life?

"You know, Dad, Evin doesn't look as bad as I thought," Babak said in an attempt to change the mood.

Shoja tugged on Babak's arm. "You haven't seen the real Evin. Most prison cells are concealed in a valley that can't be seen from the visiting area."

"You must feel lonely. Does anyone else live with you, Dad?"

"No. But, the clinic's always full of patients. Besides the prisoners, I also treat employees—sometimes even court officials. They're beginning to trust me."

The door to the visiting room opened with a crack and a bald, heavy-set, bearded man appeared.

"Doc, hurry. One of the guards accidentally shot himself."

Shoja rushed out.

"Don't worry about the Doctor, I'll watch over him," the bearded man told us.

"And who are you?" Agha Joon asked as he limped up to his feet.

"I'm the Deputy Warden. Before the Revolution, I had my own business. I gave it up to serve the Islamic Republic. Most employees of Evin are working for the cause."

Outside, they had moved the injured guard to a minibus. Shoja rode with him to the nearest hospital, where he would be able to use operating facilities that the clinic lacked. This was Shoja's first trip beyond the walls of Evin.

CHAPTER SIXTEEN

At Evin, things seemed to be improving for Shoja, at least on the surface. Starting today, our weekly visits with him took place in his room above the clinic in Building Number 9. Shoja, waiting by the clinic, came to life as Babak and I appeared. He hugged his son, and nodded at me. No wife was allowed more than a nod from her husband inside Evin. Fortunately, no one recognized Babak nor I from our previous secret visit.

"Guess what?" I tried on a smile. "They called and told us to come at five today, and here we are! We didn't have to take a number. Things must be changing for you."

Shoja grinned.

"Wow! This place looks brighter than I remembered," Babak was the first to notice as he looked around.

"We had it painted. I had the prison exterminated, too," Shoja gloated. "Oh, yeah, I forgot to tell you. We now have a cooperative store selling necessities like tea, sugar, fruits, and personal hygiene products. I'm planning to add a small operating room to the clinic. We won't have to transport patients to area hospitals for minor surgeries. You see? Just like old times, I'm actively involved."

"I wish you wouldn't, sweetheart. You worked too hard back then—and look at where it got you!"

"This isn't just my work. It's my home!" he blurted back.

I had touched a nerve, failing to realize that Shoja was making his new "home" more bearable. This was one of the first times since his captivity that we did not understand each other.

"Show us your room, sweetheart," I said in an attempt to reconcile.

Shoja took us to his room, number 13, on the second floor. Around us, security was intense. Guards with machine guns patrolled the entire corridor.

"Who lives in the other rooms on this floor?" I asked quietly.

Shoja bent towards me and whispered, "Special prisoners, and, of course, some critically ill patients."

Room number 13 was square and small. Against one wall, Shoja had a primitive bed made of a box spring and a foam mattress with one pillow. The bed was covered by a gray army blanket. A drab metal table with two chairs stood by the other wall. The table held an electric hot plate, a kettle, and a few plastic dishes. The room's small sink was stained brown from rusted pipes.

"Every night after work, I go to the cooperative and buy a couple of eggs or some cheese, and make myself a simple dinner," Shoja said. "I eat lunch with prisoners from my cell block. We usually have rice with yogurt or sometimes baked potatoes. It isn't too bad! The *Pasdars* eat the same food."

Babak pointed to a small TV on the counter. "It's so cute Dad. I've never seen one so small."

"Here, such small things are considered privileges, son."

My eyes fell on the barred windows which opened to a

walled concrete courtyard. Despite his "privileges", my husband was still a prisoner.

"Somewhere in that courtyard, the executions are carried out. Often, I'm awakened by the gunfire," Shoja said with a solemn voice.

A sharp pain hit the pit of my stomach. I masked it. "Let's have tea, Shoja."

We sat at the table, and watched as Shoja made tea.

"Sorry, no sugar," he apologized. "I didn't have enough money."

"I gave 100 touman to the prison office for you, sweetheart. They wouldn't take more."

"Hey! I never thought I'd see the day my wife would support me!" Shoja said half-jokingly. His Middle Eastern male ego was injured. The situation was worse than he admitted. Mother was supporting all of us!

"I heard that with Ramadan coming to an end, the Court will reconvene with the trials," Shoja said, looking into his tea. "Mine was the last one before the fast period began."

"Dad, I'm leaving tomorrow," Babak said softly. He caught his father's attention.

"Tomorrow? I thought it was next week," Shoja asked wistfully. He was afraid that the actual physical leaving of home and Iran would be cutting the final bonds between him and his son.

"I have to be there before school starts. I'd never go if you didn't want me to."

For security reasons, Babak deliberately did not mention "America."

Shoja tugged on Babak's shoulder. "Of course, you must leave, son. But promise to write regularly and keep me informed about your life. Just because your father is at Evin—"

"Please, Dad! You'll always be my role model. I promise to study hard so I can go to med school."

"It's a good field. If it weren't for my profession, they would've killed me," Shoja reflected. "Two nights ago, they hurried me out to treat a young man who'd been in a terrible car accident on the highway to Qom. Shortly after I arrived, he died. Do you know who his father was? That judge who gave me life imprisonment!"

"He must have trusted you, Dad."

A *Pasdar*, posted outside to watch us through an eye-level window in the door, entered abruptly and commanded, "Very sick patient in the clinic, Doc. You must come."

Shoja strode out of the room and down the corridor to the first floor. Without him, the room seemed extremely depressing. Its occupant, my husband, and I were forever separated by some exorbitant law. We had stopped touching. We had stopped sharing, even our true feelings.

The *Pasdar* escorted us out of Evin. Babak never said good-bye to his father!

From Evin, we went to visit my in-laws so Babak could see his grandparents for the last time. Agha Joon, sick in bed with abdominal pain, still raged at the world.

"I'm leaving for America," Babak told his grandfather. "I'd really like to take a few photos of you and Shazdeh Joon."

Agha Joon refused at first, but then gave in. Holding on to Babak's arm, he staggered into the next room to fetch his senile wife. I heard him screaming, "Where is that maid? How many times have I told her not to allow you to walk naked? Come now, be good. Please, get dressed. Our grandson wants to take our last picture before we die!"

A few minutes later, with difficulty, Babak managed to take one good picture of his grandparents. Agha Joon scowled and Shazdeh Joon stared into the camera with hauntingly frightened eyes. She did not recognize us.

Mother had arranged a small dinner for Babak with my brothers and sister, and their families all present. She also had a surprise for him. A photo in the evening paper showed Shoja in the clinic's pharmacy. The caption read: "Dr. Sheikh, ex-Minister, miraculously saved from execution, starts his life sentence in Evin. The doctor's office is as hectic as before, but with three differences: He practices in jail, his patients are his fellow inmates, and he works for free!"

Oblivious to the sarcasm, Babak folded the paper and added it to the contents of his luggage, along with an Iranian tape which had helped us through many lonesome nights. If the world turned its backs on us, we still had each other and the melancholic strains of "Golden Dreams".

"I don't know how you can leave three children on their own in a foreign country," Mother complained to me. "How will they support themselves?"

"They're not children any longer. They can get jobs."

"But they won't want to return to their homeland, if they stay away too long," Mother worried.

"We'll have to take that chance for their safety. I just want them to have a normal life. You understand, don't you?"

Her faint smile told me she understood.

August 30, 1979. Babak's flight was scheduled to leave Tehran at 9:00 a.m. We had been up since dawn to share an early breakfast together and to get ready. He had to fly to Paris to apply for a student visa to enter the United States. The American Consulate in Tehran had been closed for the past few months due to the strained political relationship between the two countries.

"Mom, you'd better stay here. I don't want emotional stuff going on at the airport. Let's say good-bye here, okay?"

I hugged Babak hard and he held on too. "Take care of yourself. You helped me through a lot, sweetheart. I'm really proud of you."

"Mom, tell Dad that I love him. Also, promise that you won't stay sad."

"I'll be fine," I said with a soft touch to his face.

"Grandma, I can't find the right words to thank you for everything. You're the greatest," Babak said.

Mother ceremoniously held the Qur'an over her grandson, and then kissed him twice on the cheeks. "Don't forget your family or your heritage, Babak," she advised. "A man who turns his back on either one is not worth anything."

From the street, I watched as Hushang's car took my son to his uncertain future. When the car disappeared, I ran into the yard and leaned against an old sycamore tree. Under its magnificent foliage, I allowed my tears to run freely. I had lost my last true companion.

"Someone from the office of Ayatollah Gilani's on the line, Azar!" Mother called out from the kitchen. "Come! Right away!"

I rushed back to the house, wiping my tears.

"His Honor wishes to see you at 4:00 p.m. at his residence in Qom. Please be there on time," the caller demanded.

I jotted down the address quickly and hung up. What does Ayatollah Gilani, the Tribunal Judge, want with me? Is it about Babak? Can he leave the airport? Does this concern Shoja? Is there going to be more harassment?

Since I did not have any means of transportation, Azad, the English teacher, who was visiting my sister, kindly offered to take me. This time, not on his motorcycle, but in a friend's borrowed car. However, he had three conditions: I would pay for the gas, and also his dinner at a cafe in Qom famous for *chelo kabob*. "One more thing," this atheist added, "No visits to Ma'sumeh's shrine!"

The road to the holy city was crowded with pilgrims. Azad's decrepit car moved along like a turtle. The late summer sunlight was hot and merciless. Above our heads a plane roared. It reminded me that perhaps with every passing second, Babak was farther away. Azad, finding no enthusiasm on my part to make idle conversation, started singing an old folk song:

"He, in the company of beautiful women,
Has his paradise on earth, not heaven!"

In front of us, two 18-wheeler oil trucks were drag racing. Not one day went by without a fatal accident along this road.

The ride was grueling, not only because of the dusty monotonous road, but my spirit felt cold without Babak. My mind saw the future as a blank stupor. Beyond the present pain and loneliness, there was nothing to make me plan, even for tomorrow.

An hour and a half later, the shrine's golden dome and its vaguely visible minarets came up out of the hot simmering horizon. Although I had no strong religious beliefs, I found domes and minarets quaint and romantic. Azad ridiculed me. "The whole thing is totem worship!"

The holy city had become more austere since the rise of the Islamic State. Black and gray dominated other colors in the crowds. Men took on forbidding and stern looks. Women veiled their faces. Most of the shops were closed. It was still siesta time.

Judge Gilani's house—a low brick building in a short alley—was modest. Of the two brass door knockers, I chose the smaller to indicate that a woman was visiting. The sounds of shuffling feet approached. A female figure opened the door slightly, and peeked from behind her *chador*.

"Who is it?" she asked.

"I have been summoned by Ayatollah Gilani."

"Wait here." The woman shut the door and walked away.

Azad turned to me mischievously, "I'll bet under that ugly old *chador* lurks a real beauty!"

The woman returned. "You may enter, *Khanom*. But *Agha* must wait outside."

In the vestibule, the pungent odor of mildew filled the air. Shoes had been neatly lined up at the entrance to a room. I took mine off and added them to the row.

We entered a large room in which nothing but a thick carpet and a few bolsters furnished the space, and a picture of Imam Ali, the prophet Muhammad's son-in-law, adorned the mantle piece. Several women dressed in black bent over something lying on the carpet—a human being. Someone fanned her, another offered her a drink. Her skirt was pushed up, revealing bruises on the thighs. A maid was attending to a big brass samovar.

"*Salam*," I said anxiously.

The women tossed a half-glance in my direction but offered

no response. Timidly, I sat down. This was the first time in my entire life that I had been invited to a clergyman's private residence, and was not sure of the right etiquette. Where was the Judge-Ayatollah? What was I expected to witness here?

The young woman—hardly sixteen—let her *chador* fall to expose a stunning face. Azad was right! Her complexion was a soft peach color. Her eyes—the famous Iranian eyes—were large and languorous, her hair a cascade of long brown strains dropping to her smooth shoulders. She was the Beauty among the women.

"Three days ago, my eldest brother got killed in a car accident. We just returned from the cemetery," the Beauty related sadly. "You see that young girl giving my mother a drink of water? She was my poor brother's fiancée. They were to be married soon."

"I'm very sorry! Had I known of this tragedy, I never would have disturbed you today," I said.

She walked towards the bruised woman on the floor. "Mother, this is Doctor Sheikh's wife. Father asked her here. Remember Dr. Sheikh from Evin?"

The mother half rose and shot a hateful look at me. Her eyes were red and swollen from too many tears. "Oh yes, the one brought to my son's deathbed. Good it did my son, my poor son!" The grieving woman started pinching her thighs and moaning.

"That's enough, Mother! Killing yourself won't bring him back," the Beauty pleaded.

"Maybe it was his time. We must accept God's will," the unlucky fiancée fatalistically conceded. Azad, the Leftist, would have laughed under his breath.

"It wasn't his time!" the mother screamed. "He was cursed!"

The mourning woman turned to me. Did I imagine her repugnance? Did she blame Shoja for her son's death?

The maid placed a teacup before me.

"Go check to see if the baby is awake," the Beauty told her.

The maid returned with a gorgeous baby. The Beauty held her baby tenderly, close to her breast. In this pose, they projected the innocence of a statue, the Madonna with her son.

We heard men coughing in the hallway. Immediately, the women covered their hair. Two clergymen entered, one fair and fragile, the other dark and robust. The women said *"Salam,"* and left the room, taking the grieving mother with them. I sprang to my feet.

"Father," the Beauty addressed the fair-haired cleric, *"Khanom* Sheikh's been here since 4:00 o'clock."

The other man, obviously her husband but old enough to be her father, stroked the baby's cheek as his young wife exited.

Still standing, I pulled my *chador* tighter. I felt unsafe in front of the archenemy.

"Welcome, Sister. Please sit down," the Judge greeted me candidly. "I am sorry to have kept you waiting. My son-in-law and I were delayed at the cemetery after a ceremony for my late son," he sighed. The other cleric nodded slowly. I sat down.

Gilani spoke in brief, simple, yet formal, sentences. With his light hair, blue eyes, and soft manner, the Judicial Ayatollah was entirely different from what I had expected. How calmly he spoke of his son's death! Did he have such strong control over his emotions? Or was it his faith that made him appear stoical? Didn't he have a sense of anger towards a God that robbed him of his son? Oddly, I felt less contempt towards this man who condemned my husband and destroyed our lives. His anguish was greater than mine.

"Sister! Your husband tried diligently to save my son, but he was not meant to live," Gilani continued, holding back his grief.

Now I realized what Shoja was talking about when he said he was taken to treat the son of a man who gave him life imprisonment—Gilani!

"I am extremely sorry for your loss. The death of a child is a tragedy beyond words," I sympathized.

"That is so, Sister. But since birth and death are God's will, we cannot dispute either one."

His unquestioning faith amazed me.

The son-in-law interjected, "On the one hand, we must not question God's will. On the other hand, we cannot ignore people's curses. Even the Saints have spoken of the evil eyes." He looked at me from the corner of his eye.

"So my wife believes," added the Judge pensively. "Since Dr. Sheikh's trial was the last I administered before the holy month began, she thinks that our son—"

"Is this why you have summoned me to your home, Your Honor?" I interrupted angrily. "Do you really think that, even if my husband had the power to curse your family, he would? You don't know him at all. He is neither that demon you painted in court nor the sorcerer you think him now. He is an innocent man."

The maid served another round of tea.

"Sister," Gilani interceded, "I have not asked you here to reenact the trial. God the Merciful has directed me to call you here because forgiveness is in order. "

Fanatic old man! Did he hope to break the so-called 'curse' by gaining our forgiveness?

"Could it be that your son's unfortunate accident was a sign of divine interference?" I said sardonically.

For a moment, Gilani's crystal blue eyes turned restive. He quickly regained composure. "One can never know the divine plan. But one should be fair. Dr. Sheikh has helped many people. At Evin, he works with exceptional dedication. Sister, your husband is a very kind man. You should be proud of him."

"I'm more proud of him than you can imagine."

Only a month and five days ago, this man had convicted my husband for being a 'corrupter on earth'. Now, he spoke as if Shoja were a hero! His comments were contradictory and shocking.

Through the window, a narrow slice of the setting sun fell across the carpet. Babak must be in Paris. He was safe. Gilani could not harm him.

Suddenly, I had a strong urge to speak, to disclose the underlying factors and unpredictable forces that brought us to where we were. My confined emotions had found momentum to erupt. Why in the presence of this magistrate? It was too late to petition for justice. The Judge had already tried, condemned and sentenced Shoja. My husband had not been permitted to defend himself in the court. It would not help now to plead on his behalf for mercy. Yet, I needed to speak. Perhaps Gilani's recent tragedy of his son's death had opened his heart to the truth.

"Your Honor, allow me to help you see my husband as I know him. He never got a chance to reveal his true self in the court."

I began with how I met Shoja, fell in love—and even proposed to him—and moved through the years in America, our children, our return to Iran, Shoja's private practice, my career, his establishment of the Rehabilitation Society, his work with the government, and, finally, his imprisonment and sentence. My speech was candid, bold, sometimes even startling to those religious men. How long did I go on? One hour? Two? More? Time and even place had no significance.

My *chador* had fallen onto my shoulders, exposing both my face and hair. It did not seem to matter. I was no longer a woman before two strange clergymen but a narrator of truth. The two men listened, their eyes transfixed. I was aghast at my own daring eloquence. Love and truth were guiding my words. These two could not fail.

"You see, Your Honor, our lifestyle was different from yours," I concluded after a pause. "We were Westernized and less orthodox in our practice of religion. Yes, we did belong to the upper class. None of these things made us necessarily evil. We were law-abiding and moral people, just like you, but wrongly tormented beyond description."

I stopped, my throat dry and scratchy. I was exhausted. Gilani sighed, a shadow of guilt disturbing his calm. From a nearby Mosque the melodious chanting of Qur'an filled the austere room.

The maid turned on the light and spread a tablecloth on the carpet, and placed plates of rice and beef stew on it. The Judge invited me to eat. His family had their meal in the next room.

At dinner we were an odd threesome: an unveiled female with two clergymen. One of the highest ranking officials in the Islamic Republic, who had just buried his son, played host to his guest—the wife of a man he condemned to a life in prison! None of us ate much. Emotions were too high.

"Sister, our Revolution is Islamic, and our guidance for judgment is the Qur'an," the Judge began after the dinner. "Whatever sentences we gave were based on Islamic Jurisprudence. With the help of God and the leadership of Imam Khomeini, all Moslem Iranians are forever free of oppression."

"Free? Indeed!" I blurted. "Do you know how your *Komitehs* have treated people? Us? Suppose my husband was guilty. Why did they take his old father's assets? Why were my son and I punished? Tossed out of our home like garbage? Our property confiscated? Our lives threatened? I had no choice but to send my son abroad. Thanks to your Revolution, I have neither a home nor a family!"

"Where are you staying now?" the Judge asked with unexpected concern.

"I move from place to place and live off the charity of my relatives," I answered bitterly.

No matter how I reacted, his voice remained calm. "*Inshallah*, someday you and your children will have a home again," he said.

"So, it is not a sin to own property, Your Honor?"

"Of course not. Everyone is entitled to invest money honestly earned. I will return your house back to you. Write a brief letter to Imam Khomeini explaining your status, and I will personally deliver it tomorrow."

I blinked. This could not be true.

Gilani's son-in-law, acting as an assistant, brought me paper and a pen. The Judge dictated and I transcribed the message to Ayatollah Khomeini. It was short and to the point.

The Judge took the letter from me and handed it to his son-in-law to keep. "By Saturday, I will have a reply for you, Sister," Gilani said. "Until I get your home back, please be my guest in this house. I cannot allow a Moslem woman to be homeless."

How incomprehensible! Thirty-five days after the Tribunal Judge had ordered the confiscation of my home, he was offering me his home as a refuge! Was this his conscience manifesting itself? Remorse? Perhaps, in his way, the Judge was asking for forgiveness.

"You are kind, but I would rather live with my mother," I replied. "If I don't return tonight, she will be worried out of her mind."

The host shook his head in acceptance. "After my son's death, I intended to resign from my position and ask Imam Khomeini's permission to retreat to the holy city of Najaf in Iraq where Imam Ali, the greatest of all Saints, is buried," Gilani confided sadly. "Now, as God is my witness, I will stay on to free your husband. It might take a few years. Be patient, Sister. The trial is still fresh in the minds of the people."

It was an extremely emotional moment for both of us. Tears filled my eyes. The Judge had compassion. Despite his submission to God's will, he had considered giving up his worldly position and retreating to a sanctuary to mourn his son's death. The Judge also had a sense of remorse for his last verdict. This was an indirect admittance of Shoja's innocence. Tears ran down my face. I lowered my head to wipe them.

My host coughed and looked at his watch. Suddenly, I became aware of the time and the place. Poor Azad was waiting outside.

"It's very late, Your Honor. I must go," I said in an exhausted voice.

"How are you traveling to Tehran at this hour?" he asked.

"No need for you to worry. *Allah* will look after me!"

For the first time, the clergyman smiled. "God be with you!"

Outside, Azad had fallen asleep behind the steering wheel. When I slid into the car, he woke up. "*Khanom Vazir*! You have any idea what time it is? It's almost midnight! Did you even once consider me? I tried to enter, but—" He pointed to a man with a machine gun in the shadow of a tree near Gilani's house. "I was beginning to suspect that they sent you to the same hellhole as your hubby," he yawned.

"Sorry. Couldn't help it. It's been an awfully long day. Shall we go home now?" I was not possibly able to tell him what went on at the Judge's house. He might misinterpret the whole thing.

"What about my *chelo kabob*? It's been twelve hours since I last ate," Azad complained, pulling at his mustache.

I could not possibly deny Azad's request. I owed him a lot. He had been too patient with me. We went to the only restaurant open at that hour, where Azad ate enough for two. My head was reeling from exhaustion and the unexpected experience with Gilani. How was I to interpret my conversation with the highest ranking Judge in the Islamic Republic? Even if nothing was returned to us, this meeting had been an achievement!

At the outskirts of Tehran, our car was stopped by armed *Pasdars* patrolling the area. A flashlight shone from Azad's face to mine. "Show us your I.D. Open the trunk!" the *Pasdars* ordered Azad. They were looking for weapons.

"Who is this woman?" they growled. "What's she doing in your car at this late hour?"

"This woman? Who else? My sister," Azad stuttered artfully. "We are returning from the Ma'sumeh's holy shrine!"

I trembled behind my *chador*. Accompanying an unrelated man was a punishable crime, according to the fundamentalists' interpretation of the Islamic law.

We were permitted to proceed. It was almost dawn when I reached home.

The Judge kept his word. On Saturday morning, he phoned: "Imam Khomeini has granted your request, Sister. Your home will be returned to you. The *Komiteh* will contact you with details soon. May God be with you!"

Perhaps that night Gilani slept with a more clear conscience!

Chapter Seventeen

O unbelievers, I will not worship that ye worship
Ye have your religion, and I have mine

Qur'an (Shurah 109)

For the first time, Mother was permitted to visit Shoja. It had been months since she saw him last. Not knowing what to expect, Mother reacted nervously. During the body search, she yelled, "Aren't you ashamed to frisk an old woman as if she were a criminal? What do you think I carry on me?"

The female guards stopped. Mother rearranged her outfit indignantly, and together we walked towards Building Number 9, room 13. At the sight of Shoja, Mother immediately threw herself in his arms, hiding her emotions. When she backed away, she reached into a secret pocket in her dress, took out ten 100-touman bills and handed them to him. He kissed her hands. Mother and Shoja had always got along splendidly.

"Shoja!" I said with a twinkle in my eyes. "I have some good news!"

"What?" Shoja looked at me slightly baffled.

"I got the house back! I did it!"

"I can't believe that!"

"That's not all, sweetheart," I said. "Gilani promised to stay on as Judge to free you. Soon!"

"What did you say to the Judge to convince him? Apparently, I failed," Shoja asked with more disbelief.

Mother and I exchanged smiles. "You know better than anyone how my power of persuasion works, sweetheart. I got you to marry me, didn't I?"

Shoja smiled and turned to Mother. "I owe my life to your daughter!"

The colorless room lighted up vibrantly. Shoja served tea. This time he had sugar.

"Hi, Mom! I'm finally in D.C.," Babak hollered on the phone.

I was relieved to know that he had managed to enter the States on his own. "How do you like America, sweetheart?"

"It's okay. In a couple of days I'll begin the tenth grade at the International School. I paid the first quarter's tuition. It was too late for a public school, but I'll transfer in the spring."

"Good! We simply can't pay for this private school, sweetheart. You know that I didn't even have money to pay for your ticket. Your grandmother took care of that, son."

"I know. In any event, I miss home, Mom. Tomorrow marks a year since Dad's arrest," he said remorsefully.

Babak hadn't forgotten that terrible day.

"I miss you too, son. It's not the same without you here. But, I'm glad you're safe. Are Roxana and Ramin okay?"

He hesitated. "Roxana has her hands full between school

and her job. And, of course, she has to deal with us boys. The studio is just too small for the three of us. There's no room for my stuff."

"Tell me about Ramin."

"Well, he's changed a lot. Maybe you should come and see for yourself, Mom!"

Autumn brought shorter, paler days. The void in my heart grew deeper with the succession of identical days that followed one another without hope. Reading books, helping Mother, and visiting the prison filled my hours. My once-a-week visit with Shoja highlighted my days. No one visited me. All my friends had disappeared. Hosting foreign dignitaries, attending lavish garden parties at the Shah's Niavaran Palace, dining with the vivacious Queen Mother at Sa'd Abad, wearing designer clothes: these things I never regretted. What I regretted the most was having no friends left. Even my close relatives had given me to oblivion.

My favorite aunt Mahin Banu, who helped me marry Shoja, had left Iran for England. She was one of my last strongholds on the past.

At age sixteen, my aunt had accepted the invitation of her maternal uncle, Ali-Gholi Kalantar, then the Iranian Ambassador to the United States, and had joined him in Washington, D.C.

One year before World War I, it was unheard of for any woman from the Middle East to travel alone. After a journey of several months, my aunt, as I was told, the first Iranian woman to visit the U.S., stepped off the ship dressed in exotic, pearl-trimmed veils. What she must have gone through adjusting to the New World!

Five years later, Mahin Banu returned to Iran, married and with a college degree, an emancipated woman dressed in Western clothing and full of modern ideas.

An active Nationalist, Mahin Banu detested the Shah's absolutist monarchy. After the Revolution, however, she was continually harassed for, of all things, not obeying the Islamic dress code. She would boldly strut by the *Komiteh*, wearing her Western hat, white gloves, and pince-nez. Eventually, all her property was confiscated to intimidate her. One day, with an unyielding determination not to give in to force, my aunt announced, "I put aside the veil many ago. I refuse to hide behind it again!" She flew off to join her daughter in London.

Forty days after my visit with Gilani, finally a set of house keys arrived along with a picture of Ayatollah Khomeini. The attached note offered a housewarming wish: *"Manzel Mubarak"*— Enjoy your home!

I had almost lost faith in Gilani's promise to return my house. Now, I felt rich! I had the keys. The house was mine again. What became of its new occupants? Hadn't they turned the house into a halfway home for prostitutes?

No one wanted to join me in exploring my looted, vacant home. They were afraid. This was something that I had to do on my own. As I neared the front gate alone, my courage waned. Horrible memories of that doomed day when I was thrown out of my home like a dirty dog shook me. It still hurt to remember. I turned around. Then, I stopped. Hey! You have to overcome your fear. You can't afford to lose the only property returned to you, I thought. Hesitantly, I opened the front gate. A shocking sight startled me. The once-green lawn and blooming rose garden were vanished. Mounds of dirt and deep ditches replaced them. In their greedy search for "buried treasures", the thieves had dug up all the plants and even some of the trees. My beautiful garden resembled an Iranian desert.

Inside the house, a nauseating stench welcomed me. I followed it. The toilet bowls were missing! In their place, a garbage can full of feces had been left as a memento for me. Nothing remained in the kitchen—not even the sink. A tour of the house took me through a series of bare walls, frameless windows, doorless entranceways, heaps of trash. This was no longer a home. It was a true ghost house!

I thought I had seen the worst. I was wrong. The only door spared from being torn off its hinges was our bedroom door, on the first floor. Slowly and fearfully, I opened the door to confront a dirty foam mattress. It occupied the center of the floor, exactly where our bed used to be. Next to it, a small handgun, a pair of military boots and fatigues were thrown recklessly. A pair of red nylon panties and a used condom shocked my eyes. I stepped back with disgust. Our sacred bedroom had been violated the most! The *Pasdars* had not used our home to shelter and reform the prostitutes. They had apparently indulged in their own wild sinful pleasures. We were persecuted for "immoralities." They had proved to be the sinners!

"Who the hell's in there?" a voice screamed from behind.

Panic-stricken, I dashed out to face an armed *Pasdar*.

"What're you doing trespassing here? Don't you know this house is owned by the 'Foundation for the Disinherited'?"

"B...But the k...keys were sent by the *Komiteh*. The house has been returned to me," I faltered.

"To hell with you and the *Komiteh*! This is our property now.

Gimme the keys and get lost, or I'll break your legs!" The *Pasdar* spat venomously.

I dropped the keys and fled away, taking my life with me. I swore to myself never to return to this wretched house again.

At Shoja's insistence, I arranged to take my mother-in-law to Evin, one day. My father-in-law was hospitalized for his cancer. He still, stubbornly, did not want Shoja to know. At least, he was now able to pay for his medical bills. A court decree had surprisingly released their bank assets.

All the way to the prison, my disconcerted mother-in-law thrashed herself against the car window in an attempt to get out. At Evin, a kind guard offered to carry her frail body on his back to room number 13 where Shoja was waiting for us anxiously. He had not seen his mother for over a year, and was quite unnerved by her condition.

"This is your son Shoja. And this is where he works," I tried to explain to the baffled woman.

For a sustained second, Shazdeh Joon stared at Shoja blankly. Then a tiny sparkle of recognition shone through her degenerative dementia. She slowly moved towards her son. Millions of complex nerve cells, long disconnected in her brain, suddenly started sending signals. Her face brightened. She took her son's hand. Then, to everyone's amazement, the matriarch spoke: "Shoja, my darling!"

As if making a mental connection between her son's disappearance and the nearby guard, she turned to the latter and added: "Damn you!"

Shoja encircled his mother with both arms, kissing her all over. Tears showed at the corners of his eyes.

The miracle did not last. Shazdeh Joon's memory disappeared abruptly. The personality disintegrated quickly. She reverted to her disoriented self. Anxiety and restlessness took over. The woman with the lost mind started spinning around, chanting:"Bobloboch!"

"What's she saying?" Shoja asked with confusion.

"It's all that her brain remembers of a prayer," I answered. "She's been asking God to help you."

"If I were around, this wouldn't have happened to my mother," Shoja said remorsefully.

"Don't blame yourself! Her insidious disease has no cure! You know that."

Like a caged bird, Shazdeh Joon reached for an escape, wailing : "Bobloboch! Bobloboch!" The guard blocked her exit.

"Azar, please, take her home. I can't stand this," Shoja said, burying his head in his hands. With the guard's help, I led my mother-in-law back into the car. Her first and last visit to Evin had ended.

That night, I had another terrifying dream. This time I dreamed that Ramin was dead—the worst of all my nightmares! There he was, lying on the ground, lifeless! I knelt down beside his body, shaking him hysterically. Shaking him, and calling out his name, in vain. My beloved son was gone forever! I screamed a soundless scream and woke up in a cold sweat. All night, the shiver and the fear never left me.

"As the legend goes, a dream isn't what it appears to be. It's just the opposite. Ramin will have a long life," Mother tried to console me in the morning.

"This is not a legend. It's reality! Don't you see? Something must be wrong with Ramin. Otherwise, he would call or write to me. I'm really worried, Mother. Roxana and Babak have been warning me. I'm going to America!"

"How could you leave Shoja?" Mother pressed, trying to understand.

"It's just for a short time. There isn't much I can do for Shoja here, but I can do something for Ramin there," I explained.

"Then, go! Aryan and I will visit Shoja in your absence," Mother conceded.

The most saintly quality about her was that she always practiced patient motherly understanding with her children. With exceptional generosity, Mother offered to finance my trip to America. I had no choice but to accept. There I would be able to attend to Ramin and also research a possible escape for Shoja. America could provide a refuge where I would not be under spying eyes all the time.

"Heard from Babak?" Shoja asked me on my next visit. Because our visiting time was limited, our greetings had become shorter and more robotic.

"Yes. Apparently, he's adjusting to school." My words came out aimlessly.

"Then, why this long face?"

I had the urge to tell him about my decision to got to the States. Remembering that Shoja's room would likely be bugged, instead I started jotting down quick, short notes on a piece of paper.

"Must go to the States. Brief visit. Ramin needs me."

"Can you get out?" Shoja wrote back.

"Guess so. Using my maiden name. They might not connect us."

"When?" Shoja scribbled.

"Waiting to hear from Air France. I'm on a waiting list to Paris. Too many people leaving these days."

"Wish you didn't have to."

"I must. We have to think of our son. If anything happens to him, we could not forgive ourselves. I'll come back soon," I scribbled rapidly. The letters jumbled together under my shaking hand.

Shoja paused for a few seconds, resting one hand on his face. His thoughts were pulling him in opposite directions. He wanted me to be here for him and at the same he wanted me to be with our son who needed help. Shoja slowly raised his head.

"Go! I have no objections," he said curtly. His sad eyes spoke differently. He knew he had lost me to his son.

I got up and walked in muffled footsteps to the barred window. There was an eerie stillness in the execution yard below. My ears heard the ghostly echoes of the shots. If only there were a flying carpet to whisk Shoja away from this dreadful place! But I was in the most helpless, useless position ever in my life. I could do nothing for my husband.

"Shoja, promise you won't ever risk your life for anyone or anything! Say it! Do you hear me?" I turned to him.

"Yeah," he answered absently, his mind far away.

The door opened slightly. A *Pasdar*, posted outside, peered in. "Doc! They want you in the clinic."

"You'd better leave, Azar. I don't know how long this will take," Shoja said and got up obediently from his seat.

The *Pasdar* kindly allowed Shoja to escort me halfway out of the prison before going back to the clinic. We walked side by side in silence, through the sandy courtyard and into the expanse of the compound. The *Pasdar* followed us step by step. Evin looked even grimmer at dusk. Shoja and I watched as a minibus pulled up and unloaded the last group of visitors. They moved sluggishly towards the gate.

"C'mon. We'll be late for home," a mother complained as she pulled at her little boy's arm.

"I want to stay with Baba—Daddy. Why can't Baba come home?" the little boy cried.

Some three hundred feet away from the exit, the *Pasdar* signaled. Shoja stopped. "Got to go back. So long!" he said with a sense of bravado.

Before turning in the other direction, his eyes bonded with mine, and remained so for a stretched moment. No loving good-byes with kisses or touches were allowed. Still, we could not tear our gazes away from each other. I could not quite explain Shoja's hypnotic look. It seemed to say, "You are free to walk out of those gates. I am here for the rest of my life!"

I walked through the gates, with a tormented heart. My husband and I remained separated on the two sides of the dreadful prison. The impenetrable walls of Evin seemed to grow even taller. The iron fortress gates banged shut behind me, with a hint of finality.

At home, there was an important message for me from Air France. I was scheduled to leave in three days. Granted only one visit a week with Shoja, I would have no chance to say good-bye to him. What if something happened to him while I was gone? What if we never saw each other again?

I sat down and wrote a farewell letter to my husband. No words could faithfully explain my true feelings.

Dear Shoja,

No matter where we are or what happens to us, we will always be one. And if forces beyond our control determine that we part forever, we must accept our fate gracefully. A part of you remains always with me, and I with you.

With the letter, I enclosed the Kipling poem which I had recently translated for him:

> *....If you can bear to hear the truth you've spoken*
> *Twisted by knaves to make a trap for fools,*
> *Or watch the things you gave your life to, broken,*
> *And stoop and build 'em up with worn-out tools....*

I took the envelope to mother who was busy cooking in the kitchen.

"Mother, please take this to Shoja. Also, keep my wedding band. I'll be traveling as a single woman. This could betray me. Do you hear? What's going on? Why are you cooking so much food?"

Mother took the stuff from me and said, "Surely you haven't forgotten, Azar!"

"Oh, yes!" I responded in a befuddled way. Four years ago today, on October 26, 1975, my father, Amir Mehdi Aryanpour, had passed away in his sleep with a fatal heart attack. He had been buried next to his ancestors in Kashan. In keeping with tradition, Mother observed his death anniversary by feeding the poor at the Mosque. I had almost forgotten by getting caught up with the intrigue of escaping Iran.

Father and I had a natural bond. We had developed a rather unique friendship that most Iranian girls would not have with their fathers. Father, tall and extremely handsome, would take me along whenever he could, even into the "men's world," traditionally off-limits to girls. We would go to the barber shop, where I would sit in rapture listening to him and other men discussing all the current events. Or, we would watch *Now Ruz* fireworks together in front of City Hall. Sometimes, Father took me to the old bazaar, where he would haggle with carpet vendors. He would show me meticulously hand-crafted Persian rugs, each almost perfect. Once he told me that the carpet makers deliberately would miss a knot, or flaw the design, to prove that God, and only God, could be perfect. To me, Father was perfect.

On October 29, 1979, in the predawn darkness, Hushang and I quickly packed his car and left for the airport before the neighbors could get up to discover the clandestine moment of escape. My ever-devoted mother had given me her favorite black coat, saying, "Take this, Azar. It must be cold in the States now." She had also promised to keep my trip a secret from everybody until I had arrived safely in the States. I knew she and Aryan would faithfully visit Shoja for me.

"Alborz is hardly visible today," I sighed as we drove on. The mountains steady, magical spell, now lost in the mist, was the most memorable sight of my country.

"The mountains will still be here when you return, Sis!" Hushang said in his friendly manner.

"Hushang, please explain to Shoja why I left suddenly. He truly didn't want me to go."

"He'll understand."

"Do you think they'll stop me at the airport?"

"Relax. They wouldn't know who you are. Even if you're recognized, they wouldn't harm you."

"Hushang, I appreciate everything you've done for me and my family. Really. We couldn't have made it without you."

"Don't mention it, Sis."

Mehr Abad Airport, like the rest of the government buildings, had changed face. When the Shah's images came down, the Ayatollah Khomeini's pictures went up and Revolutionary posters adorned the walls.

Anxious travelers waited in line at the Air France terminal. It was obvious that many Iranians wanted to leave, but there was no way to guess how many would be returning. As Hushang and I walked up to stand in line, I felt my heart pounding recklessly. Under a thick scarf and tinted glasses, I kept looking down to avoid curious eyes.

The attendant finally received my ticket. According to new regulations, my passport had been taken by the airline twenty-four hours earlier and sent to the authorities for approval. If I was allowed to leave the country, they would give it back to me right before boarding. The Air France agent examined my ticket and then referred me to a man with a bushy beard. He was responsible for inspecting my luggage.

"Who is the passenger?" the bearded inspector demanded.

"Me," I answered tensely.

"Then what's this man doing here?" He pointed at my brother suspiciously.

Hushang took a few steps back.

"He's come to see me off," I explained.

"Carrying any contraband?"

"Of course not!"

The inspector opened my luggage, rummaged his hands through the contents, and closed it. He stuck a label on the luggage, and tossed it onto a conveyer.

For the next stage, I entered an area partitioned into small compartments. Two female *Pasdars* were thoroughly searching a passenger, a woman with a long plaster cast.

"Can't stand on this leg too long. Please, hurry," the woman begged.

"What's the cast for?" the *Pasdars* inquired.

"Why, a fractured leg, of course! Please, may I go now?"

The cast looked suspiciously wide around the calf. The two distrustful interrogators walked off to the side. They discussed the woman's case in an undertone and with animated gestures. Beads of sweat broke out prominently on the passenger's forehead. The female *Pasdars* rang a buzzer. The panicked traveler's good leg buckled and she stumbled backward, almost into my arms. A saw was brought in and the cast was sawed open. A pouch full of gemstones fell out. The woman passenger cringed and fainted.

I passed through safely.

The final stage was to receive my passport at the security desk. Everyone on line was tense. I was mortified. This was the last checkpoint where I might be caught.

"Name!" the officer barked an intimidating command.

"Azar Aryanpour." My eyes gave a forlorn look.

The officer searched the file of passports under the letter 'A'.

"Not here! Next!"

My eyes widened. "How could that be?"

The officer raised an eyebrow. "Probably being held," he scoffed a flippant answer.

"*Agha*, please look again," I begged as a rancid taste came up from my stomach.

The officer sized me up disdainfully and then went back to the 'A' file.

I am finished! He will not find it.

"What was the name again?"

I repeated the name anxiously.

He pulled out a passport. "Take off your glasses!" he ordered.

I obeyed, giving a meek forlorn look again. He scrutinized my face and the picture. The tension spread from my jaw, through my stomach, down to my feet. The officer tossed the passport across the counter. "That way! Be quick! Plane's boarding," he commanded.

I made a desperate run towards the gate before he could change his mind and arrest me for some suspicious reason. Near the gate, I hesitated briefly only to look for my brother. There he was, standing by that column. Waving my passport, I called, "Hushang!"

"Safe trip!" he called back with a glow on his face.

It was not until the Air France jet climbed high over Tehran that my blood pressure lowered. Below, the city was concealed under thick clouds. Somewhere down there, the notorious Evin Prison engulfed my husband. So long, Shoja, my darling! Be brave. And may God protect you every moment!

CHAPTER EIGHTEEN

In Paris, I checked into a third-class hotel off of the Champs Elysees. On my previous visits here, I had stayed at the famous Hotel Inter-Continental. In the past few years, Shoja and I had enjoyed taking annual vacations to various European countries, as well as taking official trips to some other parts of the world.

As usual, the Champs Elysees bustled with life. Our Revolution had not touched it! The carefree Parisians were leisurely spending the afternoon in the quaint cafés which were loud with conversations. Unlike my casual times in the past, watching them did not fascinate me.

In my hotel room, I shut the drapes and retired to bed to make up for many sleepless nights.

"Why are you applying for a visa?" the American consul asked me coldly the next morning.

"To visit my three children."

"How long do you intend to stay?"

"A couple of months maximum."

"Many Iranians have immigrated to America recently. What assurance can you give that you will return to Iran?"

I explained my husband's situation to her. "As you can see, I could have asked for political asylum if I wanted to. But I don't intend to leave him behind. I only wish to visit with my children for a short while in America."

The consul handed me an application. "Fill this out carefully."

Around me several Iranians were also seeking visas. I went to the furthest end of the counter to complete the application. It had become my determination to avoid any Iranian I did not recognize.

The consul took my form. "Why is your family name different from your husband's?" she asked suspiciously.

"I've used my maiden name. It would have been impossible for me to leave Iran under my husband's name."

"Can anyone in France verify your statements?"

"Yes! Marie DuBois, a Parisian woman. Here. This is her address. She lived in Iran before the Revolution. I took French lessons from her."

The consul took her name and address. "You'll hear from us in a few days," she said sternly.

I bought myself a ham sandwich and went to the Tuileries Gardens to eat. Near me, children played happily. How fortunate they were!

To pass time, I spent the second day of my stay in Paris by the Seine. Tour boats carried happy passengers along the river, and an old man fed the birds on the boardwalk. Up the street, a middle-aged couple appeared. It was almost obvious from their hand gestures, their walk, and their eye contact that they were Iranians. However, there was no telling who was a friend or a foe these days. Self-consciously, I darted across the street and quickly tried to disappear down an alley.

At a newspaper stand, Ayatollah Khomeini's piercing eyes stared out from the magazine rack. He had become front-page news around the world. Although tempted, a fear propelled me past the newsstand. I constantly dreaded that our names would show up in the articles—everywhere in the world. Even in France, the nightmare of being hated for wrongful reasons persisted.

Back at the hotel, I found no message from the American Consulate in my key box. Was there deliberate foot-dragging by the government? These days, wandering Iranians were not welcomed anywhere. What should I do? I could not afford to stay in Paris too long. My funds were limited.

The following day, the silence from the Consulate continued. I passed the ticking minutes by boarding a bus to the Eiffel Tower, where I could sit and worry the rest of the hours of the day. Paris—the legendary 'City of Love and Light'—had lost its charm. Or, I had changed.

On day four, I was finally granted a visa to the States for one month! *Merci, Mademoiselle* Marie DuBois!

I arrived in the States on November 3, 1979. At Dulles Airport, I was the only passenger detained by Immigration. The officer's distrustful attitude showed strongly on his face and made me react with awkwardness. I had become the most suspicious character in the airport because of being Iranian. The officer examined my passport several times. Looking distrustful, he asked, "Is this your own passport?"

"Yes, sir."

"Wait here. I need to check something," the officer ordered.

Fifteen long minutes later, he returned with his supervisor, a serious man in a navy blazer. He held my passport and carefully scrutinized my face, comparing it with my picture.

"Is there a problem with my passport, sir?" I asked, concerned that I might be sent back.

"The picture doesn't look like you, ma'am," the supervisor said in a judgmental tone.

"Well, it's a couple of years old," I explained. "If you have any doubts as to my identity, you can call in my children, who are waiting outside. Two of them are American citizens."

How could I explain to these foreign bureaucrats that, if my picture did not look like me, it was because the Iranian Revolution had not been kind to me? It had certainly added more wrinkles and worry lines on my face.

From fear and jet lag, my legs were about to collapse. The children must now be worried. What if I was turned away?

The supervisor whispered something to the officer, gave him the passport and left. The officer, reluctantly, stamped my passport and returned it to me. My photograph was loose. Apparently, they had tested the photo to be sure it was authentic.

I exited customs and entered the terminal looking for my children, unaware of the future that was to unfold in the States.

My searching eyes caught hold of Roxana first. With long auburn hair, deep brown eyes, and high cheekbones, my daughter looked lovely as usual—except her carefree, engaging smile had vanished. Babak appeared slightly better than he did back in Iran. The old radiant twinkle returned to his eyes, as I approached.

"Mom, I never thought we'd see you again, at least not so soon," he said.

"You've not changed much since I saw you last, Mom!" Roxana sweetly lied.

I hugged and kissed them both, and looked around anxiously.

"Where's Ramin? Has something happened?"

Roxana pointed at a scrawny young man standing behind her. He looked nothing like the well-built, handsome and dynamic son I had left in the States over a year ago.

Ramin had lost at least forty pounds. His brown hair was long and unkempt, his hollow face unshaven, his eyes downcast. As I moved closer, he stepped back.

"Hello, Ramin. I've missed you so much."

"Me too," he mumbled.

These two simple words were magical. I had not totally lost my son!

On the road to their studio apartment, it started to rain. As Roxana drove a friend's car, she and Babak took turns inquiring about their father. Ramin only listened. Perhaps, waiting for the right moment, he held back his questions.

"Some of your old friends live in D.C.," Babak reported. "Maybe you'll want to visit them."

"I've only come to visit with you children for a short time. If word gets out that I'm here, I may have trouble returning home. Anyway, fill me in. What's going on in your lives?"

Roxana, who was double majoring in elementary and special education, also worked as a teacher's assistant at a school for children with learning disabilities. "Mom, I can't wait to finish this May, and go to graduate school," she said with her typical spunk.

Babak had a few complaints: "The school's too far, and I'm behind in my studies. The food's awful too."

I snickered at Babak's small complaints. Of course, I knew that he was missing his home and his father!

"You'll adjust. Give it some time, sweetheart. Ramin, what's up with you?" I asked.

"Not much."

Away from each other for fourteen months and with his father in prison, Ramin treated me like a stranger. It was obvious that having an open dialogue with my sensitive son required patience. I would be here when he was ready to talk.

The children's studio was on the sixth floor of a twenty-four-story building in Chevy Chase, MD. The room overflowed with the sorts of things students amass: shorts, t-shirts, sneakers, cassettes, books. To celebrate my arrival, the children had prepared spaghetti and meatballs for dinner, cleared the dining table, and placed some carnations in a vase.

In my rush to leave Iran, I had brought my children no gifts, only a small jar containing some soil, a token of the precious homeland they had left behind.

Ramin's serious mood continued during dinner. There were times when he was so like his father and would draw inward to be detached from others in the room. He did not touch his food.

At bedtime, the boys slept in beds on one side of the cramped apartment. On the other side, Roxana opened the sofa bed for me. She took a blanket and a pillow and slept on the floor by the dining room table.

It took some time before the exhaustion of the day brought my brain to a dead halt. As soon as I shut my eyes, the same chronic nightmare worked its way into my subconscious, with a slight change. I was back in Iran, trying to open the gate to our abandoned house, when an arm clawed me from behind. A terrorizing voice lashed out: "Get lost! Not your home anymore!"

My eyes opened to discover a lean figure standing over me. I nearly screamed.

"It's only me, Mom. I need to talk. Let's go downstairs," Ramin whispered.

"Give me a couple of minutes to get dressed, son."

The lobby was empty, except for the security woman behind the counter. We sat opposite each other.

"Mom, I quit both my job and my school six weeks ago and don't intend to go back," Ramin dropped the bomb.

"Why? What do you want to do with your life now?"

"I don't know. At this point, I don't care."

"But you have already finished one year of college. It's a pity to—"

"I know, but I can't help it," he confided in me.

I laid my hand on my head. "Apparently, I can't force you to do something that you don't want to do. If you don't care to go back to school, you'll have to look for a job. With all the major changes in our life you can no longer depend exclusively on us for support," I paused. "You also have to take your health more seriously. Any eating disorder could become life threatening, son!"

He pressed his lips. His sunken eyes wore a mournful expression.

"Now, tell me what's really bothering you, sweetheart," I continued in a softer tone.

"You don't know?" Ramin snapped. Then, he let down his guard. "Everybody speaks of my father as if he were the Iranian 'Al Capone.' It's common knowledge, the Sheikh anathema. I don't know who or what to believe any more!"

My son was carrying the weight of guilt and shame for his

father and his family. I knew he trusted I would give him the honest answers, even if it meant cross-examining me at one in the morning.

"Your father is simply a victim of circumstances, a convenient target. You should not see him as someone with a criminal past, or judge him politically incorrect. If he were dishonest, we would be rich now. Instead, we rely on your grandmother's charity."

"You mean we have no money of our own?" Ramin wondered.

"All we have is what's in our bank account here. A few thousand dollars." We talked some more. Ramin asked about his father's public and private life, and I answered at length and in detail. A few times he interrupted me, requesting further explanation. I responded with patience. At the end of our long conversation, my son seemed less confused. Then, he looked away, biting the side of his index finger. Obviously, Ramin was fighting within himself. Finally, he spelled out his most troubling thought.

"Mom, if Dad's stuck in prison forever, what would you do? I mean, would you look for a new life? Another man?"

I reached out and took his hand. "I'll always wait for your father, son," I answered without hesitation. "And, I'll always be there for you!"

For the first time, Ramin's sad face lightened up. My words had tipped the balance in his mind. He had found a new light in his life in regard to his father and me. He realized he was not in the presence of the enemy. This seemed to be an important discovery.

"Let's go back to bed, Mom. You must be exhausted," he said tenderly.

By the time we got back to bed, it was 2:30 a.m. In Tehran, it was 11:00 in the morning. Shoja seemed millions of miles away!

On November 4, 1979, the American Embassy in Tehran was seized by some radical students and its personnel held captive. The Iranian Government had totally ignored the immunity of American diplomats. This was an act of retaliation for America's approval of the deposed Shah's recent trip to the United States. The Shah was to receive treatment for cancer. The captors were demanding the Shah's return in exchange for the freedom of the hostages. In a strange way, their families and I were sharing the same helplessness. More and more wives and children, whether Iranians or Americans, were becoming victims of a frenzied Revolution.

"Oh, my God! This incident may lead to a war between America and Iran," I warned Ramin, who was lying in front of the television.

"Will this affect Dad?" He asked with concern.

"It will affect every Iranian's life, not just your father's. Now, get dressed. We have to leave for the bank. Hurry up! I have to act quick. Things may never be the same for Iranians again here in the States."

Ramin left for the shower. I opened the refrigerator to prepare breakfast, but found only French's Mustard, Heinz Ketchup, pickles, and, of course, a six-pack of soda. There were also a few cans of pork and beans, and a pack of milk. How "American" my children had become!

I returned to the living room and waited despondently. Ramin reappeared in a short-sleeved T-shirt.

"Aren't you going to be cold like that?" I asked him.

"I'll be okay," he answered casually.

"We need to do some grocery shopping today. You kids must begin to eat real food. Now have a glass of milk before we go."

"Please, don't treat me like a child, Mom. I'll eat when I feel like it."

At the bank, the teller gave us a balance of $7,250.

This couldn't be! I knew we didn't have much money, but $7,250? That would not last for more than a few months. What would we do when the money ran out?

I turned to Ramin, "Still have doubts about your father?"

"Mom, what do you want from me? You want me to get a job? I can't concentrate. Or, do you expect me to go back to school? I've missed too many classes to catch up," he said in a defensive tone.

"You're smart. You can do it. Go talk to your advisor. They will understand your situation. What do you say?"

He put his hands to his forehead. "Mom! I'm confused enough. Don't push me. I don't promise anything. But I'll think about it. Okay?"

"Okay. But please remember that I've come all the way here for you. I can't help you unless you let me, son."

News reports of the American hostages overshadowed all the world news. The media further accentuated the crisis by making inflammatory remarks about "Iranian terrorism." Fears of a possible war, of violence towards Iranians, and of being deported from the very place where I sought refuge for my children, compelled me to seek immediate security for them. Time was critical.

The first item on my agenda, was Babak's school. The

principal of the International School, Mrs. Walker, received me warmly. Tall and thin, she had an air of authority about her. "Nice to meet you, Mrs. Sheikh. When did you arrive in the States?"

"November third."

"You were lucky. One more day and you might not have made it. I hope you don't intend to go back, especially after this hostage crisis."

"I'm here to help my children only. My husband needs me back home."

I briefly explained our situation to her, and asked if she could arrange for Babak's transfer to a public school. "We simply can't afford to pay the second quarter's tuition," I concluded.

Mrs. Walker sympathized. "To be honest with you, Babak's chances for a transfer to a public school are minimal at this point in the school year. And we don't want to lose a bright student just because he can't pay tuition," she said. "At the next board meeting, I'll discuss his case and request a full tuition scholarship."

Considering the hostage situation, Mrs. Walker's kind offer was touching.

Not all Americans were so understanding. Quite frequently some Americans displayed their patriotism and anger towards us at the same time: "You f—ing raghead terrorists! Leave this country. Go back where you came from!"

"Nuke Iran!" was spray-painted on most street walls! Even here in America we were faced with new dangers. We could be spat upon and attacked by an angry American mob. Our insecurities intensified.

The second item on my agenda was to provide some temporary income for the children. For this purpose, I flew to New York City to meet with Dr. Shahin. The ex-Minister now resided in a high-security apartment on the Upper East Side. Several thousand miles away from Iran, Shahin kept a low profile because of Ayatollah Khomeini's alleged secret agents. Yet, he had gotten rid of his physical disguise and returned to his natural look—no beard, silver gray hair!

"It's so good to see you, Azar! My wife will be sorry to have missed you! She's out visiting our son. You've changed! Lost weight?"

"Maybe. It's been hard, you know."

"Are you going to stay in the States?"

"No! I'm just here to see the kids and-well-to explore possibilities for Shoja's escape."

"There are always options for such things. Of course, it would be expensive, not to mention dangerous. If you want me to, I'll ask around," Shahin suggested.

"I'd appreciate it. But, please hurry. My visa runs out in a few weeks."

"Why don't you at least plan to stay until the hostage crisis is resolved?" He raised his eyebrows with anticipation. "Isn't Roxana an adult citizen? You can apply for permanent residency in the U.S. through her."

"I wouldn't dare. The Iranian Government might find out and have me arrested when I go back. I came only to help the kids. They may have to quit school, unless I can find a source of income for them," I confided.

"I heard you got the house back," Shahin said with a slight smile as he held a match to his cigarette.

"News travels fast! One *Komiteh* gave it back and another took it," I answered.

Shahin blew out a smoke ring while choosing his words carefully. "You may've heard that Mr. Ansary, former Chairman of the National Iranian Oil Company, is here in New York. He has occasionally asked about Shoja. Would you like to see him? Maybe he'll help you."

"It's difficult for me to ask such a wealthy man for help. Besides, he is on the Ayatollah Khomeini's black list. It's not wise for me to be seen with him."

Shahin laughed nervously. "I'm on the same list! Don't worry. No one will find out. Go, talk to Ansary. I can arrange a meeting, perhaps for today."

I accepted. After a phone call, he returned to tell me a luncheon had been arranged for the same day.

At the French restaurant on Madison Avenue, Mr. Ansary was cordial and, as always, immaculately dressed. The Revolution had left no apparent marks on his appearance. We ordered lunch, and talked about Shoja.

"Is it true that Admiral Madani saved Shoja's life?" Ansary asked.

"Shoja's alive because he's innocent," I answered calmly.

"So, what do you think of the new regime?"

"It doesn't matter what I think. If the majority of Iranians are happy with the change, then we must accept it, even though this means the demise of our lifestyle."

"You don't really believe that," the former NIOC Chairman said. "Iranians had a rather good life before the Revolution— but did they appreciate it?"

"They may have had many things, but they didn't have freedom."

"*Khanom* Sheikh, you seem to have been brainwashed by the Revolutionaries!"

From the beginning of our luncheon, it was obvious that my host and I would never agree as to the underlying factors of the Iranian Revolution. I just hoped I had not insulted him.

As I silently debated how to initiate discussion of a loan, Ansary saved me the trouble of making an embarrassing start. He asked, "Before you return to Iran, is there anything I can do for your family?"

Ansary must have assumed that I wanted to see him for some reason and that this was not just a social visit. With difficulty, I told him about our financial situation. Would he believe that the wife of a former Minister was almost destitute?

"Would a few thousand dollars do?" he inquired with an air of formality.

Asking for a loan would have been an impossible thought to Shoja and I a few years ago. A loan was not an everyday event. It was an act of desperation and this fellow countryman showed me enough respect to grant my request. I swallowed hard. "Yes. As soon as I can secure an income, I'll return the money. I'm sure Shoja would appreciate your loan."

Back in D.C., I felt no sense of jubilation. The money only bought a little more time until the children could get jobs. Ramin was furious about the loan. "How could you lower yourself to accept money from an outsider?"

I had been through enough humiliation. I did not need Ramin acting in an uppity way as if we did not need the help. These were not ordinary times and our children had to understand it.

"It's just a loan. I did what I had to do. Now, it's your turn. Are you going back to school? Or, are you getting a job, son?" I asked impatiently.

"I'm considering going back to school. Just don't push me," he said with some disgust.

"Good. Now, eat your dinner."

Ramin reluctantly obeyed. He did not have to admit it but I could see that my being there for him was working.

The International School had exempted Babak from tuition. He was adjusting to the new country. Someday, I dreamed that he would be able to put the nightmare of the Revolution behind him.

Ramin too returned to school, although he was not very enthusiastic about his studies. His sense of helplessness for his father and his country persisted.

When Mr. Ansary's deposit arrived, I decided to look for a larger apartment.

The new apartment, an unfurnished two-bedroom, was one block away from the studio. We used some of our savings to buy a few items to furnish it.

After we had moved and settled in, I received a letter from an old American friend, James Moore, in Nevada. An architect, Jim had spent several years in Iran in the early 1970s as a consultant to the government. He met Shoja while designing modern hospitals for the country. He wrote:

Dear Azar,

Glad that you all survived the Revolution. I was especially worried for Shoja. It's a pity that the Iranian Government rewarded his

honest dedication with life imprisonment! He was one of the few
Iranians who actually placed the welfare of his country before his own.

I am aware that your assets have been confiscated. Let me know
what I can do to help your family. Surely, your husband would do the
same for his friends.

At the climax of the crisis between Iran and America, the
offer of help from an American friend was encouraging—but it
came too late. I had already indebted our family to someone else.

Later in the day, in the nearby park, I happened to meet
Samadi, the former Iranian diplomat and my children's
guardian in the States. He had suddenly grown a thick bushy
beard and carried prayer beads in his hand as a gesture to
appease the Islamic community in Washington, D.C.

"Azar, you come to America without calling on your
friends?" he complained.

"Friends? It's been over a year since you last checked in on
my children. Shoja and I trusted you to be their guardian in this
country!" I rebuked him.

"My dear, the Revolution has taken a toll on me, too,"
Samadi said. "But, tell me, what's new in Iran? We hear that the
Mullahs go on arresting and executing people. Killing your
own people is bad enough, but to take American hostages?
Insane—outrageous!"

He made no reference to Shoja.

"Of course, if Carter wants, things can change in a month.
Problem is he's indecisive. Nevertheless, if you have a large sum
of money in the bank, withdraw and transfer it to Switzerland.
In retaliation for the hostages, the American Government may
seize all Iranian assets in this country," Samadi warned.

I gave him a cold stare back. "Don't worry about us! We have nothing."

"With no assets, how do you arrange for your rent?"

"I'm sure that you'll find out soon."

A year ago, I would have never tried to insult someone in this way. But Samadi had proved not to be a solid friend.

"Have you applied for a green card? Better get on it before it's too late," the ex-diplomat advised. "Things are getting tense between the U.S. and Iran."

"I'm going back. Shoja needs me there."

"In that case, perhaps you could help your people."

I looked at him, puzzled.

"Rumor has it that you know Admiral Madani from old times," Samadi said. "As you know, he's Khomeini's Defense Minister. He's also a candidate for President and may win the election. Madani can help us restore the monarchy. I'm not speaking about the Shah coming back to power. He lost any chance of returning when his closest allies, including General Fardoust, betrayed him. However, his son, Crown Prince Reza, is quite capable."

"There's no monarchy to restore! Iran is a republic now."

I could not envision another revolution. Ayatollah Khomeini was in power, whether the Western countries liked him or not.

"Rubbish! The present regime is illegitimate. With 'our' support, a strong leader could easily overthrow it."

By "our support", was he referring to the C.I.A. or to the Monarchists? Had the man gone bonkers to think a coup was possible?

"Azar, if you take a message to Madani, you will help both

your country and yourself. Once the regime changes, your husband will be freed."

"I doubt very much that Admiral Madani wants anything to do with people like you," I said firmly. "Besides, I have no interest in politics. You'd better find somebody else. Now, if you'll excuse me, I must leave. My children are expecting me for dinner."

It was Thanksgiving Day—my favorite American holiday, one celebrated by all regardless of religious or ethnic backgrounds. It was also my birthday. Shoja had turned forty-seven three days ago. Had he received the birthday card and the poem I sent him? Twenty-nine days had passed since our last visit without any letters from him. I missed him terribly.

I had just put the graceful turkey on the table when the phone rang.

"Is this the Sheikh residence?" a man asked in Farsi.

"Yes. Who is calling?"

"No one special. Just a call to remind you that even on this side of the world, you will pay for your crimes!" the voice threatened.

I hung up quickly.

"Mom! The food's getting cold. What's keeping you?" Babak called.

My enthusiasm for eating had been lost. The caller's threat had distorted my relative peace of mind, but Babak's impatient calling jolted me back to my children. I should not let the relentless threats destroy us. We would enjoy this day together.

CHAPTER NINETEEN

O cameleer, for God's sake, help me on
Heartache and need led me to this caravan
Hafez (Fourteenth Century)

Early in December, Roxana took the day off to go with me to the Immigration and Naturalization Office in Baltimore. A large crowd—mostly Hispanics, Orientals, and many Iranians—waited patiently for their numbers to be called. We took a ticket and joined them.

After nearly two hours, I was called by a female officer.

"I would like to have my visa extended for another month, please," I asked politely.

The government clerk looked at my visa and frowned. "According to this, you must leave the U.S. today."

"I know, but my son, an American citizen, is ill. I need to stay a few more weeks."

"You don't get it. You must leave today. Go back to your 'Ayatollah' and burn American flags!" the officer said loudly. She was letting out her personal venom against Iranians at me.

Everyone's eyes in the crowd were riveted on me. With the

mention of the word 'Ayatollah', they were probably waiting for me to throw a bomb in the room. I walked back to Roxana in a confused state. "You heard her. What should I do now?"

"I don't think you have any other choice but to apply for a green card, Mom. Why don't you go back and find out about the procedures?"

Thankfully she had a clear head and gave me the encouragement I needed. I took another ticket and waited an additional hour and a half. This time a kinder and less prejudiced officer received me. "Through your American-born daughter, you may petition for permanent residency any time," he informed me.

The immigration officer gave me some applications to take home, study, complete, and return with necessary documentation. It would take eight weeks to process my file. During the filing with Immigration, I was not allowed to leave the U.S. My dilemma was to stay the extra two months without endangering my chance to return to Iran and to Shoja.

A letter from Aryan solved my dilemma:

....Shoja wants you to stay as long as it takes for Ramin to recover and suggests that you apply for a green card. It may be impossible for you to reenter America in the future. Life here is still the same, if not worse. The government attempts to keep the euphoria of the Revolution alive, but it's not as strong as it used to be. People are disenchanted. You should appreciate being away from it all. By the way, Shoja received his birthday poem and loved it!

The poem was a nostalgic cry for my lost home, Iran:

Tell me of my home,
That ancient beloved city,
With twisting alleys,
Inharmonious houses,
Where simple-hearted people lived,
At the foot of the magisterial Alborz.
Tell me of my people,
Of those ragged children,
Bathing their little bodies in the ample sun,
On the unfriendly pavements.
And of the quintessential street vendor,
His wealth strapped to the back of a sickly mule,
Bartering for a loaf of bread.
Or, that wandering dog,
Yelping for food,
Target of the passersby's boot.
Who occupies my home,
My sanctuary,
That white edifice enfolded in a rose garden?
Do the noisy sparrows still nest,
In the tall, proud, poplar tree?
The lofty weeping willow,
Rinses her long hair in the pool?
Does the glossy black Raven,
From the old fir's pinnacle,
Proclaim the changing seasons?
Are my children's light footprints
Engraved on the lawn?

Their pictures on the mantle piece —
Roxana's generous smile,
My sons' mischievous twinkles?
Does Mother, serene and selfless,
Prostrate herself towards Mecca,
As the Muezzin calls,
From the Mosque with turquoise minarets?
And my husband,
My raining light —
Without him,
Where is my home?

A few days later at the Immigration Office, I was granted a temporary permit. I would have to stay in America until I received my alien registration card, commonly called the 'green card.'

By now, a few of the hostages had been released, but the rest remained in captivity in Iran. All diplomatic negotiations for their freedom had been unsuccessful so far. Even President Carter's punitive measures—economic sanctions and the holding of the Iranian Government's assets in the United States—had not worked. As the crisis deepened, so did anti-Iranian sentiment in America. Iran had become a pariah in the world community. In such an atmosphere, we struggled to settle in the United States, which even under normal conditions would not be easy, considering the differences of our cultures.

My first Christmas in the States was not a happy one. Ramin complained of stomach pains and stayed in bed. He might have developed ulcers from his eating disorder. The other two children had shut themselves in their rooms because I had not allowed them to join their friends for a Christmas party. Despite their age, I had to protect them. It was not just Ramin's health that worried me but the safety of all my children. We had been receiving hate letters and threatening telephone calls in D.C. Who were our enemies? The Communists, the Islamists, the Monarchists, and now even some Americans, despised us equally.

I sat by the window, watching the silent snow and feeling lonely. The only refuge I had was poetry. I reflected my sadness into a poem:

> *Christmas!*
> *Chiming bells,*
> *Rainbows of celebrating light,*
> *Snow, crystal white,*
> *The hymn, the beautiful hymn*
> *Of Mary's innocence,*
> *From St. Someone's church,*
> *Interpreting, for all,*
> *Christianity in simple terms:*
> *The miracle birth, the Trinity.*
> *Jesus Christ is born again—*
> *For the umpteenth time!*
> *Hallelujah!*
> *Under the pine tree,*
> *I open the parcels of grief, alone.*
> *A refugee, solo wanderer.*
> *Seized of my past by tyrants,*
> *Lost to my present by pain.*
> *Tomorrow, time to surrender unto Death!*

Jesus speaks of the angelic heavenly peace.
Nice promises, for the faithful,
For me—a suffering cynic—irrelevant!

In Iran's presidential election, Abolhasan Bani-Sadr, an ambitious French-educated economist, had defeated his rival, Admiral Madani. Although a devout Moslem, Bani-Sadr was secular and rather moderate in his views. People waited anxiously to see what he would do in regard to stabilizing the political situation, releasing the hostages, and saving the failing economy.

Due to the hostage crisis, the deposed Shah of Iran had been forced to leave America for Panama. It was easy to imagine that his fears were greater than ever before, and certainly more than ours.

As I continued my vigil to wait for the response from Immigration, there was an unexpected visitor, Jamshid, one of a handful who claimed credit for saving Shoja's life. He was a short stocky man in his late forties who gave an eerie appearance because of his bulging eyes and two missing front teeth. He presented me with a huge bundle of flowers.

"We haven't met before, *Khanom*, but consider me your friend."

"How did you find us here?" I asked.

"Oh, I have my ways," Jamshid laughed while assessing the living room with disapproval. "Those S.O.B.'s who destroyed you should see the dump you live in now! Jeez! All that slander, and this is what you ended up with? God, you must hate those assholes!"

"I don't hate anyone," I responded, unnerved by his candidly raunchy profanity. "There was a Revolution. We were not the only victims."

"Hey, how much do you pay for this crummy apartment?"

His direct questioning took me off guard a second time. "Five-fifty a month," I answered. What did it matter to him?

"You working?"

"This is the kids' apartment. My daughter works."

"Yeah? But you must have another source of income. America's expensive!"

Was he collecting information for the *Komiteh*? My face must have betrayed my suspicions to make him change his tone.

"Guess it's not any of my business. Well, *Khanom*, you're not the only one whose life has been turned upside down. I've had my share of troubles, too. During the crazy Shah's time, I was sent to jail for five years. I bribed my way out. Now, about this new regime, I first supported them. But then, poof! Things changed. If I hadn't split a few months ago, I might've been back in jail. Get your husband out of that hell. He might not luck out the next time he's up for execution."

"Have you heard something?" I asked anxiously.

"Still have my contacts in Iran. Fact is, everyone thinks that they'll kill your husband sooner or later. I can help him escape."

Dr. Shahin must have sent him, I thought.

"How? Be more specific, please," I asked for details.

"Same way I recently helped a former commander of the naval forces to escape. As we speak, he is safe in Turkey, on his way to the States," he boasted.

My attention was aroused. "But my husband's case is different. He's confined in Evin."

Jamshid lighted a cigarette. "With money, anything can happen!"

He looked at his watch and handed me his business card. "I'm late for a meeting at the State Department. Think over my proposal, and let me know if you want my help."

Could I trust him?

A week later, Hushang phoned from Tehran. "Good news! You can speak to Shoja tomorrow at 1:00 p.m. sharp. Just dial 293017, and they'll connect you to Evin. Please, don't use any names," he ended his brief conversation, leaving me with much anticipation.

The next day the children stayed home to speak with their father. They had not heard his voice in a long time. Luckily, we were connected the first time we dialed. "*Salam*," I nervously said.

"Who is it?" an anxious voice answered.

"I'm calling as scheduled."

"One moment."

I turned to the kids and whispered, "I think he went to call Dad!"

From several thousand miles away, Shoja's voice was heard: "Hello, love!"

I cleared my throat. "It's so good to hear you! Are you okay?"

"Okay. You and the children?"

"We're fine. As soon as I take care of a few problems, I'll return."

"I miss you all so very much," Shoja sighed.

"Any changes?" I asked.

"No. Just as it was. Now put the kids on. Tell them to hurry. Not much time."

One by one, the kids said a few words to their father.

"Hang in there, Dad," Ramin said. "We're proud of you."

There was a delay in hearing and speaking between Shoja and us, but his voice sounded encouraging. In the given circumstances, words could not be exchanged instantaneously, without strain.

The line was abruptly cut off.

"Only three minutes and two seconds," Babak complained. "You'd think that they would be more generous, considering the special arrangements!"

"At least we know Dad's okay," Roxana remarked.

"Please! Let's not pretend. How could anyone be okay in such a prison?" Ramin protested.

However frustrating and inadequate, this phone call caused quite a commotion when a Leftist Iranian newspaper printed an article with this headline: "Ex-Minister's Secret Phone Call to the States!"

The piece portrayed our simple conversation as Shoja's discussion with the C.I.A.! We apparently had miscalculated in thinking things might be improving for Shoja. Once again, he was, as the rest of us, a pawn in the changing game of chess within Iran. Was the entire thing a setup to bring our name back into the public focus? Whatever the answer, the incident could only make Shoja's confinement more difficult. Weeks later, he wrote:

My beloved wife:

This is my first letter to you in weeks. My visitation and communication privileges were both suspended. To write this simple letter, I had to go through so many approval channels. Judge Gilani helped.

I'm now head of the entire medical facility here. It all keeps me very busy, seeing over 200 patients daily. Hard to believe! The good thing is the work actually keeps me sane.

I received one of your letters with the kids' pictures. How much they have changed! Azar, stay where you are for a few more months. I would feel more secure.

Reluctantly, I postponed my plans to return, despite receiving my alien registration card which officially identified me as a U.S. permanent resident.

"*Khanom* Sheikh, since I didn't hear from you, I decided to follow up on my recent visit," Jamshid said on the phone. I had little time and no interest in his further intrigues.

"Sorry, but I've been quite busy."

"I can imagine. The S.O.B. media can be brutal. Didn't I warn you that things could change, eh?"

He had read the recent article against Shoja.

"It's been pretty awful," I said.

"Well, why not come to visit my wife and me in Stamford, Connecticut? We'll make your stay enjoyable. Guess what? The naval officer I helped to escape will be there too. He'll be hiding out at my home for some time. You can ask him any questions you have regarding escape from Iran. Maybe you'll even learn to trust me, eh?"

This was the first time he gave me any reasons to ignore the ominous feelings I had previously felt around him. After all, my mission for coming to America was not just to look out for the kids, but to plan for Shoja's escape as well.

"I'll be glad to visit you and your wife," I accepted cautiously.

"*Khanom*, just one thing: No mention of this conversation to anyone. Okay?" Jamshid demanded.

Why such secrecy? Who was he trying to protect? The naval officer or himself?

On a nice sunny morning in March, Jamshid met me at LaGuardia Airport in New York City, and drove me to his house in Stamford, Connecticut. His attractive wife had prepared a pleasant lunch.

"Where is your long-term guest, the Admiral?" I asked.

Jamshid scowled. "Didn't make it to America this week. Hopefully next." Noticing my disappointment, he added, "I'll answer any questions you may have about the escape."

His wife's calm presence gave me reassurance that his 'escape' connections might still be legitimate. In the far back of my mind, I knew he would eventually ask for money. The price had to be negotiated later. Although I had no idea where I would get the money from, still, I decided to plunge into the purpose of our meeting. The thought never came to my mind that our conversation could be tape-recorded, and I had no interest in playing the game too long. So, I asked, "How do you plan to get my husband out of prison?"

The host gestured at his wife to leave the room. She immediately excused herself. Jamshid turned to me. "Fact is, once in a while Dr. Sheikh performs surgeries outside the compound. Usually, he is escorted by no more than two guards. My 'friends' could arrange to kidnap him."

"Don't you think that the authorities will wonder what happened?"

"We've thought of that. We'll blame the 'kidnapping' on Communist radicals, who hate your husband's guts. The final step is to take the Doctor across the border to Turkey. How do you like to be in your hubby's arms in a couple of weeks? Sounds good, eh?" Jamshid laughed heartily, exposing the gaps from his missing front teeth. He spoke with conviction. His willingness to carry out what appeared to be an easy kidnapping closed my eyes to the loopholes in this James-Bond-type scheme. So, to my mind, there were no dangerous consequences. Jamshid's plan seemed simple, shrewd and perfect.

"How much do you charge for your services?"

"*Khanom*, don't insult me. I'm not in this to make money but to help a friend. My Oriental rug business here in Connecticut is doing pretty well. And, one of my brothers is a bank president. We're quite reputable people."

"Please, I need to know how much your plan will cost me," I asked again, knowing that friendship to a person like him still had its price. Escapes simply were another source of income for a daring entrepreneur.

Avoiding eye contact, my host replied, "One million touman! My 'friends' usually charge much more. We're giving your husband a break!"

"One million touman? That's 100,000 dollars. I can't afford it," I said.

Jamshid became obnoxious by tossing out a new suggestion with an air of cynicism. "Ask your millionaire friend Mr. Ansary to lend you the money. He's sitting on a king's ransom. Shouldn't bother him to share a little with you."

Had Jamshid's contacts informed him of my visit with Ansary? Had he heard of the loan?

"No one just gives away a million touman," I said.

The man pushed down and twisted out his half-smoked

cigarette. "No money, no escape. Tell you what we could do, though. You make two payments. Pay my 'friends' in Tehran 300,000 touman to spend on obtaining a fake passport and other necessities. Once your husband reaches Turkey, give me the second payment in U.S. dollars. With the new exchange rate, that would be about thirty grand. I'll distribute that among 'the guys' later. See? I'm even reducing the fee. The best deal you'll ever get!" he grinned broadly.

The art of the negotiator. The more he made concessions, the more I trusted him!

I started to think that the escape plan could work for Shoja. I would call Mother tonight and ask her for the 300,000 touman. Once I was assured that Shoja had crossed the border safely, I would worry about the rest of the money.

"You seem to have this well worked out. But, what happens if, God forbid, your plan fails?" I stared into Jamshid's eyes to see if he was really trustworthy.

"Don't even think of it," Jamshid said. "At the slightest hint of failure, my 'friends' will abort the mission. They'd never endanger themselves or Dr. Sheikh. If they quit, I'll return all of your money in U.S. dollars. I'm an honest man, *Khanom*."

Despite an air of uncertainty that hung around this man, my love for my husband made me accept his proposal. All that mattered was Shoja's freedom.

Our conversation continued for another half hour as we discussed the details. When we concluded, Jamshid gave me his typical warning: "Everything is to be kept a secret. Get it?"

On the flight back to Washington, I felt like a heroine.

"You need 300,000 touman? For what?" Mother asked on the telephone with dismay.

I had no choice but to lie. "A man here will pay me a very good rate in U.S. dollars, but for no less than that amount. We need the money."

"I have no more savings, except for a few bonds that I could cash," Mother said.

"Please, Mother, loan them to me. An elderly man will collect the money from you. His son will pay me the dollars in America."

Ever kind, accepting and generous, Mother promised to have the money available as soon as possible. How I hated myself for lying to her. My mother was innocently being involved in the kidnapping of my husband.

I spent many sleepless nights. How would Shoja react to his own kidnapping? Suppose he was safely taken across the border, then what? How was I going to raise the rest of the money? Afterwards, where would we go to hide? Which country? What continent? Would we be targets on the run forever? And, what if the plan failed? No! I should not even consider that.

Twice I tried to contact our American friend, Jim Moore, and ask him for a $30,000 loan. He was on a cruise in Scandinavia, out of contact with everyone. No one else was in a position to help.

I could not unburden my mind by sharing the secret even with my own children. The truth was too dangerous. I continued to live in duplicity.

The second *Now Ruz* went by without Shoja's freedom. This

was a particularly gloomy holiday for us. Mother had been hospitalized for her chronic asthma, obviously acting up as a result of nervous exhaustion. That was not all. Hushang had also gone into hiding. The *Komiteh* was planning to take over his ship-building company, Shenaveh, just as it had been nationalizing others. Worse than that, Hushang had campaigned for Admiral Madani, who had recently fallen out of favor with the present government. He was accused of secretly contacting the American Government. Both Hushang and Madani could become targets for assassins.

Shoja's *Now Ruz* card was scarcely uplifting:

Happy New Year to my family, from Evin! I celebrated the occasion with a small box of candy that a patient gave me. The authorities' opinion of me is improving. One recently implied that my life sentence might be reduced to fifteen years. A remote suggestion of freedom, but my hopes are higher now!

Shoja could do nothing but hope to get out. The reduced sentence meant another thirteen years and five months of lost time for an innocent man in prison. It was like being buried alive. I was going to take Shoja's life into my hands. I wanted him out sooner. No, it was stronger than wanting. I would have him out much sooner!

According to Jamshid's call late in March, everything was going forth as planned. "We're on our way. Get the rest of the money," he demanded.

"Is my husband out of Evin already?"

"Nope. Not yet."

"What's taking so long? You said two to three weeks!"

"Don't try to corner me. Things are unpredictable. Just get the thirty grand together, lady. Your mother did her part, now it's your turn."

"We agreed you would receive the $30,000 once my husband reaches Turkey."

"Maybe we did, maybe not. Fact is, if the money's not ready on time, my 'friends' may have a change of heart."

"What does that mean?"

"Lady, no one can outsmart smugglers, so don't try, eh?"

I hung up the phone, sat down and placed my head in my hands. It was good my children were not at home. No one could understand my feeling that I would go insane—the money, the smugglers, the change of plans, lying to my mother. I had to get more money. But how?

My spirits were lifted a few nights later when Aryan called from Tehran to tell me that Mother had been released from the hospital. The other good news she had for me was that the keys to our former house had been returned, again! The *Komiteh* had finally conceded to Ayatollah Khomeini's decree.

"Is it for real about the house? Can we trust what they're promising? Or, do they take the house back next week, Aryan?"

"This time, it seems real, Azar. The keys came with a document from the Court. No one can take the house away," her voice rose with each word.

"Even so, that house is useless. We can neither sell it nor live in it," I said pessimistically.

"You may officially be still barred from selling it, but the Mullah who delivered the keys knows of a potential buyer. The buyer will take your house for two million two-hundred thousand touman," Aryan said.

"What? The house was worth five times that!" I erupted.

"Maybe at one time. Now, it's uninhabitable. Besides, half of it is in Shoja's name, and he's barred from selling. Here's the deal: The buyer will pay only for your portion, but he'll get the entire house. He's willing to take a big risk."

"What does Shoja think?"

"He wants you to get rid of the house," Aryan advised.

Desperate for money for my greater plan, I surrendered to Aryan's suggestion. At least Shoja was aware of this option and apparently in agreement.

"Okay. You have power of attorney, please sign the papers for me. I can't leave the States. Not yet. Just send the money fast. I really appreciate your help."

"Good news. Mission accomplished! A perfect job! Your husband's across the border," Jamshid called ten days later. It was mid-April.

"Can't believe it! When?" I shouted.

"We set the plan in motion a week ago. This morning they got to Ankara. Now, your husband's in a safe place until he gets political asylum from America. If you don't hear from him, it's because Khomeini's secret agents are everywhere. He just can't run the risk."

My excitement settled and skepticism moved in. "Isn't it strange, though—a week has gone by since Shoja's rescue without any mention in the media?" I asked.

"Nope. Not at all! The government isn't crazy enough to publicize a notorious prisoner's escape and embarrass itself,"

Jamshid replied. "Just think how the people would react! Trust me, *Khanom*, the Iranian Government will keep it secret as long as it can. Now, send the thirty grand right away."

"Until I speak to my husband, I can't be convinced of his safety," I said doggedly. "And, I won't pay the remaining money."

"Oh really?" Jamshid yelled. "Then, I'll telephone my 'friends' to cancel our contract and send your husband back to jail—and certain death!"

"But you promised that—"

"Don't talk to me about promises," he cut off my words. "If the thirty grand is not in my hands within two days, Dr. Sheikh will be returned to Iran."

"Please—give me a few more days. I haven't raised the money yet," I pleaded.

"No money, huh? Okay, then make out a check. Because I'm a soft touch, I won't deposit it until you tell me to. Oh, one more thing: Khomeini's spies may have you and your kids under surveillance, so be alert!"

I made out a check for $30,000.00 and signed it. My logic? Before the check was cashed, I would hear from Shoja and he would advise me how to raise the money. Or, Aryan might come up with the money from the sale of the house. In either case, Shoja's freedom would be guaranteed.

As I mailed the check, a vision of the future for Shoja and I came to my mind: a stone cottage in Australia, with a scene of goats, sheep, and a vegetable garden. A new life!

Three days later, I grabbed the phone at the first ring, hoping to hear Shoja on the line.

"Hello?" It was Aryan's voice. I was disappointed more than she would have understood.

"Congratulations! Your house has been officially sold," Aryan said with excitement. "After paying the taxes; the bill for the utilities not paid by the intruders; your recent debt to Mother; and the required 'donation' to the Mosque, you have 1,700,000 touman left. Not bad, huh?"

If the touman was exchanged to U.S. dollars, the money would sustain my family for a few years. And, Shoja's escape would be finalized!

"You can't imagine how happy you've made me, Aryan. I'm grateful to you forever."

"Well, for the first time in a long time, Shoja was happy too when he found out about the house today," Aryan said. He asked me to—"

"Wait a minute! Stop! Did you say that you saw Shoja today? That's just impossible!" I exploded.

"I visit him every Wednesday. You know that."

"But when did you actually see him last?"

"Today! I just told you. What's the big deal? He said to have his brother transfer the money to you."

"Aryan, swear that you saw Shoja today."

"Okay! I swear," she said in a confused voice.

My heart stopped dead. "Oh God, I've been deceived! The entire plan was nothing but a scam. I should've asked you to check in on Shoja. You'd have told me he was still in prison," I lamented.

"What on earth are you talking about?" Aryan shouted.

I realized that I was talking to my sister about a secret plan, and this on a call to Iran. I stopped myself.

"I can't talk any more. Please try to understand. I must go now! I'll explain everything to you some day."

"Azar!"

I dropped the phone as a panic attack took over me.

All night, I paced the floor and cursed myself like a mad person. Idiot! Fool! You not only failed to rescue your husband, but you gave away half the family savings. How will you ever confront them with the truth? I wished I had never seen Jamshid's face. A man who had no morals and preyed on the weak like a vulture.

The children wondered what was wrong with me. I told them I was worried about their father. I used the faint excuse that some days were worse than others when I wanted this all to be over.

At the break of dawn, I left for New York. The 300,000 touman was gone. Perhaps Dr. Shahin had some suggestions about retrieving the $30,000 check. I had to try to recover that money from Jamshid.

"Why didn't you consult me before giving that crook money?" he scolded.

"I was told not to say anything to anyone. Anyway, I thought you trusted him."

"I knew the guy was a shrewd businessman. But, I had no idea he would double-cross people like this," Dr. Shahin said.

"What should I do now to get the $30,000 check back? I'm desperate," I said with a great sense of shame.

While smoking a cigarette, Dr. Shahin contemplated the problem. "Well, you can put a stop payment on the check, but to prevent further trouble, I suggest a gentler approach."

He decided to phone Jamshid's office and arrange a meeting.

Jamshid met us at two o'clock in a coffeehouse on York Avenue. He shook hands with Shahin.

"Nice to see you, Doctor. Please, have a seat. Waiter! Two more coffees. And bring some pastries," Jamshid said out loud. He acted as if he had nothing to hide. The man practically ignored me.

"*Agha*, Mr. Jamshid, I've been told about the rescue attempt," Shahin explained. "I want to thank you personally for your courageous effort. It's good to know that there are still kind people around, who lend a hand to those in need without taking advantage of them. But since your plan has apparently been postponed, *Khanom* Sheikh is here to ask for yet another favor. She has not been able to raise money to cover the $30,000 check. It would be most gracious of you to return it to her. Her intention is not to cancel the arrangement altogether. She just needs more time."

Jamshid's facial color changed. "Too late, Doctor. The check covers payments to those involved."

In spite of Shahin's previous warning, I could not keep quiet.

"But you made me a promise."

"We had a deal, *Khanom*. Nothing further to discuss," Jamshid said, avoiding my eyes. He was not a man to surrender gracefully.

I clenched my fists.

Dr. Shahin took a more intimidating tone. "*Agha*, it would be better for both parties to settle this misunderstanding in a friendly manner, rather than in court. I advise you to think about it."

Jamshid started to break up his cigarette into little pieces. Shahin and I could see his mind working, looking for a way out. He was in a corner and the threat of a court lawsuit was a sword he did not want hanging over his head. Finally, thanks to Dr. Shahin's wise intervention, Jamshid conceded: "*Khanom* can have her check back."

He continued to act noble. "As for the 300,000 touman paid in Iran, she'll get another check at the government exchange rate, by mail. Roughly thirty grand. I consider the contract broken. We'll be even. But let me tell you, Doctor, it'll be a cold day in hell before I even think about helping anyone again."

Jamshid's second check arrived two weeks past its promised date. Two problems arose immediately. The first was that the check was only for $8,500, instead of $30,000. The second problem was that it was drawn against a bank in the Philippines and my bank was unable to collect the funds.

I was ready to take this con artist to court for fraud when Jamshid's name suddenly appeared in the American press with stories of illegal arms sales to Iran. Jamshid's brothers were also mentioned in the articles. Apparently, their Oriental carpet store in Stamford was a front for more serious dealings.

When Jamshid disappeared, and his oldest brother was found dead under mysterious circumstances, I knew that I would never see my $30,000.

To compound matters, Shoja's brother was negligent in sending the proceeds from the sale of our home. Didn't he realize our situation? With Iran's poor economy, the longer he delayed, the more the touman lost value. How long could I continue borrowing money?

CHAPTER TWENTY

In Tehran, my cousin Sohrab Sepehri succumbed to cancer. News of his death filled my heart with melancholy.

Sohrab was one of the most talented contemporary poets and painters of Iran. What specifically distinguished him from others were his originality, and his carefree attitude. Unlike some artists of his time, he never yielded to the pressures of commercialism, but followed his own path. A nonconformist and self-directed artist, Sohrab was not even swayed by the criticism of some intellectuals who found his work lacking a social message. I could not decide whether his paintings or his poetry were more expressive. His paintings I saw as poetry on canvas; his poetry, paintings in words:

> *I am from Kashan.*
> *Content with life:*
> *A loaf of bread,*
> *A little intelligence,*
> *A tiny bit of talent,*
> *And a mother more tender than the leaf on the tree!*

From the age of twelve, I was fascinated by Sohrab who

was ten years older than me. His lean bony frame, deep flaming eyes, and humble manners mirrored the image of an ascetic hermit. To attract his attention, I would take him my school compositions or short poems, hoping he would discover a hidden talent. He always encouraged me to work harder.

When I became engaged to Shoja, Sohrab expressed surprise that I should think about marriage so young. "Why?" he asked. "You were just beginning to mature."

I explained that I fell in love.

"Falling in love is one thing, but getting married? You are sacrificing your identity and talents to become an ordinary woman," he warned.

So, the artist had detected some talent in me! No matter what he thought about marriage or his position against it, I was in love with Shoja and committed to be his faithful wife.

A few years later, the sight of my three children reconciled our differences. "Azar," Sohrab teased, "I always thought you would create beautiful works of art, but not living ones!"

As a belated wedding gift, he offered any of his paintings that I liked. Since I found it difficult to select one out of the eight that I favored most, he gave me all eight. Those precious paintings were seized and forever lost when my house was confiscated by the Revolutionaries.

I visited Sohrab just before my exile began. On one side of his large and bright studio, he had his easels with uncompleted paintings; on the other, a plank bench which doubled as a bed, and a few hassocks he had tastefully upholstered himself. The shelves were filled with books, the walls with paintings.

His profound eyes shone with enthusiasm as he showed me his latest work, an oil painting of Kashan, our ancestors' city with many white-domed clay houses in the heart of the desert. During what turned out to be my final visit with Sohrab, he did not once refer to Shoja or to the Revolution that was quickly changing the face of the city outside his window. In his presence, I also forgot about life beyond his studio. We absorbed ourselves in his works. I temporarily escaped the real world which offered me hate, war and destruction, and entered into a world of beauty and intellect.

As I was leaving, my cousin gently held my hands in both of his and said, "There are better days to come." And so he shared my sorrow. I would miss him forever.

So far, the attempts of the United Nations and the discussions with President Bani-Sadr had not settled the hostage crisis. With the growing fears of an American air attack on Iran, more people were leaving the country. The Iranian population in the Washington area was on the rise. Many Iranians, in search of a second home, kept on the move from town to town, state to state. The wealthy preferred to settle in metropolitan areas. Others went where their jobs took them. Since the beginning of the Revolution, over one million Iranians had fled the country with nearly half of them ending up in the United States.

My own life in exile centered around my children. With the first transfer of money from Iran, I paid back Mr. Ansary's loan in full, and carefully budgeted the rest around the kids' expenses.

Roxana was starting her graduate work in education, specializing in children with learning disabilities. Between her job and her studies, she had little time for the young men who showed interest in her.

Ramin, who was a member of the football team in high

school, had taken the varsity sports in college this time. His health was improving.

Babak was studying seriously at school, yet finding time to make new friends.

Our dysfunctional family was on its way to recovery through determination and hard work. Unfortunately, our life was never free from pain. Late in spring, Agha Joon passed away. Shazdeh Joon quietly joined her husband in death, shortly after.

Shoja's latest letter was colored with sadness:

....*The man and woman I loved and revered, have left me forever. My prison sentence was a great blow to my parents. I can never forgive myself!*

The first time I ever saw my in-laws was on my wedding day. I could not tell by their expression whether they liked me or not. After all, they did not choose me. Their son did. I never got to know my mother-in-law very well. She was a woman of few words and little opinion. Yet, she respected me. My father-in-law, however, enjoyed my spontaneity and sense of humor, so as a consequence, I felt closer to him. Within the family, he was the guiding power.

Every summer, Shoja and I would take the children to Tabriz to visit them and to escape Tehran's heat. The ancient city of Tabriz was famous for its cool breeze, winding cobblestone alleys, and boulevards lined with poplar trees and petunias.

My brother-in-law, Zia, and his family lived with my in-laws. His marriage was arranged by them. It was not a happy one. The family had assumed that Shoja would marry Zia's wife's sister—a plain, undereducated, and unsophisticated girl, almost his own age. Shoja had refused blatantly. Our marriage was very disheartening to this girl, but no one could blame Shoja and I for falling in love.

In July, after eighteen months of exile, Mohammad Reza Pahlavi, the deposed Shah of Iran, died in Egypt. Ironically, the Shah's death coincided with the first anniversary of Shoja's conviction.

Still in turmoil, Iran was far from the utopia promised by the rhetoric of the Revolution. The new leaders, mostly clergy themselves, had assigned high positions to young zealots. Within the first year, it became evident that the euphoria and zeal of the inexperienced men was in ways hurting the country. The extreme orthodoxy of the leaders and the lack of competent technocrats had turned the world against Iran, and had stagnated the socioeconomic development of the country. The citizens lived in constant fear of a government that did not respect its own laws. Khoshkish, the former Director of the Central Bank under the Shah, received a change in his sentence. His life imprisonment had been "commuted"—to execution! It seemed impossible to trust the verdicts of the Revolutionary Tribunal. How could we be sure that Shoja's fate would be different?

Obviously, Shoja could not express his concern in his most recent letter:

....The clinic keeps me so busy. There is not enough time to tell you about my daily activities. What does count are the things that bring

temporary solace to me. First, a stray cat gave birth to three kittens in the clinic. Remembering how much Roxana loved cats, I made a home for them in my closet. One day my new roommates were discovered and removed. Prison regulations do not permit inmates to have pets. I hope they found a better home.

The second incident was the birth of a baby. I delivered her. The mother, a German prisoner, was charged with smuggling drugs. When the baby's cry echoed in the clinic, I remembered the time when my own children were born, and cried. I pray to God every night to let me see them one more time.

In the face of possible death, Shoja had reflected an increasing spiritual dependence—an indication of his social environment and personal loneliness. He was also more demonstrative, and showed sensitivity to simple things that he seemed to overlook before. The prison was changing my husband.

On September 22, 1980, Iran was suddenly air raided by Iraqi missiles. The Socialist Ba'thist regime of Saddam Hussein, unhappy about Iran's rights to Shatt al-Arab waterway, and apprehensive of the spread of Ayatollah Khomeini's Islamic fundamentalism, had started displaying its military might. Saddam denounced his 1975 treaty which gave Iran partial control of the Shatt al-Arab, Iraq's only sea outlet in which rivers from both countries merged before reaching the Persian Gulf. The Islamic Republic, already involved in a civil war with the opposition groups, mainly the Leftists fighting for power, was being forced into a more fatal war. Two neighboring countries, sharing an historical and cultural heritage, were turned into enemies.

Most Iranian expatriates perceived the war with Iraq as the

final stage before the collapse of the Islamic Republic. Some even joyfully predicted that the monarchy could resume power. They were proven wrong. Hundreds of thousands of teenage Iranians volunteered to be sent to the front lines to defend the motherland. In some ways, the war had reunited the nation. Patriotism had rekindled the dying fervor of the Revolution.

In Tehran, my family had abandoned their homes to seek shelter outside the city, away from the missiles. There was no word of Shoja. My concerns were mounting with the possibility that a missile could land at Evin. How ironic if Shoja should die from an Iraqi missile after escaping an Iranian fire squad! What if I could never return home? What if Shoja and I never saw each other again?

Washington, D.C., did not remain immune from the infighting among diverse Iranian political groups. They constantly challenged and fought each other. Recently, a pro-Shah activist had been shot to death in broad daylight. The day before, students affiliated with the *Mujaheddin-e-Khalq* or People's Warriors, a "Marxist Islamic" group, had threatened my children at the university. The *Mujaheddin* were not to be dismissed easily. My family's blood could be spilled in an insane moment in America by one zealot whose mission was to destroy his political organization's "enemies."

It had become unnerving to go to a store and be afraid of being shot when we came out, or jumping every time we heard a car horn sound or a door creak. The children and I needed to get away to a safer place so we could disappear into a quiet life. Plans had to be made quickly.

Babak had been investigating educational opportunities at Princeton University. Several of his teachers had recommended

Rutgers University as a second choice. Perhaps New Jersey could provide the anonymity we desperately sought for our lives and our peace of mind.

I watched the passing of rows and rows of evergreens and bare trees that shook in the cold December wind as the Amtrak train sped along in New Jersey, nicknamed "The Garden State."

At the small New Brunswick station, I asked a cabdriver to take me to the administration building of Rutgers University. He realized I was new to the area.

After driving through a street of old, drab town houses, we crossed a small bridge.

"Raritan," the driver called out the name of the river. "And that tall white building overlooking the river has some nice apartments, if you're looking. Not bad, yeah? Especially with the park and all. Rest of the city? Not much to see. Just a college town. Where you from? You got some kinda accent."

Haphazardly, images from my home passed before my eyes. I dared not blurt out, "Iran." Americans mistrusted Iranians. I gave him a safeguard answer. "Oh, I come from the other side of the world!"

The driver dropped me off at the administration building. I got some information, and then rode a campus bus to different areas. The several campuses comprising Rutgers overwhelmed me.

From the center of town, I took a train twenty miles south and visited the fifth oldest university in the United States, the prestigious Princeton University. The campus's tree-lined paths, sculpture gardens, and imposing architecture made Princeton far more attractive—and also much more expensive.

Back at our apartment in Washington, I reviewed the literature with my children. Our personal safety had become my priority for choosing a school. Iranian students would have problems with funding, especially at an "Ivy League" school. Rutgers was more affordable, and despite its huge size, was located in a small town—not the type of place to attract many Iranians. My children would be safe there.

Following Ronald Reagan's swearing in as the fortieth President of the United States, the American hostages were freed after 444 days in captivity. Contrary to our expectations and hopes, this did not improve relations between the two countries. America was not ready to forgive Iran for its anti-American campaign and "act of terrorism." In retaliation, Iran condemned "American Imperialism" and America's support of Iraq in the war.

I had had no letters or communications with Shoja for three months since the Iraq-Iran war started. My only information came from my sister who continued to keep her weekly visits to him, even though her own life was threatened by the Iraqi missiles. Shoja's short letter arrived after the New Year:

Times are bad. Like other Iranian patriots, I'm appalled by the enemy's invasion of our homeland. I see many war casualties daily at the clinic. I'm also teaching first-aid classes for the Pasdars so that they can assist me. My contributions never seem to be enough. At least you are safe!

An enclosed photo showed Shoja holding a machine gun. On the back, a short note read: "Don't be alarmed—no bullets!"

"There's probably another gun held to Dad's head forcing

him to smile," Ramin commented wryly. He still found it difficult to accept his father's imprisonment.

Following many letters and calls, Shoja's brother finally transferred our remaining money from the sale of the house. The exchange rate had declined drastically to our disadvantage.

Late in January of 1981, Babak was called to the Immigration and Naturalization Office for an interview. On the way, he passionately spoke of his plans for the future. Attending Princeton University was on the top of his list. His happiness was contagious. I also began to think of the future.

The immigration officer, stiff and frigid, seemed to take an unnecessarily harsh approach.

"How long have you been in the States?" he asked.

"A year and five months," Babak answered.

"Why do you want to become a resident?"

"Because my family's in America, and I want to be with them. Besides, I go to school here."

The officer looked at my son intensely with cold, glassy blue eyes. "Have you ever committed a crime?"

"No, of course not!"

The officer continued his interrogation. Then, he browsed through Babak's file. What was he looking for?

"Where does your father live?"

"In Iran."

"How come he's not with his family?"

Babak blushed. "My father is a political prisoner."

"They're holding your father hostage? Iranians abuse their own people too?" the officer mocked. Babak and I exchanged anxious glances.

Finally, the interrogator opened Babak's passport and stamped it. Then he invited him to raise his right hand to take an oath. Without sincerity, the officer congratulated Babak on becoming a new immigrant. Babak glowed.

"Young man, starting today, you can work. Do you have any skills?" he asked.

"I'm still a student, but I have a lifeguard's license," Babak answered proudly. "I even helped my brother at a pool last year for a week. Perhaps I'll go back to the same job this summer."

"You worked last year? Foreigners cannot work without a permit." The officer had suddenly stumbled upon what he had been looking for. "You have violated the law. As a result, your status as a permanent resident, and even your student visa, become void."

Lightning struck me. Babak's eyes began to twitch.

"Excuse me, sir. What did my son do wrong?" My desperate voice rang in my ears.

The officer tore a couple pages from Babak's passport.

"Your son has broken the law. He must leave the country within a month!"

"Where will I go, sir?" Babak stuttered.

"Where? How about Ai-Ran? Take your oil money and go home! People of your kind are appreciated there." The man was blinded by his own prejudice.

"Sir, my son worked only a few days, helping his brother— a naturalized American citizen. His total income was less than one hundred dollars. Even if he unwittingly committed a crime, it was so innocent—can't you overlook it? Especially with his father's situation? The war? There is no way that my son can return to Iran. They'll arrest him, or send him to the front to be killed. Please, have mercy." I was pleading to a stone.

The officer tossed the passport, and pointed to the door. Babak was motionless, shocked into disbelief. America, the land of freedom and opportunity, would throw him away for a minor infraction.

"Let's go." I pulled his arm.

He stumbled and nearly fell from the chair as we walked out.

Outside the Immigration building, we were both dazed to find our car, which was parked in front of us. As we got into the car, I screamed, "I hate laws!"

The callousness of the officer and his final judgment had pushed Babak into a silent quandary. His eyes were lusterless and void. My poor son was just beginning to put the nightmare of the Revolution behind him. Iran had taken away his past. America was taking away his future. Where could he go from here?

A thin wet snowfall covered the road adding more hazards to my driving along with my unfocused attention. Babak and I were buried in our thoughts. Neither of us had any idea where we were. I stopped at a gas station and asked if we had passed Washington.

"Jeez, lady! You're way off. It's in the other direction."

I turned the car. Babak's prolonged silence was frightening.

At home, I took a sedative to calm my nerves. Roxana and Ramin were not back yet. Babak laid on his bed, staring at the ceiling. I sat beside him and held his hand. It felt cold.

"Son, we've lived through greater crises than this one. You have another month. We'll figure something out. They can't just deport you like this," I tried to reassure him, though I was as scared as he was.

Babak broke into tears. "I have no country! No home! And forget college! Without the stupid alien registration number and the student visa, no university will consider me! My life is ruined," he cried.

When Roxana and Ramin returned home after their classes, I took my frustrations out on them. "It's late! Where've you been? Couldn't you have phoned? Don't you know how much I worry, especially with all those threats?"

"Mom, what's your problem?" Ramin asked.

"Babak has been deported," I held my hand to my forehead.

Roxana dropped her books. "What? That's ridiculous! How?"

"Just because he had helped Ramin with his lifeguard job for a few days, without a work permit."

"We've got to help him!" Ramin said. "We'll hire an attorney, Mom, the best!"

After two days of agony and research, we discovered a well-known immigration lawyer. He sympathized, but said that no one could nullify the decision. All we could do was apply for extensions on a month-to-month basis. In the meantime, Babak should resubmit an application for permanent residency. This time, however, his file would be sent to the American Consulate in Canada. If approved, he would be called to that country for an interview and returned as a resident of the U.S.

The lawyer acted promptly and filed a petition with the Immigration court. The court agreed to extend Babak's stay for another month. He also filed for Babak's permanent residency at the American Consulate in Toronto. The lawyer's actions gave us some mental relief, especially for Babak. He went forward with his life and sent his application to Rutgers University, thinking that it might be hard to enter Princeton with his uncertain immigration status. Ramin also applied to Rutgers.

It was our third *Now Ruz* without Shoja. Mother wrote:

Our Now Ruz *carols are the roaring of enemy planes overhead and the wailing of mothers mourning the death of their children. As if fighting with Iraq is not enough, the government wages a civil war at home. Just yesterday, twenty prisoners—women included—were executed.*

Your cousin Farid is in prison, awaiting a trial for corrupting the morals of youngsters by operating an ice-skating rink!

My children, too, are in danger. Hushang had no choice but to escape the country. He is on his way to the States—penniless. Amir Ashraf, who tried to join his wife and daughter in Germany, has been stopped at the airport. His passport is confiscated for no clear reasons. I fear for his life.

The same month, an article appeared about Evin in the Washington Post, with a surprising reference to Shoja. According to the reporter, the jailed ex-Minister of Health and Welfare was responsible for treating 150 political and 450 criminal inmates.

Those presumed numbers seemed to be skewed by the Iranian authorities. The Islamic Republic's opposition estimated thousands of prisoners at Evin, and many more in other prisons.

Ramin and Babak had both been accepted by Rutgers,

despite Babak's immigration status remaining in limbo. The projected move to New Jersey had elicited mixed feelings for us. Though only 150 miles apart from Roxana, who was going to stay in Washington to finish her graduate studies, the distance still meant separation. We would also miss Hushang, who had settled in D.C. with his family and was searching for a job. I knew no one in New Jersey. Our safety required us to leave Washington.

On my second visit to New Brunswick to look for a place to live, the town seemed drearier in a drizzle than before. The damp April air crept under my skin and gave me a chill as I stepped out of a cab to spend the night in the nearest motel.

I negotiated a quick transaction with the motel manager. He asked for a credit card. I had none. He accepted thirty-eight dollars in cash. I got a room at the end of a long corridor. When I entered the motel room, the door squeaked. A stale odor of cigarette smoke and mold pervaded the air. The carpet and the wallpaper were discolored and shabby. Obviously, this was not the Hilton. Of course, one gets what one pays for and pays for what one can afford!

In the adjoining restaurant, two men dined amid bold red drapes, dim lights, and Naugahyde chairs. I decided I was not so hungry and returned to my room.

Lying down on the bed, I took out a paperback copy of *The Scarlet Letter*, which had remained unfinished for months, wrapped myself in the frayed blanket, and began to read. The concentration demanded by Hawthorne's prose evaded me. I remembered the few letters that I had picked up from my mailbox before leaving for New Jersey. I rummaged through them, finding only bills, until I came across an unexpected treasure.

My Beloved Wife:

I received your letter of the good news for the boys. Rutgers is a good school, but New Jersey seems so far away! Why are you leaving Washington? Your daughter, brother, and all your friends are there. I hope you know what is right for you and the kids.

Life is the same at Evin. An inmate, an Indian Dervish, taught me to perform hypnosis. He believes I have a natural talent. Already I have put several Pasdars *to sleep at their request.*

I was taken out of Evin to attend to a Pasdar *who fell into a deep ravine. His leg was hurt bad. He could not move. I rescued him from the ravine and we took him to Pars for major surgery. This was my first appearance at my own hospital since my arrest. Obviously, I was nervous as hell.*

After the operation, a few former colleagues spoke to me. What a shock for them to find me still alive! Too bad we did not have enough time to chat. I suppose, the guards presence made things more tense. Before leaving, I found the doorman, Akbar, who had joined in spreading lies about me. I kissed his cheeks. He was embarrassed.

Some good news, I hope. Judge Gilani advised me to petition Ayatollah Khomeini for a retrial. The chances are slim, but he suggested I might get a reduced sentence. I sent in the petition. I'm waiting for the response.

Azar, get the boys established in New Jersey. Then I need you to return to Iran. We must accept there is no near end to this war. I won't survive, unless you come back. I need you!"

In this depressing room in a strange place, Shoja's words were not the brilliant lights of hope. After the joy all his letters had given me, this one brought bitterness. How little he understood my situation or considered my feelings! Leaving friends? Which ones? All those in Iran turned on me because of him. Did he think that I had become a socialite in Washington? And, his hopes for a retrial! Didn't he realize that the response to his letter could be death? Didn't they kill Khoshkish, former Director of the Central Bank, after he received a life sentence? Hmph! Some good news, indeed!

Outside, the cold rain continued to fall, accompanied by a wailing wind that lashed the trees, the roofs.

Once more I read the letter, this time with rage. From Evin fortress, thousands of miles away, my husband was trying to control me. Was I not already living in an invisible cage, which he unknowingly constructed around me? Why was he constantly reminding me of his need for me? What about my needs? Did I still know this man who talked of an Indian Dervish and hypnotism? Outside of his clinic, he had no responsibilities. The care of our family rested entirely on me. He demanded my return, giving no thought to our children or how I would manage to live in war-torn Iran. Did he expect me to depend on my mother forever?

Storm winds whipped through the cracks in the windows, shaking and rattling the blinds. I crumpled the letter and threw it aside. Such news! Shoja had risked his life to save an injured *Pasdar*, who probably had killed many innocent people! Didn't he promise me once not to take any risks again? Indeed, this is a privilege to be escorted by armed guards to his former hospital and allowed a brief moment with his old colleagues! Ha! He further humiliates himself by embracing the doorman who has spoken against him. Does he have no self-respect?

The storm screamed with a roar and pounded against the

window with full force. A sharp forbidding noise followed. Had a window blown open? Could someone be breaking into the room? The light flickered, and went out. It turned dark, utterly dark.

Anger gave way to fear, fear to sadness. I buried my head in the safety of the pillow. The past three nomadic years flashed across my mind, each memory more painful than the last. Wherever I went, loneliness and the weight of Shoja's life imprisonment followed. I would never free myself of his sentence. Tears began to roll down and soak my face. I felt betrayed, abandoned, lost and unprotected in a world that showed no mercy. I cried and sobbed for a long time. Until there were no more tears to shed. Then, I fell into a fitful sleep.

Sometime later, I opened my eyes to a profound tranquillity. Both the violent storm outside and the one within had vanished. Despite the jet-black environment of the ugly motel room and my life, my mind experienced a clear, lucid brightness. As if in a sweet dream, or a subtle trance, I was lifted like a feather. I felt weightless—a supernatural sense of harmony with life. Had God come to my rescue? I slept the rest of the night peacefully.

The brilliance of the morning sun matched my inner mood. My eyes were red and puffy, but my heart felt light. I left the motel, without breakfast. I walked briskly, last night's serenity buoying my steps. The fragrance of blooming lilacs in the air awoke me to the spring's dramatic presence.

At the traffic light I asked a passing motorist, "How far is it from here to Rutgers University?"

"Where in Rutgers? It's a big place!"

"The Summer Session Office, please."

He tried to conceal his smile. "Rather far to walk. Jump in. I'll take you there."

"Thanks!" I got into the car. There was something reassuring about this gray-haired gentleman that made me trust him.

"You have a curious accent. French?" he asked.

"Sorry to disappoint you. Actually, I'm Iranian," I said with caution.

The older man smiled and drove on, apparently not fazed by my admission.

He pulled up before a yellow frame house and said, "Here you are." I thanked him and got off.

Inside the building, I asked the secretary if I could see the Director.

"Take a seat, Dr. Austen will be with you in a moment," she said.

When I entered the office, I was startled to see Dr. Austen was the same man who dropped me off in front of the building. How embarrassing! What must he think of me? Not only an Iranian but a hitchhiker as well!

"How can I help you?" he asked.

I placed Ramin's and Babak's enrollment forms before him. "My sons are interested in taking these courses for the summer, if it's all right."

"Why didn't they come themselves?" he asked as he spread out the documents.

"They're still attending classes in D.C. I've come to look for a house so that we can move to New Jersey before summer classes begin."

"I see," Dr. Austen mumbled, looking over the papers. "These courses seem appropriate. I'll sign off, and you can take this to the

Cashier's Office. While you're there, look at the university bulletin boards for rentals. Come back and let me know how you make out." He spoke with respect as if I was an ordinary American. I thanked him and headed to the Cashier's Office.

Later, I returned to Dr. Austen hungry and exhausted.

"So, how did it go?" he asked.

"Okay, except I couldn't find a decent house within my budget. Only a two-bedroom apartment in a high-rise by the river, which will be available at the end of the month."

"Did you take it?"

"No. I'd rather discuss it with my sons first."

"What about your husband? Doesn't he have a say?"

In such a short time, I had come to trust Dr. Austen enough to tell him a little about Shoja. He listened patiently as I encapsulated the years into a few words.

"I'm so sorry to hear that. You and your children must be devastated," Dr. Austen said kindly.

"We do our best."

"Listen, when you settle in New Brunswick, stop by my office again. Let me know how things are going," he advised.

At least now, I knew someone in New Jersey!

CHAPTER TWENTY-ONE

With them the seed of wisdom did I sow
And with my own hand labour'd it to grow:
And this was all the harvest I reap'd-
"I came like water, and like wind I go!"
Omar Khayyam (Rubaiyat/Twelfth Century)

On May 29, Ramin, Babak and I left Washington for New Brunswick. Our entire "estate" was squeezed into a small U-Haul truck. Nomads in search of a promised safe land! It was hard to say farewell to Roxana and leave her behind at the American University to finish her studies. She was the strong and confident one among us. Without her optimistic moral support, we could not have survived as a family through so many stresses and ongoing ordeals. She pledged to join us in New Jersey after her graduation.

Our new apartment in New Brunswick was spacious and bright. The boys occupied the master bedroom. Neither one seemed happy about leaving a cosmopolitan area for a small town atmosphere. But they understood and accepted the reasons for the move.

The following day, the boys went to discover the campus at

Rutgers for the first time. I went to see Dr. Austen in his office. He asked me, "Have you settled in?"

"Sort of," I responded with little enthusiasm. My life to me seemed to be in the turmoil of one readjustment after another.

"I've been thinking about your situation. I'd like to help you. Tell me, what is your education?"

"Well, I have a master's in education from the States, and two years of graduate study in Persian literature. Right before the Revolution, I was planning to enter the doctoral program in literature at the University of Tehran."

"Are you looking for a teaching position?"

"Who would hire me? Anyway, my stay in the States is only temporary," I said, my mind, as usual, thousands of miles away.

"You seem depressed. Have you considered taking some classes while you're here? That might help."

"It would be difficult to pay the tuition," I admitted.

"We have some grant money left for women in Library Sciences. You may qualify for a summer scholarship. Classes start in a week. What do you think?" Dr. Austen suggested. The idea seemed so easy and acceptable to him.

Why start something new, when the future was so uncertain? I thought. I ended the meeting without a firm commitment to Dr. Austen. My children, however, were more persuasive.

"Do it, Mom! You always wanted to continue your education. Here's the right opportunity," Babak encouraged.

"At least until the war with Iraq is over, keep yourself busy, Mom," Ramin persuaded. "I'm sure Dad would want you to do it."

"Mom, do it for yourself. You deserve it," Roxana convinced me on the phone.

Slowly, I began to realize that I should do something more positive with my time. A new door had been opened without my knocking on it. All I needed was the courage to walk through the door.

In July, I joined my sons in starting summer classes at Rutgers. In spite of my love for learning, I found myself going through the rote work of being a student without excitement. My mind was always preoccupied with home and Shoja.

Other doors had been opened for us. Babak could study and work in America without fear of being deported to Iran. He had been classified a permanent resident. Ramin and Babak had both qualified for financial aid at Rutgers in the fall.

In Iran the power struggle continued. President Bani-Sadr's efforts to gain more control ended in losing favor with Ayatollah Khomeini. Bani-Sadr, like many other leaders of the new regime, eventually became the target of the Ayatollah's wrath. He fled Iran and found asylum in France, as Madani had earlier. Others were not so lucky to get away. Sadeq Ghotbzadeh, the Iranian Foreign Minister, was accused of conspiracy against the Ayatollah and put to death. Abbas Amir Entezam, the Iranian Ambassador to Sweden, was convicted of espionage and given life in prison. The Revolution granted no mercy to hundreds of its own children.

The large number of executions were followed by a wave of terrorism attributed to the *Mujaheddin* network, including a massive explosion that left seventy-three leading officials dead in Tehran. Another powerful bomb destroyed the government headquarters, killing newly-appointed President Mohammad Raja'i and several other top officials. The government responded with greater violence. The nation's streets were turning blood red!

Shoja wrote:

A host of new misfortunes! Our warden, Kachui, was shot inside the prison. Ironically, his assassin was the same Pasdar I risked my life to save from the ravine. The Pasdar then attempted suicide. Both men were rushed to the hospital. The warden died. His murderer lived.

Our new warden imposed new restrictions: no newspapers, books, or radios. Even our exercise periods are curtailed. In the wake of other assassinations, Evin's population grows rapidly.

Terrorism was contagious. In Egypt, President Anwar Sadat, an ally of America, fell to the bullets of an assassin.

Back in 1975, Shoja and I had had an opportunity to personally meet the Sadats when we attended a formal state visit to Egypt, one of the most dazzling historical countries in the world. We were equally impressed by the Sadats' friendly courtesy. The President and Mrs. Sadat were particularly close to the Shah and Queen Farah of Iran. At a reception, a few guests commented on Jahan Sadat's physical resemblance to me. I was flattered. Mrs. Sadat had our photograph taken together. Unfortunately, the picture was lost in the chaos. Now, Jahan Sadat had suddenly become a widow. I still had hopes of being with my husband again.

Shoja wrote:

My beloved wife,

No word on my retrial yet. Yesterday Judge Gilani and a few other high officials visited my new dialysis center I recently added to the prison clinic. The Judge praised my good work. He thought it's time for Imam Khomeini to reconsider my situation. The authorities agreed.

Judge Gilani asked me privately when you are returning from America. I told him you are supervising our children. He said from what he knows, our children were not minors and did not need their mother. He suspected you have other reasons for not returning.

Azar, I miss you. Come back to me!

Come back? To what? Prison? Bloody extremist purges? A prison society? Even if the war with Iraq ended, the government's war with us would continue.

Just as I tried to take the right steps to prevail over the confusion around me, Shoja made me feel guilty. Did he not realize I needed to finish my studies in order to get a job? Our savings were nearly depleted. If I went back to Iran while he was in prison, what work would I find as a prisoner's wife?

Downhearted, I went for a walk along the Raritan River which changed colors as the sky and trees reflected in the water. A light rain came and went quickly. In the pale autumn afternoon, the Raritan took on the golden brown color of the oak trees above it. For me, a Middle Easterner who grew up in a semi-desert land, the river and the trees were an oasis, pointing to the Eden.

A young couple, obviously in love, walking hand in hand, fired up my imagination of long suppressed physical desires. Under all the rage and pain, separate from my outward appearance as a docile student and patient mother, I was still a passionate woman who yearned for love. The couple had triggered a nostalgic longing for familiar scents and sounds. I tried to recapture glorious memories from the past. But, a memory was not the same as the real touch. I thought again of the letter that had brought me out here. For the first time, I was afraid of the possibility of losing my husband. I was not sure whether Shoja would want to stay in Iran more than he would want to be with me.

For Shoja's fiftieth birthday, I sent a card, the numbers "five" and "zero" prominent on its cover. Inside, I jotted:

Happy birthday, sweetheart! Don't worry about getting old. I'm just a few years behind you! We will grow old together!

I also sent him my latest poem, reflecting loneliness, a mood that had come to dominate my life:

The sky,
Empty of its celestial occupants.
My heart,
As dark as the sky,
And God far away!
The house,
Bare of all living sound,
But my breath,
Heaving in and out with sorrow.
The caged bird batters herself,
Against the bars of captivity.

Other birds far beyond the horizon.
Where can she go,
With wounded wings?

Through the wall of fantasy I fly,
Soaring past scenes of childhood gone.
A song of the old times I sing:
Wind whips the barren trees
Pomegranate branches blossom snow.
On the verandah,
Lonely shoes huddle together,
Against the cold.
Behind the window,
Familiar, smiling faces—
How handsome Father looks,
In his cashmere, paisley robe,
Almost mystical as he recites Hafez.
Mother's unceasing flame,
Warms the winter night.
Her table,
A still-life painting:
Round copper tray,
Enclosed by folds of taffeta.
Ruby red pomegranates,
Orange tangerines,
Dark roasted pistachio nuts.
The cat, swollen with sin,
Lazing upon the satin cushion;
My brothers, growing to manhood,
Tall and solid as the poplar tree;

My sister doing homework,
Spills trails of black ink,
On the intricate floral carpet.
The spout of the china teapot
Snores sweet dreams,
Atop the brass samovar.
Nanny and the butler chat by the fire.
Blind Aunt Touri laughs,
Predicting a wedding soon:
The butler needs an heir,
My nanny, a husband!
Aunt Touri senses light.
She is full of stories —
Ghosts, goblins, and fairies —
All in color.
Father says:
"After the next snow,
"We should buy new shoes for the girls
"To wear at Now Ruz.*"*
Mother has asked the merchant's wife
To send bolts of velvet and lace
For our New Year's dresses.

The soft, melodic memories,
Take me to that dreamland
Where spring has arrived,
And Now Ruz *has begun!*

Six weeks later, Ramin came running back to the apartment, breathlessly. "Dad's been retried! He's been condemned to death." He laid the evidence down in front of me.

A shocking cold feeling came over me that matched the freezing January day outside. "That's impossible, Ramin! Your father's request for a retrial was never granted," I said, trying hard to convince both my son and myself.

"Not according to this Iranian newspaper. Here, look for yourself. We haven't heard from Dad for weeks! How do we know he's alive?" he said in a frantic voice.

I glanced at the newspaper. Although it had yesterday's date, its reliability could be questionable. Then I glanced at Ramin. His face reflected his fear. I took his hands in mine. "Let's call Mother to find out, son," I decided.

Alas! There was no answer to be gotten. Recent Iraqi air raids had disrupted all telephone communications to Iran. All we could do was wait for a reconnection.

"I hate this war!" Ramin said in an angry voice. "To hell with the governments. I want my Dad alive!"

The nightmare of the day became my dream at night. I dreamed of my ancestral farm in Kashan. Near the pond, along the pomegranate trees, there was a gallows. From the distance the body hanging at the gallows was that of my grandfather— the 'outlaw' who had rebelled against a ruthless king many years ago. At a closer look, it was not my grandfather—Shoja swung from the rope, lifeless!

CHAPTER TWENTY-TWO

Shoja was still alive! His letter from Evin read:

> *The Iraqi war escalated. We were cut off for weeks from the out-side world. I had no news from you. It was hard.*
>
> *One flicker of hope. Judge Gilani decided not to ask for a retrial. He will seek a full pardon. One more good news. Starting next month, a few of us prisoners will spend one day a week with our families. I wish you could be there!*

The letter arrived January 30, 1982, on our twenty-fifth wedding anniversary! On that wedding day, I wore a beautiful ivory organza dress, with a fresh carnation in my hair. I looked into a silver mirror, Shoja's gift to me, and discovered an ecstatic face. Then, as a dreamy eighteen-year-old girl, I knew how to walk on clouds. Now, in my mid-life, I needed to stand on solid ground.

My memories were interrupted by the telephone's loud ringing.

"Shoja is free!" Aryan yelled at me from halfway around the world. Her words were incomprehensible to my brain.

"Did you hear me? Your husband is a free man, Azar!"

"Don't tease me! It's not fair," I shouted back.

"Who's teasing? Today, Shoja's life sentence was reduced to five years!"

"But you just said he's free."

"He will be. . . soon. Shoja is being released in two stages: First a reduction of sentence, then a pardon. He'll be out by *Now Ruz*—just seven weeks away."

"Why not now?" I asked with a hint of suspicion.

"Because the public must be prepared slowly," Aryan explained the logic of the idea.

"From life to five years? And then right into freedom? That's hard to believe, Aryan."

"Shoja himself called us with the good news. He wouldn't lie," Aryan assured me.

I breathed deeply and exhaled slowly as if a tremendous weight had been lifted from my chest. So, this was no dream! My husband would be free in seven weeks! If they kept their promise, Shoja might be with me soon and we could plan for our future together. Our future! It sounded so wonderfully right!

When Shoja's letter arrived with the details of his new sentence, my hopes were crushed again. He wrote:

....Judge Gilani considered my services in prison. He has reduced my life sentence to five years. As he told me, 'It is only fair that you serve the same number of years in prison as you had served the Shah. But, of course, your five months imprisonment under the Shah does not count, so you still have twenty-four more months to serve.'

I told Judge Gilani that I am innocent and should not spend another day in prison. He said he would try to let me free much sooner, perhaps by Now Ruz. *Of course, I had to pledge not to flee the country and set aside enough time to supervise Evin Clinic.*

"Your father should not have accepted such restricting conditions!" I complained to my sons.

"But Mom! Dad's going to be out of jail by *Now Ruz*. Why can't you just be happy about that just like us?" my sons told me, their eyes shining with hope.

Being out of Evin on conditions was not enough. Shoja should be given unconditional freedom. He was an exemplary citizen of Iran, not a criminal.

Another spring arrived, but not a new beginning for us. The Iranian New Year passed without Shoja's freedom. The officials postponed his release date, pending Shoja's response to a new treacherous ultimatum: "Either your wife returns, or you stay in prison!"

The officials were afraid that Shoja's love for his family would compel him to defect. He turned to me for an answer in his latest letter: "Azar, my future's up to you. Help me!"

My first reaction was to do anything for Shoja, without questioning the outcome. To get him out of Evin—that dark, bloody pit—had been my primary goal for years. I wanted him free! But the way the judges played with the laws at the spur of the moment only made me more skeptical. What if the ultimatum was just another trick to keep Shoja there longer? What if the judges wanted to imprison me now? A few years earlier, they had threatened to activate some fake dossier against me. Who knows what they might do now? And if they did not arrest me, and did free Shoja, we would still remain their prisoners in Iran. What else, if we could not leave the country at our own will even to visit our kids? More importantly, would those Iranian officials stop with me, or would they demand the children's return too?

No! I could not risk going back to a country where laws and promises changed with the sunrise and sunset, where human rights were disregarded and women were denigrated to being a lesser person.

Before I gave my answer, Shoja managed to send a short letter secretly through my mother. Under tremendous pressure, he had made a shocking decision for both of us:

Azar, I understand your reasons for not wanting to return at this time. A divorce would solve our problems. In our hearts, we will remain married. The divorce would be on paper only. The government will be assured I won't defect. And you will not jeopardize the family's safety. Things will work out, eventually.

A divorce? The unthinkable had happened. How could my husband of twenty-five years fall for such a trap and ask for a divorce? How casually he puts it: a paper divorce! How could a relationship which has already suffered a long separation, survive after a divorce?

The reality of a paper divorce represented our second marital crisis. Our first crisis came when I turned thirty. At that significant age, I realized that most of my life had been consumed in the small and dull details of existence. My identity was solely defined by marriage and family. My marriage, like most marriages in Iran, was not the union of two complete, independent adults. Shoja, totally involved with his career and male ambitions, had no understanding that I wanted to do more and be more too. I felt I had become expendable to him. This awareness disturbed me. He even neglected his children. Sometimes, he would look at them with an expression of surprise and ask, "How did they grow so fast?"

By the time Babak started school, I felt myself an outsider in a changing world. I had not moved much forward mentally or professionally. Our house was immaculate, and the children seemed healthy and happy—which would have fulfilled and contented my mother. I needed more.

I took a bold step and decided it was time for me to go away for a while and reassess my life. Shoja, not truly understanding my motives, objected. He feared that I would slip away from his male control. We had several arguments. I insisted, and this time, I won the battle of wills. Shoja gave in reluctantly. In my parents' home, I had struggled to make my own decisions. Then I had married and compromised my views to fit Shoja's needs. This was my first opportunity to prove to everyone—and to myself—that I could be independent. My old nanny, Soqra, offered to come from Mashhad to care for the children.

I departed for England, alone. The first few days were miserable. Separation from my children, the cold, damp London weather underscored my depression. I felt lost. All the other trips had been arranged by Shoja to the last detail. This was the first time that I was on my own, totally responsible for myself.

As my health improved, I began visiting museums and libraries, traveling across London to see historical monuments. I discovered that I could enjoy doing things without a man's help. I also used the time to evaluate my talents, education, career and opportunities. I could not accept myself if these were wasted any longer.

Two months later, with a renewed sense of myself, I returned to Iran and immediately began a job search. Within a year, I held a part-time position as an instructor at the College of Shemiran and, later, at the National University. I also continued my work with the Iranian National Television, writing lyrics and stories for a children's weekly program. I further planned to enter the doctoral program in Persian literature at the University of Tehran—something that I had always dreamed of. The Revolution ended so many of my dreams!

As time passed, Shoja gradually accepted my relative independence. However, the male-dominant society of Iran and Shoja's domineering personality continued to keep me in the background. His job and status, whether being an orthopedic surgeon or the Minister of Health, had always been the focal point of our identities and lives.

Now, his present situation left me no choice. I forced myself to write the request for divorce. I knew that my letter would be inspected by Shoja's captors. So, it had to convince them that I had no intention of ever returning to Iran, even if it meant ending our marriage. After a week of feeling forlorn, I gave in to Shoja's suggestion and went along with his ploy. I wrote:

My Dear Husband,

I find it necessary to express my feelings openly in regard to your impending freedom and invitation for me to return. I hope that after reading this letter, for the sake of our many years together, you will consider my response objectively.

Throughout our twenty-five-year marriage, you always placed priority on your goals of serving the people, while your family remained in the background. Because of that, you are now in prison, and I am without a home or country. Although I admire your dedication, I can no longer live with it. No doubt, after you are freed from prison, you will again risk your life—and mine—for the same humanitarian ideals. I cannot allow you to compromise our family's well-being more than you already have.

Please do not expect me to return, but rather accept my request for an end to this marriage. As long as I live, my love for you and Iran will reign in my heart. But the time has come for me to seek a safe and quiet life for myself and our children. I hope you understand. Love forever, Your Wife."

I looked up after signing the letter and cried. This letter seemed a bitter reminder of how the Revolution kept tearing away at us. I hoped we knew what we were doing.

In a few weeks, Shoja responded by letter:

....I passed your request on to the officials. I'm still waiting for their decision. Your letter seemed so sincere. It frightened me. I hope you will never feel obligated to choose between your happiness and me.

On the fourth anniversary of Shoja's imprisonment, the issue of his freedom was not yet resolved. Were we even still married?

In America, the competitive life had inspired more self-confidence in me. I had learned to deal with the myriad details that were part of my daily American existence. There were disappointments, too, as I struggled to cope with the complexity of a new culture—the constant inevitable loneliness, the social isolation, and the occasional, painful prejudice for being an Iranian.

In Iran, meanwhile, the hellfires of retaliations were the way of life. The war with Iraq, terrorism by the opposition groups, and government counterattacks raged on. The new reign of terror had consequences on almost every family. My cousin, Mariam and her fiancé, both in their early twenties, had been executed by the firing squad. Their charges? Sympathy with an opposition group. Family members were not even told where the bodies of the two young activists were buried. The government sent a last mocking insult: the grieving parents had been billed for the bullets used!

Judge Gilani's two younger sons had also paid the high price of their lives for turning against the government—and their father. Gilani's religious faith and political ambition had taken precedence over his own family. The Judge, who had already lost one son in a car accident, lost two more to the Republic. The safe house where Gilani's sons were hiding was destroyed by a bomb. When it came to the Islamic Republic's security, no one could be spared, not even the young sons of the highest-ranking Tribunal Judge. Gilani must have accepted this new family tragedy as God's predestined will.

Fear had caused some people to testify even against their own children. Dear God! One would think the apocalypse had come!

Amir Hosain, who had moved to the outskirts of Tehran to keep a low profile, had been forced to go deeper into hiding.

Recent arrests and executions of some Iranian intellectuals had threatened his safety. His wife and only son lived in a deplorable state of persistent fear. Each knock on the door brought shudders to everyone.

My second brother, Amir Ashraf, was still forbidden to join his family in Germany. Reasons for the detainment were never provided. My sister Aryan and her husband had their own misfortunes. Their son, Armin, had been expelled from medical school for listening to jazz music—a big sin, according to some extremists! Fearing that their son would be forced into the meaningless war, a generic problem of so many Iranian families, Aryan and her husband arranged for him to hide in a distant town. How long could people go on hiding in their own country?

For me, time, itself, was counted only by the number of years Shoja had been in prison: four years, three months!

In December of 1983, I received a Master's degree in Library Sciences and began my new career as a librarian at the Center for Urban Policy Research within Rutgers University. Considering my lack of experience, the job represented an achievement.

Roxana was adding to her credentials by taking a crash course in Montessori education. She had made up her mind not to think of marriage until her father was free to join the family in the States.

Ramin, however, had fallen in love with a lovely American girl. This relationship had encouraged him to plan more seriously for his future.

Babak busily prepared for his MCAT examination in order

to get into medical school. With his high scholastic achievements, he seemed to have no difficulty. We all worked vigorously towards new goals and hoped continuously for a reunion with Shoja. So far, there had been no definite news on his release. Perhaps another *Now Ruz* would go by without him.

Suddenly, American bookstores sold thousands of copies of Ken Follett's *On Wings of Eagles*. Based on the experiences of the two American representatives of EDS imprisoned in Iran, the book described their miraculous escape with the aid of EDS President Ross Perot. Because those two men had known Shoja as Minister of Health and Social Welfare, the book portrayed him as an honest, progressive technocrat who wanted to bring the health and welfare of his country up to American standards. EDS flatly denied bribing anyone at the Ministry of Health and Social Welfare in Iran.

In a court within the United States, Ross Perot and EDS proved that they had done business honestly in Iran and their computer company was not a house of corruption.

The book was a major accomplishment in my fight for Shoja's freedom. My husband's innocence was made public for the first time.

Shoja's ninety-ninth letter arrived in mid-July:

Great news! My five months imprisonment under the Shah has been taken into account. I guess they ignored your divorce request, Azar, and decided to wait for my five-year term to be up in September—two more months! Just hope that my bail will not be higher than our family can afford. Please, pray for me!

There was good news on other fronts too:

Amir Hosain had returned home safely; Amir Ashraf had finally been allowed to leave the country to be with his family in Germany; and Armin had been given a second chance at the medical school, although the conditions for his readmission were stringent.

CHAPTER TWENTY-THREE

Live, be joyful with a delightful friend
For the world is nothing but a breeze, a legend
Rudaki (Tenth Century)

At 7:04 a.m., September 8, 1984, Shoja's triumphant voice surged through the phone lines: "I'm free! Free—as of an hour ago! Forget about the conditions. Never mind the details. For now, celebrate. I'm a free man!"

Five years, five whole years—no, to be exact, four years and 363 days—I had waited for this moment. Shoja was free! There really was a God! A God that had the power to open prison doors!

The "details", as they appeared in Shoja's first letter after freedom, spoiled my festive mood:

Last Thursday morning, my release form arrived. After so much waiting, the date was set for Saturday, September 10. The condition of working in the prison had been eliminated.

However, I had to get together five million Touman collateral. The family arranged it immediately. Since the money arrived at Evin by twelve, the officials decided to release me that afternoon. I guess cash bought two days reprieve!

The toughest part was saying good-bye to my fellow inmates and then to the guards, some of whom had treated me like a brother.

With my few belongings, I left Evin, a free man. As the iron gate closed behind me, I choked with emotions. I vividly recalled the first day I was brought here to serve my life sentence. I suppose, a part of me remains behind those prison walls forever.

I'm living with my sister. She has moved with her family to Tehran to find work. Her house is not far from the hospital where I work. The flood of new patients all tell me I'm a more well-known doctor now than I ever was.

I feel wonderful, except for one thing: I can't leave the country for a year!

Another year? Another 365 more days and nights of waiting and loneliness?

My children and I could not put our lives on hold. We concentrated on the present. Our jobs and our studies remained productive distractions. Ramin had just landed a good job in a general contracting firm after graduating from Rutgers. They would pay for him to continue his education. Suddenly, he had become interested in civil engineering.

One month. Two months. Three months. Twelve months— another year passed slowly. It was now 1985. Incredibly, Shoja was denied a passport again for another year!

"Another year? Oh God, no! How long can we continue to live apart?" I cried bitterly on the phone.

"Well, we don't have to, Azar. You can come back. The war's still going on, but we could manage. . . everyone else does," Shoja suggested resignedly.

"Has everyone else been treated as we have? I'm afraid to

return. So many things could happen to us again." I paused a moment. "Besides, I have to wait for my vacation time. I can't jeopardize my job. You understand, Shoja? Don't you?"

"You mean that your job is more important than seeing your husband after six years?"

"Of course not, but I need this job."

"And I need you!"

His words sounded hollow, almost insincere. My husband was disappointing me. He was not trying hard enough to be with me. He did not understand my need for security and freedom. Neither did I understand his futile pleading to come back to an imprisoning society, no matter how noble his reasons were. I had begun to develop a ruthless resistance to anyone planning my life for me, whether my husband or the Revolutionaries.

Before the year was over, Iraq launched a heavy aerial bombardment on Iran, leaving behind extensive casualties and destruction. The hospital where Mother was fighting the shingles, an excruciating disease, was targeted and badly damaged. Miraculously, she was not hurt. My family managed to get Mother on the last plane for Germany before international flights were canceled. From there, she would fly to America for special medical care. The rest of the family left Tehran for a safer place.

Iran retaliated for Iraq's attack with a severe counteroffensive. The bravery of the Iranian soldiers was admirable but resulted in another stalemate. All attempts by the United Nations to establish a cease-fire failed. Ayatollah Khomeini adamantly proposed peace on three conditions: Iraqi soldiers completely evacuate Iranian territory, the Iraqi Government should pay 350 billion dollars in war reparations, and Saddam Hussein should step down from power. Of course, the Iraqi government, who was Hussein, would not agree to these terms, and the blood of the Iraqi and Iranian people spilled over each other with new intensity.

A perky, blond flight attendant pushed a wheelchair towards me that carried a gray, bony figure. It was a warm day in late May. Mother, extremely haggard and emaciated, clutched a blanket and was shivering. At seventy-five, she looked as if she were one hundred.

On the way home, completely disoriented, Mother leaned against me and rested her head on my shoulder. She was burning with a fever. I rushed her to the emergency room. After a preliminary exam, the doctor recommended a hospital stay for tests. What were they looking for? The tests indicated colon cancer. With her previous medical history of uterus cancer and chronic asthma, and her extreme frailty, surgery might be too risky. She was discharged to come home with me.

I phoned Shoja to discuss Mother's condition. "I won't be able to come to Iran while Mother's here. She's seriously ill."

"Well, my dear, at least now you have a good excuse," Shoja said half-sarcastically.

Ramin, Babak and I took turns looking after Mother. Strangely enough, she showed some improvement. I watched her at daily prayers, completely at peace with herself. Since Mother could no longer do her *Nemaz*—prayer—standing, she did it in bed, with no sign of pain or grief on her face. Mother's faith in God and in her family was indisputable. She would easily give her life for God and her children.

"Mother, how old were you when you first began *Nemaz*?" I asked her once.

"I must've been around nine," she talked slowly. "For me, praying five times a day has been a momentary spiritual escape from this material world."

"Mother, tell me how you and Father met. I'd love to hear it again," I asked her another time.

"Oh, it seems like another lifetime. Well, they showed me his photo when I was fifteen and said, 'This young man is going to be your husband.' After the wedding ceremony, when they left me alone with this strange man, the groom, I cried—you know, being shy and nervous. But your father was understanding—and dashingly handsome!"

"You must've been pretty good-looking too!"

Mother took a pause to breathe. "I suppose I came up to his expectations."

How drastically Iranian customs changed during her life! Mother had only eight years of formal education. I was allowed to go on to graduate school. Mother's marriage was arranged. I chose my own husband. She never worked outside her home. I was a career woman. Still, Mother was always liberated in her heart.

There were so many more stories that I wanted to hear about her life, but time was running short.

By midsummer, mother was hospitalized again. The doctor warned that her heart was failing and her life hung by a thread.

At dawn, Shoja called. "I've got a passport. I'm coming to America!" He sounded overwhelmed by excitement.

"When?"

"I don't know the exact time, but soon. Perhaps, in a couple of months, hopefully. There are still a million things to take care of. You can't imagine the bureaucracy here."

"Shoja, what if they disappoint us again?" I revealed my deep fear.

"They won't. The authorities seem sincere this time."

The mockery of fate! What should have been one of the happiest days of my life became marred. Shoja was coming as Mother was slipping away!

Refusing to be an imposition when Shoja arrived, Mother left the States one month later. Of course, the children and I realized that she preferred to die in her beloved homeland. I pressed her tightly against my chest for a long time, hoping to immortalize the moment. Mother broke away from my embrace. She took my hand and slid a gold wedding band back on my finger. "This is yours. You gave it to me for safekeeping. Wear it. Your husband is coming home soon!" she heralded.

Then, calm and resigned, Mother left me for the last time.

Two days later, Babak also left home for Columbia Medical School.

From the first day I arrived in the Unites States, a real basic fear kept me from making new friends. I had lost all my Iranian friends. They were either jailed, scattered in hiding places around the world, or driven away by my husband's situation. Along with losing friends, I had lost faith in people.

In America, the strained relations between Iranians and Americans, which at times reached a boiling point, made it difficult for me to find a friend. My colleagues at the Center for Urban Policy Research were nice and sympathetic. However, the people I really trusted were my children. Amidst all that we faced as a family and as a nationality, the children were going on successfully with their studies and lives, which mattered most to me. I felt especially proud that my youngest son, Babak, had made it to Columbia Medical School in New York.

There was one other person that I could consider a friend, Victoria, an assistant professor of psychology. Although a few years younger, she took me for what I was, without bias or much expectations. With her, I learned to trust a new friend. We also shared a common sense of uncertainty. She had just ended the security of her marriage. I was trying to save mine.

One evening, Victoria met me for dinner at the newly built Hyatt to celebrate her birthday. We dined. We chatted. We laughed. Then, the conversation turned to my life, as it usually did.

"So, when is your husband coming, Azar?" Victoria asked as we drank our coffee. Under the low restaurant lights, her fair, delicate face reflected concern.

"No date's been set. As usual, everything's uncertain. We never know. The Iranian authorities might find reasons to hold him back... just as they've been doing these past years," I said with frustration.

"Still, he will be coming. You must be excited."

"I am, but scared too," I admitted. I was startled by my own confession. The fear, lying deep in my subconscious, had manifested itself.

"Why scared?" Victoria asked.

"Well, for many years we've had a long-distance marriage. You know, messages exchanged in and out of prison can't hold real feelings. We wrote to each other about things, places, and people but never intimate feelings. Can passions deprived for so long survive? My life, like Shoja's, had become one of censorship, that is, censorship of all my feelings and emotions for all these years. If Shoja was in prison, I, too, had been serving time in another type of prison, simply one without the walls that Shoja faced every day."

"Do you still love him?"

"Of course!"

"Is it love? Or sympathy?"

"What difference does it make? I need him," I said hastily.

"I detect some resentment, don't you?" Victoria asked.

"Can you blame me for being resentful after everything he put me through? Our safety has been constantly threatened. I feel that someone's always after us. It will be worse when Shoja comes. You know, the fanatics are still out there. All I want is to be happy."

"Azar, one's just got to fight for her own happiness. It doesn't come easily. Be truthful to your own feelings about what you want for yourself. And be truthful in what you expect from your husband," Victoria advised.

My friend's words were the mirror that reflected thoughts in my soul.

At night, Shoja phoned. "Are any of the children home?" he asked with concern.

"No. Ramin will be working late tonight. What's wrong? You sound strained. Are you okay?"

"I'm fine."

"Then what is it? Please tell me."

"Something terrible has happened."

"Mother?" I asked spontaneously.

"She passed away a few hours ago. Azar, I know how much you loved your mother, but she was never going to get well. She's at peace now."

For a moment, I was paralyzed by the sad news. Then, denial came. "It can't be true. She was doing better!" I cried.

"I realize it's hard, but it's true. Your mother is gone!"

I continued to cry throughout the night. The most precious person of my past was gone forever. As unbearable as Mother's death was the sense of guilt that I could not be there for her burial. At mid-life I felt like an orphan. Would there ever be a kinder, sweeter and more devoted mother in this world?

In December, while still mourning my mother's death, The Washington Post printed an article under the title: "*Atrocities of Khomeini's Iran.*" The *Mujaheddin*—the strongest opposition force against Iran's Islamic Republic—had compiled and published a blacklist of alleged torturers working for the Iranian Government. Shoja's name was on it! The *Mujaheddin's* list could put our family in grave danger!

In a letter to the editor, I repudiated these false claims and explained that the *Mujaheddin* carried cyanide pills. If arrested, they would rather die than be forced to betray their organization. Many of them had taken their own lives. A few had been saved by Shoja at Evin. As a physician, he could not have possibly refused treating those patients brought to him, despite whatever might have happened to them later. Shoja had taken an oath to save lives.

The damage was done. Our name was back in the gossip

circles. We were black-listed again. The threatening phone calls and hate letters were renewed. I had our phone number changed and unlisted, but could not conceal our address. Where would we go? There was no safe haven where my children and I could retreat.

The stress took its toll on me. My health deteriorated. I developed sleep disturbances with more frequent nightmares. I also began to suffer from shortness of breath which eventually manifested itself in asthma. My periodic abdominal pains became serious problems. I felt the whole world had turned against us again.

Ironically, despite Shoja's unjust sentence and his great work at the prison as a physician, the *Mujaheddin's* blacklist had further isolated us from all Iranian groups—the Monarchists, the Leftists and the Islamists. After this damaging publicity the more serious question for me was whether the Islamic Republic would allow Shoja to come out. The backlash had already begun.

CHAPTER TWENTY-FOUR

"I am finally out!" Shoja's excited voice boomed through the telephone.

It was Friday, March 7, 1986. The Iranian authorities had actually allowed my husband to come out. It was a miracle!

"Shoja! Where are you now?" I asked in a state of shock.

"Geneva."

"Oh, God! It's really happened. You're out. Free!" I expressed, my voice shrill with happiness.

"Yeah! You don't want to know how much I had to stake," Shoja responded with less enthusiasm.

"Tell me."

"No, not now."

"Sweetheart, I'm sure you want to be among people, but please keep a low profile in Geneva. Okay? You never know where your enemies might be. The *Mujaheddin* are after you. Please be careful," I warned.

"I'll be fine. Don't worry for me," Shoja said with his characteristic confidence.

"When are you coming to the States?"

"I'm going for a visa first thing Monday morning. I'll try to catch a flight the same day. Can hardly wait."

"Neither can we. Hurry home, sweetheart!"

Shoja's first attempt to get a visa had not been successful—too many people ahead of him. He had decided to spend the night in front of the American Consulate in Bern, determined to be the first in line tomorrow.

On the second day, Shoja's request for a visa had been rejected.

"I spent a night in the car with temperatures below zero only to be turned down," Shoja complained on the phone. "They said I could enter the U.S. as a permanent resident only since all my family's there. Do you know what that means? It means I should apply for a green card and wait here for months to receive it. I can't do that. If the Iranian Government finds out about it, I may get into serious trouble. You'd think Americans would have more sympathy for people like me! It's hard to keep the faith! Perhaps we're just not meant to be reunited! I'll go back to Iran."

"Shoja, no! You can't go back without seeing us. Please! Wait just a little longer. I will try to get help at this end. The American Government can't ignore its own position on human rights by not allowing a man to reunite with his family. I'll find a way to help you," I said.

Shoja heard and believed me. I immediately got to work calling a distant relative, a former Iranian diplomat. He graciously agreed to contact his American friends at the State Department. In the meantime, I engaged my lawyer, to see what he could do. He promptly sent a telegram to the American Consul in Bern, emphasizing the humanitarian aspects of this case and requesting reconsideration. I sent telegrams to Senator Frank Lautenberg and Senator Bill

Bradley of New Jersey about the situation, and appealed for their intervention and help.

On Thursday morning, a man from the State Department called the library. The unsympathetic bureaucrat advised, "Your husband may enter America only as an immigrant."

"But, sir, my husband has been a political prisoner for many years. The Iranian Government demands that he return. He'll be in great danger if they find out that he has become a U.S. resident. Please, isn't there anything you can do?" I pleaded to this stranger. "My husband and I may never have another opportunity to see each other."

"You may hear from me later this morning, but I can't promise anything," the State Department official told me frigidly.

I tried to resume my current research project—a bibliography on low-income housing in New Jersey—but could not focus on my job. If Shoja's request was rejected again, I knew of no one else who could help us.

The State Department bureaucrat called back. "Mrs. Sheikh, tell your husband to reapply for a visa first thing tomorrow morning. The American Consul in Bern might give him another chance."

At 3:30 a.m., 9:30 Geneva time, Shoja phoned ecstatically. "I'm on my way, love! What do you want me to bring you from here?"

"Just you!" I shouted back.

God! Don't let another calamity befall us!

March 14, 1986. Once again, I studied myself meticulously in the washroom mirror at J.F.K. International Airport. The

Revolution had separated my husband and I for eight years. Tonight he would see me and the children after all those lonely, struggling years. Physically, I was in rather good shape, but emotionally I had the anxieties of a silly schoolgirl on her first date. Would I still attract Shoja? I could not turn the time back eight years and pretend that I was the same young woman.

It was even hard deciding what to wear. After changing several times, the final choice had come down to a gray wool skirt, white silk blouse, and a cashmere sweater. I poked at my short hair. I was not ecstatic about it. It had lost its luster and Shoja had loved my hair long and straight. But would that alone make the difference for him? Would the new me attract his eye and help rekindle that glow of love which he had previously kept for me in his kind brown eyes? As the romantic people believed, would love really overcome the worst of times?

In the airport waiting with the three children, we took turns standing, sitting, pacing anxiously and watching the arrival board for any possible change of Shoja's scheduled arrival.

At 6:15, Swiss Air flight number 110 landed without delays. I quickly posed everyone beneath the huge electronic clock to capture this moment on film. Then we dashed to the arrival area, with Babak leading ahead of us. I kept up by holding on to Roxana's arm.

"How do we know Dad's on this flight?" Ramin asked.

Roxana, carrying a bouquet of flowers in one arm, used the other to reassure her brother. "He is!"

At 7:00 sharp, the customs gate opened to reveal the first passenger, who dragged a large suitcase.

"It's him!" Roxana burst with excitement. "Dad! Dad!" she called and waved her arms to get his attention.

"Can't be," Babak said curtly. "No one leaves customs that quickly, particularly Iranians."

I was not sure. Was the approaching figure really Shoja? Didn't love require that I recognize his face among a million people, after a million years?

The passenger's searching eyes discovered Roxana. Dropping his luggage, he rushed to his daughter and wrapped her in his arms. "My beautiful daughter! Look at you! You're a woman!"

"Dad! You look great!" Roxana said as she placed her head on his shoulder. Magically, all the years slipped away and she hugged her father as if she were a young child again. She simply accepted him as he was.

Shoja reached over and extended his arms towards his son. "Ramin, how I've longed to see you."

"Me too, Dad, but I'm Babak!"

Shoja once more embraced him. "Oh, you've grown so big!"

Babak seemed to appreciate the compliment. "Dad, it's wonderful to have you here."

Ramin hesitantly stepped forward to his father. Shoja said nothing, but grabbed him and held him tightly, tears running down his cheeks. Passersby looked on and smiled as they watched this family being reunited.

The three children surrounded their father, as if to insure he would not disappear again. Shoja, absorbed by them, did not sense my presence. Transfixed by—yet oddly alienated from—their intimacy, I dared not interrupt.

This was my moment to absorb Shoja after these years. He had changed. Enveloped in a dark, ill-fitting suit, his body was stooped. His thin hair had fallen from the top of his head; it had turned gray on the sides where it used to be a clean black. The deep lines of his face and a short bushy beard that he had grown presented a harsh image. Then, I saw his eyes! The eyes had lost their kind and reassuring look. Even his gentle smile had hardened. This man was unfamiliar. Or was I seeing him differently? How did he feel for me in his heart?

Our eyes met and froze. Awkwardly, I smiled. Did he smile back through that thick beard? We were two perplexed minds and hearts. He gave me no command to move forward and to give him a wide-open-arms endearing welcome, as I had hoped. Still, I graciously remained silent, accepting what I thought might be his male Iranian reservation that avoided showing emotions publicly.

Shoja broke the impasse by walking to me. He brushed his beard across my cheek, while he gave me a light hug. I reciprocated, my kiss bouncing off his face. Not a romantic embrace by any means.

"Finally, you are here, sweetheart!" I said softly.

"Seems like a dream," Shoja responded.

That was all. Nothing more was said between us. As the children and their father started walking towards the terminal exit, a dark figure, briefcase in tow, pushed into the line, bumping Shoja's side in the process. An assassin? I thrust myself forward. "Shoja!"

Shoja and the kids did not hear. The man turned left and went about his business. My subdued fears had revealed themselves, this time wrongly.

I followed behind my family, feeling like a second-class member. I had no kind thoughts for myself either. I blamed myself all the way back to the car. Fool! This wasn't the grand welcome you planned for your husband! You screwed up. This man has just come back from hell. Give him time to breathe, to come back to life. You will have your turn soon to share in his deeper emotions. Be patient!

A brand-new blue Nissan Maxima waited for us in the parking lot.

"Wow! What a car! Whose car is it?" Shoja asked, his eyes lit up.

"Mine! I just bought it!" I said mischievously.

Shoja seemed too surprised to say a word. He merely shook his head. On the road, the children chattered nonstop, trying to fill their father in on the stories of their lives. When the discussion slowed, Ramin asked about life in Iran.

"Well, it's difficult," Shoja confessed. "The war, food shortages, lots of other problems. But the government seems in control, despite what you might hear."

He stopped and looked over at me, making me more conscious of my laugh lines and the slight gray tingeing at my temples. Beyond these changes, did he still find me desirable?

"Azar, thanks for helping with my visa. The American Consul in Switzerland was impressed by the support you were able to gather," Shoja said. He sounded so formal.

"We're glad you're here, sweetheart. We would've been extremely disappointed if you couldn't make it here."

"Me too," he said.

Before we reached the apartment, we gave Shoja a brief tour of what had become our American hometown, New Brunswick.

"Of all the great cities in the States, what made you choose this one?" Shoja asked with a hint of curiosity.

I wanted to tell him bluntly that his situation forced me to hide my children and myself away from the *Mujaheddin* and all the other enemies. Yes, he was responsible for us to seek a place like New Brunswick where we hoped to live quietly. In fact, our lives were still at stake because we were related to him. Instead, I said, "We came to this town mainly for the children's schooling. Now, of course, I have a good job, nice colleagues—even a few friends. There's a sense of community in this university town—important for a family uprooted and transplanted."

Inside the apartment, Shoja scrutinized every room. The apartment could not compare to our former house in Iran, but with simple modern furniture and lots of flowers, it looked cozy and comfortable.

"When I arrived in America, we didn't own a thing. Little by little, we pulled all of this together. I hope you feel at home here, Shoja," I sincerely wished.

He patted me on the arm. "Azar, someday, I'll get you a new home and furnishings even better than those you lost."

"I'm quite content with what I have, especially now that you are here," I remarked. "Are you hungry? I'll get dinner."

Shoja ate voraciously, not waiting for others to begin. Each plate of food took on an immediate and great satisfaction. "This is delicious! You've learned to cook," he commented.

"Yes. And other things, too. Like most Iranian women in America, I've become self-reliant and found confidence to stand up for my rights," I boasted. "Women have adjusted much better than their husbands to the challenging life here."

"What do you expect?" Shoja said with a full mouth. "In their own country, those men were big shots. It's hard for them to have no social status in America."

"Sweetheart, after living in prison, you, of all people, must understand that there's a lot more to life than social status!"

Shoja got up from the table, wiping his lips with the napkin. "It's late for me. I must get some sleep. Babak, would you mind if I slept in your bed tonight?"

I blushed with embarrassment. Maybe, my response sounded too harsh for my husband and he decided to reestablish his male preeminence over the household. What if he had lost his need for human touch, my touch? Almost eight years had passed since we shared a bed.

When I got up in the morning, my first thought was that Shoja was here. As I quickly put on my robe and went to the kitchen, I tried to remember what he used to like with his black coffee. Right! Plain toast.

Shoja was already up, looking out the window.

"Good morning, Shoja. Did you sleep well last night?"

"I slept only for a few hours. Too excited to sleep, I guess." He then pointed to the Raritan. "At Evin, I often tried to visualize this river as you described it in your letters."

"Which is better, your imagination or the real thing?" I asked.

"Oh, neither is free from shortcomings," he answered philosophically. "Sometimes, you long for the real, only to find it an illusion."

Was it time to hug him and bring him back to the reality of being with his family? And with me? I had no time to react before Shoja changed his tone.

"Now, how about a good old-fashioned breakfast? Some scrambled eggs, maybe?"

I complied immediately and started to cook. Shoja heaped four or five teaspoonfuls of sugar into his coffee, and added milk.

When I served his breakfast, he gobbled his food as if he were still living on a rationed prison diet. At least, he enjoyed my cooking. I sat down with a cup of coffee. "Talk to me," I asked him.

"Don't know where to begin," Shoja answered, finishing his last bite of food. "There're so many stories! Why don't you tell me about yourself?"

I told him select episodes of the last eight years, leaving out deliberately the most troublesome events. We would have plenty of time to talk about them, later. "It was difficult, Shoja," I concluded.

He raised his eyebrow. "Difficult? Maybe in some ways. But your life wasn't threatened! I never knew from moment to moment if I would live."

I did not want a confrontation with my husband this morning. But, he was not facing the reality. My own life was threatened during the Revolution, in Iran. And, we could all be stalked and killed by the *Mujaheddin* here in the United States.

"How long can you stay, Shoja?" I asked, trying to keep us both calm.

"Three weeks."

"Only three weeks?" I placed my cup down. "After all the trouble you went through to get here, why not longer, why not forever?"

"Because my family will go to jail."

"What?"

"Listen, they wouldn't let me out without assurances.

Perhaps in the future the government will be more lenient. For now, I have no choice," Shoja said.

Dispirited, I got up and poured my unfinished coffee down the sink. Shoja sensed my intense disappointment, and left the kitchen.

Who is Shoja's family? I thought to myself. In Iran, an unkind brother, and a sister who had contacted us only one time since Shoja's arrest. They had practically disowned us. Two selfish people who only needed Shoja when they wanted his money. And, now, he is worried about them when his real family is right here, in this apartment?

If I did not reveal my thoughts to Shoja, it was not because I intended to be the passive Iranian wife that he expected me to be. Rather, I did not want any arguments with my husband on the second day of his arrival. We would solve our problems in time. I thought.

As a family, we spent part of the day strolling in the local park. While casting nervous glances to the right and left for the mysterious enemy, I proudly showed off my man to my neighbors. We walked side-by-side, but did not hold hands. I reached towards him, nearly touching his finger. He pulled away.

Suddenly, an obscure picture enlarged in my mind. Lines of inmates shuffled into the execution yard, drained of life. Shoja lived watching the dead, the dying and the hopeless men in captivity for many years. These ghostly images must have changed him, forever. He could not be expected to have tender feelings. My own feelings for him were also contradictory. As if his misery was contagious, I was afraid to get too close to him. Yet, I wanted him. We both needed time to rediscover our passions.

In the afternoon, we all went to the shopping mall. Shoja needed to be completely outfitted with new clothes.

"Dad! Buy this red sweater; it'll look great on you," Roxana suggested.

"Oh no! I can't wear that color. How about this nice gray one?"

"Then take this neat tie," Babak advised. "It goes with gray."

"Absolutely not! We can't wear ties in Iran anymore. Too Western!" Shoja exclaimed.

The Islamic Republic had remained uncomfortable with foreign influences. Shoja seemed trapped in a cultural revolution within Iran and his own mind. For some reason, he was not willing to break away from either one.

Ramin's contribution to his father's wardrobe was a sweat suit.

"This I can use!" Shoja said. "I play volleyball with my friends on weekends. You should see me. I'm pretty good. Now, you know what I'd really like? A large ice-cream sundae!"

We all laughed.

In a few days, Shoja finally felt more at ease and seemed willing to talk about his prison life.

"So many nights I didn't think I'd live to see the dawn," he said thoughtfully.

"Please, tell us about them, Shoja. We need to know," I encouraged him.

Shoja relaxed by placing his arm around Roxana. "Well, you probably don't know about the time after the unsuccessful Nojeh coup. It was a few years ago. Some army officers had intended to take over Nojeh Air Force Base, near Hamadan, in the West. From there, they planned to attack the Capital. Of, course, they never made it. Many were arrested, a former guard at Evin among them. He confessed—under duress—that he'd spoken of this coup with a few other prisoners—including me."

Shoja stopped, disturbed by the recollection. We watched and waited in silence.

"They took me in handcuffs from the clinic to the court convened to try the traitors," Shoja continued. "The Prosecutor told me that I had escaped death before, but not this time. I told him the guard mentioned something vaguely, but I didn't give it a thought. The guy seemed unbalanced. Who in his right mind would talk of such a sensitive plan with strangers? The Prosecutor said I still should've reported the incident. But my job was to give medical assistance, not to report on others! Besides, who would've believed me?"

Shoja looked down in anguish. "They kept me in a cell. All night I waited for the death sentence."

"How did you get out of it, Dad?" Ramin asked.

"Judge Gilani—he believed my story," Shoja answered quietly.

How many more untold chronicles did Shoja carry within him? My husband had come through the hellish fire and needed special affection. But what could I do for him when he would not allow me to pass through the invisible wall he had drawn between us?

By the end of the first week, I felt we were almost a complete family and ready to celebrate *Now Ruz* together. To my astonishment, Shoja extended the existing wall between the two of us by announcing that he and Ramin would go to Lake Tahoe for a week's trip.

"Can't you just stay put for a while, Shoja? The *Mujaheddin* are after you."

"Please, stop protecting me. Don't worry so much. I know how to take care of myself," Shoja reacted strongly. "Most of the *Mujaheddin's* leaders have been executed in Iran. The remaining ones have little power in exile. Besides, I get bored here. I don't know how you can live such a quiet life!"

I held back my resentment. "Perhaps, you and Ramin need some time together. Go to Lake Tahoe!" I said. But, didn't Shoja and I need a vacation too?

While Shoja was away, a man came to the apartment, claiming to be a one-time major general in the Iranian army, and a former inmate at Evin.

"*Khanom*, I drove up from D.C. just to see Dr. Sheikh. He is in America, isn't he?" the stranger asked.

"My husband's not home," I said, eyeing a parcel the man had put down. "I don't expect him back soon."

"Too bad! I really wanted to see him. Would you give him this for me?" He pointed to the large brown item.

"Sorry, but I can't accept it," I said nervously, suspecting it to be a bomb.

The man read my thoughts, and began to untie his package outside the door. "Look, *Khanom*. It's only a rug." He lowered his voice. "During a moment of despair in Evin, I attempted suicide. Your husband saved me. This is a token of my gratitude."

"That's very kind of you, but who should I say left it?"

"He'll remember," the stranger responded before disappearing.

When I phoned Shoja in Nevada and discussed the rug incident, he laughed. "Oh yes, him! I remember. But, if the man prefers to remain anonymous, I shouldn't disclose his name, even to you."

If that man knew Shoja was in the States, I wondered, who else knows? How can I protect him?

The last few days were spent sight-seeing in New York, where I felt comfortable trying to disappear among the crowds. We moved through the museums quickly, mostly because Shoja showed little interest for art. At a Broadway show, he fell asleep. Walking along the famous Fifth Avenue, Shoja looked at his watch and nagged, "When can we go home? Haven't we seen enough?" Even at home, Shoja was restless, pacing from room to room, as if waiting for something unexpected to happen. He flipped through my mail. "Nothing for me? Well, of course not! I don't live here, do I?"

The three weeks were up in a wink. When the final day came, Shoja packed his luggage with a somber face.

"Here. Put this picture frame on top so it won't break," I suggested while giving him a picture of me and the children.

"I know how to handle my own things!" Shoja protested.

"Are you still planning to live with your sister when you get back?"

"Who else? Obviously, you won't be there."

"Can you guarantee our safety if I return?"

"There are no guarantees," he said, raising his voice slightly.

"In that case, I'll wait for you here, sweetheart. They can't keep you in Iran forever."

In frustration, we said good-bye at Kennedy Airport.

"So long, sweetheart! We'll see each other soon," I said with conviction. Shoja grasped my hands and held them for a moment, gazing tenderly into my eyes. For a second, it felt like the old times. Then, abruptly, he dropped my hands and walked away. What held him from displaying his emotions more openly? I had hoped at least for a hug.

Somehow, somewhere, we had to meet again to get our feelings and our lives settled.

CHAPTER TWENTY-FIVE

One group are in thought of religion and the devout
Another in a quandary of certainty and doubt
Suddenly upped a messenger from his hideout
You fools! The way is neither this nor that about.
                    Omar Khayyam/Rubaiyat (Twelfth Century)

A few weeks after Shoja's departure, I met with my American friend, Victoria, to sort out my feelings about my husband and my marriage. I was confused. I needed to talk to someone who would listen objectively.

"How did things go between you and your husband?" she asked me.

"Not so good. Nothing turned out as I expected. Shoja's changed—in every way. He had developed new second traits in prison. He was restless and inattentive. Shoja even had the habit of walking at night, and not getting enough sleep. That made him nervous. Of course, who would not lose sleep after what he had been through? Anyhow, we just didn't seem to have any fun together."

"What about intimate relations?" She tossed her short blond hair to the side.

"Oh, well," I blushed, "to be honest, we parted total

strangers. The ice between us didn't seem to break. Shoja seemed unsure of his needs for me, and mistrusting of my feelings for himself. Maybe his family had turned him against me. You know, they are all jobless, and see me as a threat to their security. Maybe it's not those things, and we've just lost passion."

"Maybe you needed more time," Victoria suggested.

"Perhaps we should give it another try," I reflected. "You know, I still have this strange faith in our marriage. That's why when Shoja called to tell me that things have been arranged for me to come back to Iran for a short visit, I accepted. Judge Gilani has promised that I'd have no problems. What do you think?"

"Go for it," Victoria encouraged me.

Whether it was her inbred American confidence or a woman-to-woman determination, my friend helped me see what my heart and my mind were thinking. I would go back and see for myself what was left of my marriage, and my country.

On July 13, 1987, after eight years, I returned to Iran in an attempt to be reconciled with my beloved country, and my precious husband.

At Mehr Abad Airport, I felt the trickles of sweat that come from impending fear. Having suffered so much within my own country before, I was afraid that the custom officer could be the first of several steps where things would go wrong. After a few minutes of checking and double-checking my passport and papers, the official scrutinized my wardrobe from head to toe to see if my attire was acceptable to the Islamic dress code. My black trench coat and large head scarf were approved. At the next stage, a half-awake guard asked me, "Do you carry any cassette tapes?"

I shook my head. "No!"

The guard sluggishly searched my luggage, yawning a few times. Finding nothing to be labeled contraband, he motioned for me to go. I was allowed to enter my own country!

A porter helped carry my luggage through a small crowd of austere figures gathered near the exit door. I missed right away the gaiety of people greeting one another in the States. There were no smiles, no flowers to greet me. And, no sign of Shoja. I tipped the porter and ended up out on the sidewalk, waiting alone. The perimeter of the desolate airport was black. It felt so strange. Was I really "home"?

Shoja suddenly appeared. He gave me a nod and a smile, took my luggage and rushed off ahead of me back towards the parking lot.

"Hey, slow down. Wait for me. I was afraid you'd forgotten me."

"Sorry, I was just waiting in my car," Shoja gestured to a car. A large ten-year old black Cadillac sat waiting for us.

"You know, I don't like to appear in crowds," he confessed.

"The airport was so unusually quiet and dark—almost frightening," I remarked, trying to make a conversation

"What do you expect? There's a war. The airport's a target. Anyway, how was your flight? I hope they didn't bother you at customs."

"Surprisingly, everything went well. How have things been for you, sweetheart? Do they still have you under surveillance?"

"The regime no longer considers me a threat," Shoja said matter-of-factly.

"Oh? Then, why do they keep you in Iran against your will," I asked.

I still held resentment that Shoja seemed stuck in a country that, in a sense, held him hostage.

"Please, let's not discuss that now," Shoja said firmly.

For a moment, the marble Shahyad Monument appeared before our headlights and disappeared again into the blacked-out cityscape as we turned onto the expressway.

"I've got a suite at the Hilton. It's now called *Isteqlal*—Independence. Hilton is far from downtown and fairly safe."

It felt strange to stay in a hotel in my own town, but with no home of our own any more, a hotel was the only place left for some privacy. Perhaps at the hotel, freer lines of communication would open between us.

The rest of the time on the road was spent talking about the children—a safe, neutral subject.

The Hilton lobby was empty and dismal—no flowers, no music, no finely dressed men and women. The grand piano, once the source of romantic interludes, was draped in black, and pictures of martyrs and other war mementos sat on top of it. There was nothing around me like that glamorous night when Shoja and I had played host to Frank Sinatra, who came to Iran to attend a charity ball for the disabled. Those were images that belonged to another life.

Shoja returned with a key, and together with my luggage, we got on the elevator, escorted by a hostile *Pasdar* yielding a machine gun. He followed us suspiciously all the way to our door, as if we were up to something sinful. A tension knot swelled up in my throat.

We entered a suite as drab as the lobby, consisting of a sitting room, a bedroom with two double beds, and a full bath. The furniture, drapes, and linens were clean but starting to show their age. Only one of the four lamps had a dimly lit bulb. Without drawing attention, I took a long look at myself in the mirror. The distorting glass reflected a drawn, tired face. My confidence was shaken.

It was late and time for sleep, so I undressed and got in my nightgown and robe. I went to one of the beds, slipped under the covers shyly and waited for my husband. My heartbeat quickened. Shoja undressed, got into his pajamas, and promptly went into the other bed.

I blushed with chagrin. *He is not in love with me any more,* I thought. Suddenly, my physical desires melted into anger. I took a deep breath to calm myself. "If Iraqi missiles attack, what do we do?" I asked, as if nothing had gone wrong.

From the darkness, his voice answered, "There are not very many shelters. People usually hide in their cellars or pour out into the streets."

"Do you think the suite's bugged?" I whispered.

"Probably not," he yawned. "But it's safer not to discuss politics." He yawned again.

All was quiet for a while. Eventually, Shoja's steady, deep breathing indicated he had fallen asleep.

I stayed awake all night to think about my ultimate goal— trying to keep our marriage together. Sometime past midnight, I quietly went to the window to look out. Above, the lucent Milky Way seemed sprinkled against the murky sky. Below, the city was in a black veil, no lights except for occasional headlights sneaking through the darkness. This was not how I remembered Tehran. My thoughts were beginning to be almost as dark as the city.

What was becoming of our marriage? Had our old passion been replaced by mistrust? Was there something that Shoja feared? Would our distressed relationship survive? What further sacrifices would be required? Had I not already been through enough? Could the wall of strangeness that stood between Shoja and I be torn down?

Early in the morning, exhausted and disoriented, I stepped out on the balcony to look at the Alborz Mountains which seemed to float in the mist against a grayish dawn. The mountains' snowy peaks protruded through the valley's smog, caused by thousands of old cars polluting the air. Still, Alborz seemed majestic, a reminder of ancient Persia.

"Cover your hair!" Shoja yelled from inside. "You'll be in big trouble if someone sees you like that." Some morning greeting!

Annoyed, I returned to the room. Through the window, Shoja pointed at the valley to the left. "You see those tall stone walls? That's Evin."

"Have you ever gone back there?" I asked gently.

"No, but there are times I think I never left it," he said sadly. I felt a pang of sympathy in my heart, and reached out for his hand. He quickly pulled himself aside. "I'm going to order some breakfast," he said flatly. "What do you like with your coffee?"

Silent, an hour later, we left the hotel to visit with my family. The city seemed a little more like home when I saw the tall sycamore trees lined on both sides of what used to be Pahlavi Street, now called Valiasr.

"It's so quiet today! Where are the people? I heard that Tehran's population has tripled since the war."

"Yes, but today's *Ashura*, the tenth day of the mourning period," Shoja explained impatiently. "Have you forgotten? Every *Ashura*, except for the parade of mourners, almost nobody comes out."

Memories of that last *Ashura* flooded my mind. Eight years ago, millions of Iranians had demonstrated on such a day, not to commemorate the Prophet's grandson's martyrdom—but calling for the downfall of the Shah. Eventually, the Islamic Republic had been born. The political climate seemed to have changed dramatically since. The Revolutionary fervor had vanished. People were more concerned with everyday survival.

"I hope we don't run into religious processions," I sighed.

"No one's going to bother us," Shoja assured me.

He turned the ten-year-old Cadillac onto Shemiran Road. Here and there, heaps of rubble and steel were painful visual testaments to recent Iraqi bombings. Hundreds of thousands of homeless people from the war-stricken provinces had poured into Tehran, occupying every available building, and numerous campsites. The once lavish International Hotel was now like a tenement apartment building housing some of the homeless. Clotheslines were strung across the hotel balconies and clothes dried in the morning breeze.

Our old neighborhood seemed shabby and decayed, with one exception—the Mosque. They had constructed a larger courtyard around it.

Shoja slowed down to catch a glimpse of the former house where we had lived for ten years, before it was confiscated by the Revolutionaries. Its gates were closed. The once white walls around the house had turned gray, and the old bright-red roof had weathered to a rusty orange. Did anyone occupy it?

The sight of our old house brought back painful recollections, submerged deep inside me. There was no sense living in the past. I turned my head away. "Shoja, let's go, please, I'm anxious to see my family."

My sister's garden was not as colorful as it used to be. Shahri—the old gardener—had passed away. Aryan, her husband, my nephew Armin—now a physician—Amir Hosain and his family greeted me at the front door. For a moment, I forgot and looked around for Mother. How I missed her!

It was a comfortable reunion. I felt safe to speak within the confines of my sister's home. We all had so many stories to exchange and not enough time to talk. Everyone was so different, not just in appearance, but more resigned, more disillusioned. Time and Revolution had worked against them. It was sad to learn that those around me had suffered so much. I respected and admired them for staying behind in Iran where they hoped to build a new nation, a democracy. Of course, all they had harvested so far, was a brutal war, and unending grief.

The next day, Shoja drove me to Behesht-e-Zahra Cemetery to visit my mother's grave. We left the city at dawn to avoid heavy traffic.

The past six years of war had caused the borders of the cemetery to expand and stretch with the graves of hundreds of thousands of young martyrs. From a gigantic fountain at the center of those new graves, red-colored water flew freely, signifying the martyrs' blood.

Shoja and I watched with sadness as a large crowd of mourners—men, women and children—buried another martyr. The deceased had been washed in water and rubbed with cedar and camphor, then wrapped in three layers of white shrouds while special prayers were chanted. He was carried by four male relatives on a casket to the grave. The young martyr's shrouded body was removed from the casket and laid down into the ground, facing Mecca. Two men unwrapped his lifeless face and rested the back of his head on a mud brick, symbolizing an old religious belief: from dust to dust!

The Islamic Republic of Iran had honored the young martyr for dying while defending his homeland with a symbolic key to heaven. Before the first shovel of dirt was poured on the body, the key was placed on the Martyr's chest. The women began to wail as the final prayer was read: *"On this day, no soul shall be treated unjustly...."* The father, stooped with grief, held his tears back courageously. His son was going straight to heaven. He felt no need to cry. The martyr's grave was covered, and adorned with white and yellow chrysanthemums.

Not far from the mourners, another family was having a picnic around the ghastly red fountain.

"How could people enjoy themselves in a cemetery, especially near that bloody fountain and these mourners?" I asked Shoja with dislike.

"Well, Iranians have accepted death as part of their everyday life and have learned to go on," he answered philosophically.

My mother was buried in our family mausoleum under a marble stone engraved: "Fakhri Sepehri Aryanpour, Devoted Wife and Mother." I lay a bouquet of flowers on her grave. "Hello, Mother, I will never forget you!" I wept, missing her. I realized that I might never be buried here with her.

Agha Joon and Shazdeh Joon were buried, side-by-side, in

another section of the cemetery. Shoja helped me place flowers on their graves before leaving this cemetery to visit another.

We drove 150 miles south, through heavy traffic and smog, to Kashan where my father was buried in the shrine of the Imam Habib Musa, a descendant of the Prophet. This humble shrine, which had been financed by an endowment from my grandfather, had a quaint informal appearance about it which suited my father. After paying our respects to Father, we left to have lunch.

Kashan—an old desert city with a rich civilization—was the birthplace of both my grandfathers. The restaurant owner, an old friend of Father's, recognized us and went out of his way to serve us the best rice and *kabob* one could find during wartime. At the end of the meal, he insisted that we join him for tea at his house which was located in a dirt alley, behind a deep muddy ditch. We walked over a plank, through the shoddy front door, into a splendid living room out of the *Arabian Nights*.

Shoja and I exchanged smiles. The host laughed mischievously. "I know what you're thinking," said the host. "I could afford to have the ditch filled and the alley paved, but that would attract attention and provoke envy. Before too long, the *Pasdars* would be at my door, extorting funds."

So, the *Komiteh* continued to invade homes and to terrorize.

Our next destination was the remote village of Ardahal, surrounded by miles of sandy mountains. In this land of thornbushes and desert sand, my beloved cousin, Sohrab, was buried in the yard of a small mosque. The land's mystifying emptiness and its solemn quietness where spirituality reigned must have attracted Sohrab.

Strangely, Sohrab who had died young of cancer during the

Revolution, was now considered the most famous of Iran's poets and painters. His daily visitors were mostly the villagers who admired his simple philosophy of keeping the earth and water pure. Sohrab had wanted no tombstone on his grave. In keeping with his wishes, a blue mosaic tile, symbolic of the desert's sky, remained his only grave marker.

As we left Ardahal for Tehran, the spectacular desert sunset reflected in the turquoise and cream-colored tiles of the mosque, created a sensual delight. Sohrab! Rest in peace!

For my homecoming, Aryan arranged a family get-together. Everyone had changed. The elders had aged more noticeably—grayer, hunched over, despondent. I listened intently to stories of how their lives had been disrupted in Iran. There were so many combinations of problems at the same time—the devastating war, the skyrocketing inflation, the raging unemployment, the national demoralization. One aunt mourned the execution of her twenty-two-year-old granddaughter along with her fiance. Her crime? Opposition with the government! A relative's husband had been imprisoned without any news from him in months. A friend's son was missing in action. Then, there were those young couples who expressed deep concern about raising children in a rigid society. "My small daughters must wear a chador to school," one mother said tartly. "I'm not even sure most of what they learn is useful."

So many sad stories! So many broken lives! People had become fatalistic. I heard over and over: "Why make plans, when at any moment the war or the *Komiteh* may rob us of tomorrow?"

In an attempt to escape reality, every Iranian had become a

poet. Poetry easily expressed and disguised their suffering. Had Iranians lost their last chance to be free?

On the second week of my stay in Iran, Shoja left me at the Hilton to go back to work at the hospital. From all accounts, he was still a very dedicated physician, and much more popular than ever before.

I hired a taxi to do my own exploring around the city.

"Life's tough, but at least everyone shares in the hardship," the driver remarked as he took me through a maze of heavy traffic and hordes of people. Since the war, Tehran's population had jumped from three million to approximately ten million. I noticed many foreigners among them.

"Afghan refugees," the driver explained. "Hundreds of thousands of them here to escape Communism."

In the center of town, the evidence of war was most conspicuous—bombed out buildings and bomb potholes caused by the Iraqi missiles.

"Is the opposition's voice still strong?" I asked the driver.

He eyed me suspiciously. "Wouldn't know. I only mind my own job."

Even after the Revolution, small talk among people was tense. Nobody wanted to be accused of saying the wrong thing and taken off to jail.

Downtown, business went on, more or less, as usual, and the people went about their lives with indifference—faces hollow, eyes empty, no spontaneous happiness. On Ferdowsi Avenue, known for its gold and money exchange shops, several *Pasdars* grabbed a passerby woman and threw her into a small gray van.

"Her hair's showing," the driver said, half-mockingly. "Big offense!"

"What will they do with her?" I asked with concern.

"If lucky, she'll only be fined. Could be imprisoned, though—up to two months—and, of course, flogged seventy-four lashes," the driver commented without much emotion.

I immediately pulled my scarf down further on my face covering every strand of hair. Women had become victim's of a man's world. What kind of ideological age had Iran entered?

"Will you take me to the old bazaar?" I requested.

"It's not at all what it used to be, *Khanom*. Besides, just a few days ago, a bomb went off in that area," the driver warned.

The sights and the smells of the old bazaar were still alive in my mind: the cadence of blacksmiths hammering on hot metals, the glittering gold of jewelers, and the aroma of exotic spices. The shops had been housed under elaborate domes of brick and mosaic ceilings. Now, the intricate traditional bazaar, the progenitor to modern shopping malls, had undergone a change too. It was not a safe place to shop.

The driver drove me to another part of the city to see the neighborhood where I had grown up. The street had a new name, face, and mood. My childhood house had disappeared, along with every other familiar thing around it. Even my favorite candy store was gone. I remembered how I used to press my little face against the window of the candy store to look covetously at boxes of chocolate with Alice Fay's picture on them. Or was it Betty Grable?

My sweet memories of Tehran had been superseded by the realities of a brutal war and the mounds of debris that lined the sidewalks.

"Please, take me back to the Hilton. I've seen enough," I instructed the driver.

That night Shoja and I dined in the almost empty hotel restaurant.

"So, tell me about your day, Shoja," I asked in a desperate attempt to make a silent man talk.

"Not much to say. I saw lots of patients. You know, many doctors left Iran when the war started. Even if the government let me, I could never leave now when people need me so much," he explained in a resigned way.

I was shocked by what I heard. Shoja, the personification of all innocent citizens who had been victimized unjustly by different Iranian governments, was willing to stay in Iran and provide medical care to his countrymen no matter where he found himself in the inferno! He should be seen as a remarkable survivor.

"Many of your colleagues have come to America and started life over," I finally managed to say. "What makes you so adamant that Iran is the only place to serve people?"

Shoja found no time to respond. At that exact moment, the air raid sirens penetrated the room with a monstrous shrill and shook the walls. The panic set in. Our conversation and our hopes died down instantly. We raced to the lobby, and found ourselves among a dozen frightened Asian businessmen. Overhead, there was the dreadful thundering of jet engines and the quick whoosh sounds of missiles. We all fell to the floor to protect ourselves. The hotel shuddered. Lights went out. Instinctively, I grabbed Shoja's arm tightly and prayed that we would survive.

For twenty minutes, the sirens blared. How many more

would be killed tonight? How much longer must this war drain the blood of innocent people?

The sirens stopped suddenly, but the shrieking noise reverberated in my head. The danger seemed to be over—for now.

I had a whole afternoon to spend with Amir Hosain. I needed my loving mentor's advice.

We drank tea and talked about his life. Amir Hosain, the archetypal scholar, whose political dreams of a democratic government had been vetoed many times, still believed that his place was in Iran. Although he was not teaching at the university for political reasons, his home was open to those who sought his knowledge. Despite many obstacles, Amir Hosain was mentally more active than most Iranians. My brother's real joy, however, remained raising his only teenage son who had been born to him late in his life.

Amir Hosain asked me about my life in America, my job in the library, and my children. I filled him in on the essentials.

"So, what are your plans for the future?" Amir Hosain asked.

"Well, I feel estranged from both my country and my husband," I confessed. "When it comes to Iran, I have no illusions. I can't live here again—not as long as I have a choice. My place is near my children, in America. In regard to Shoja, however, I have mixed emotions. But, I still love him, and don't want to give up."

"Perhaps, you two blame each other for your misfortunes," my brother wondered. "Shoja can't forgive you for leaving Iran while he was in prison. And you hold him responsible for your exile. Such problems may only be settled in time with compromise."

"Compromise! Haven't I done enough of that already? I can't compromise the freedom I have fought to gain—for myself, my children, and even for that hardheaded Shoja!"

"Then, do what's right for you and your family. You are a brave and resourceful woman, Azar. Use your talents. Follow your instincts. Be happy!" he advised in his simple eloquent manner.

My brother understood me, even though Shoja did not.

The last few days of my stay in Iran passed quickly and quietly. I first began to read from the great works of the Sufi mystics, mainly Rumi, in the poetic Farsi language. Then, I tried to familiarize myself with Iran's post-revolutionary ideology and literature, published solely by the *"Vezarat Ershad"*—Ministry of Guidance. What I read seemed enlightening and promising on paper. Without question, I had no regrets for the downfall of the Shah's dictatorial regime. But Iranians still lived under the iron hands of another autocratic government. Freedom of speech, so essential to a democracy, was almost non-existent. All news was subject to the government's tough censorship and propaganda. It was sad to see that the new Republic with all its inherent potential was ideologically entrapped in the past.

Since there was no nightly entertainment, Shoja and I often dined with my family. My sister was unhappy about my coming departure.

"Azar, it's good to have you back. Won't you stay?" Aryan implored one evening.

"I don't think so. My three-week vacation's almost over. I must be back at work next Monday. I want to stop in Frankfurt for a short visit with Amir Ashraf on my way to America."

"If I were you, I wouldn't leave my husband so long," she warned. "The war's left many widows, all shopping for good husbands. Shoja's a prime candidate."

"I don't doubt my husband's love," I responded with a frown. "He would never be swayed by another woman. Shoja has never given any hint that he was unfaithful."

"I'm sure you're right," Aryan said portentously.

Shoja and I spent our last evening together at the Hilton, making small talk. Evin had left its strong mark on how we expressed ourselves. We were not allowing ourselves to touch or be romantic.

"What should I do if they stop me at the airport?" I asked, knowing the unpredictability of the Iranian authorities.

"Nothing! Then you'll just stay here with your husband where you belong," he answered bluntly.

"Shoja, it's not that simple."

"It is—if you want it to be."

"We can't pretend things are the same. Look around! Everything's changed," I tried to reason.

"But my feelings for you haven't."

Now I felt quite perplexed. This statement was the closest he had come to some 'romantic' expression. Still his tone lacked tenderness.

"You may not be aware of it, but your feelings have changed," I said.

"And what about yours?" He threw aside the newspaper that he pretended to be reading, a temporary wall to keep his feelings hidden, and stomped out of the room.

I ran after him. "Please come back, Shoja. Let's talk."

"What's the use? You are not going to change your mind," Shoja said angrily. He seemed so distant, so untouchable.

Early the next morning, Shoja drove me to the airport. Neither of us had much to say.

With a heavy heart, I boarded the plane, leaving Iran—perhaps never to return. However, I knew my life with Shoja was not over, yet.

CHAPTER TWENTY-SIX

During a simple ceremony, I pledged an oath and became a citizen of the United States, although a part of me would always belong to Iran. At least I could claim to have a country now.

Autumn and winter passed quietly. Like a patient recovering from a long illness, I tenaciously clung on to each moment of living. The future was a mist way ahead of me, so time had no meaning except what happened in the present. I worked hard and read vigorously. I also began to travel within the States to discover my new country. Coming from a much older and more arid land, respectable for its ancient civilization, I found America's freshness and stunning scenery rejuvenating.

Meantime, Roxana had moved to New Jersey, where she was teaching at Princeton Montessori School, and working on a doctoral program at Rutgers University in educational administration. She was also seriously dating a charming physician.

Ramin had moved to an apartment close to his work. His enthusiasm for his work, studies and life had changed remarkably. My proud son had regained his health and his self-confidence.

The children's growing independence was an encourage-ment and my delight.

On a perfect fall day, with sunny and glorious warm col-ors, Roxana got married. Although the groom was many years her senior, Shoja and I accepted Roxana's decision and gave her our blessings. Shoja had been permitted to attend her wedding only on the condition, again, that his family in Iran would be arrested should he decide not to return within the promised time! We were not going to let this threat destroy a very special day for us. We would enjoy our daughter's wedding together.

At a beautiful villa in Southampton, we prepared with joy for the wedding ceremony, following a tradition that originat-ed several thousand years ago in Iran. On paisley shawls with gold threads, we placed a silver mirror facing two candelabra, symbols of purity and light. A miniature censer held aromatic seeds to ward off the bad fortunes. The ceremony included a platter of bread—the staple of life—along with a bowl of sugar crystals and a small jar of honey that meant a sweet beginning. There were also brightly colored eggs, signifying fertility. Mother's antique Qur'an sat at the end of the display. She had written everyone's birthdays and added her comments of wis-dom about living, on the inside cover.

Of course, we all knew that keeping tradition was nice, but it took much more effort for a marriage to be successful.

Roxana put on her ivory satin and lace wedding dress. The only jewelry she wore was a gold chain that Mother had given her once. Her beauty was complemented by her bouquet of white gardenias and tuberoses.

"Mom, how do I look?" Roxana asked the universal question, before leaving for the ceremony.

"Gorgeous. Just smile," I replied with every mother's universal answer.

The music started with an old Persian wedding song that had also been played at my wedding. Bridesmaids held a silk canopy over the bride and groom as they sat under the candlelight facing the mirror. Above the cloth, I rubbed two sugar cones, and whispered, "Forever be happy."

The clergyman began with a simple prayer. When he concluded, he asked, "Roxana, do you consent to be married to this man in the presence of God and all these witnesses?"

Roxana remained silent. Traditionally, the bride must wait to be asked three times. The custom was for the bride to play "hard to get" and for the groom to offer gifts to get her answer.

By the third question, Roxana answered, "Yes!" The rings were exchanged. Our daughter was pronounced married!

I looked at Shoja and saw a glint of tears in his eyes. Like me, he was thinking of Roxana's happiness.

Shoja was still in America when, once again, Iraq resumed its extensive missile attacks on Iran. Many Iranians fled the target cities for their lives. Shoja reluctantly decided to postpone his trip until it was safe to return home. His written request for an extension on his stay in the States was approved by Judge Gilani. Nevertheless, Shoja was irritable in America with nothing to do. I advised him to apply for a green card. I also encouraged him to study for the Federal Licensing Examination of physicians.

With a green card and a medical license he would be

allowed to practice in the States. He could find no more excuses to go back to Iran. I thought.

To my surprise, Shoja accepted. While waiting to hear from Immigration, Shoja began to study diligently for the exams. During this period, I tried to make him feel comfortable and to recreate old times by serving his favorite foods, stocking the house with fresh flowers, and dressing up for dinner. Nothing made him interested in me. He acted like an outsider in a temporary environment. Our relationship did not seem to improve. In fact, it deteriorated. The long hours of studies and the pressures of the coming exams were too much for a man who had already endured a great deal. My relative independence added to his unhappiness. It became a source of constant threat to his male ego.

For a man who pretended he did not need me, he frequently asked, "Where were you when I called your office this morning? Or, "At fifty-five, I have to put in fourteen hours of study to take the FLEX, just because my wife doesn't want to live in Iran! Why? I don't know!"

He manifested his complaints through his stern looks and daily pointed questions. It was like he was saying, "See? You are creating all these problems!"

Had his family tortured him by telling lies about me, out of envy? In Shoja's case especially, the prison authorities had every reason to brainwash him against me. Hadn't they already attempted to break our marriage and force us into a divorce? Didn't they demand my return to Iran in order to release him?

Shoja's captors must have worked on his jealousies repeatedly. I could hear them, all the way to America, singing a chorus of lies in his ears every day: "A disobedient wife is no good.

She must be living a sinful life in that satanic America if she is not willing to return to her husband!"

The people around him must have destroyed his trust in me. Unknown to any of them and to their lies, I lived the life of a nun—shutting the doors to all pleasures in exile. I even told him so. Didn't he believe me?

During Shoja's three-months stay in America, I came to realize that it would be impossible to have any deep intimacy with him. My husband saw me as his foe, while I saw myself as his victim.

Shoja was successful. He received his green card and passed the physicians' exams the first time. Without hesitation, he made immediate plans to return to Iran to quell down the rumors that he had defected.

I asked him not to leave. "It's not safe to go back. Stay! You can help people here. Remember, your first commitment is to your family. Don't leave! They will not hurt your family in Iran."

Naive as I was, I thought that if I held on to him a little longer, he would come around. We could never become lovers again. But, as husband and wife, two faithful companions, we could protect each other against the hostile world. Whether I was deluding myself or not, I was still emotionally committed to Shoja. He had his family, his green card, and his license to practice orthopedic surgery in America—three major reasons to stay. No matter what he said, I could not believe he would give up the opportunity to start a new life with me, here in the States. My blind confidence in our long relationship proved to be wrong. My pleas did not work. Shoja repeated his standard excuse:

"At this point in my life, I can't reestablish my career in a new country," he said with coldness. "I conceded to take the exams only to prove to myself that my mental faculties were not damaged in prison. Otherwise, you and the children don't need me. Roxana's married. Ramin's a corporate vice president. Babak will soon be a doctor. And, you've got your career, your friends. You don't need me!" He took a pause. "Once, you told me that things have changed. You were right. We have changed in the way we perceive each other, and ultimately, in how we see our destinies. Our life will never be the same," Shoja concluded in an embittered tone.

I stepped towards him. "Listen! I know we can never go back to where we were, Shoja. But we can move on together. I want us to have a safe life. I don't want us to be hunted down again. That's not much to ask, is it?"

He took a step back. "There's no more to be said. I've made up my mind in regard to the future," Shoja said firmly, avoiding my eyes.

Blood rushed to my head. "Am I a part of that future, Shoja?" I asked nervously.

He looked more distant than ever. As he began to talk, a presentiment of something ultimate hovered over me. I knew beforehand that what he was about to say would change my life forever. To this day, I remember our last dialogue word by word.

"It depends. Will you come to live in Iran? Things are changing," he answered.

Was he offering me *carte blanche* a safer life in Iran, despite his wrongful imprisonment and mental tortures? How could he? He had no power to protect us from the deadly whims of the next government leaders.

"I left Iran because of you, remember? My whole life is here now—my children, my career," I replied predictably.

"If you return, I'll provide everything you need," Shoja pretended a promise.

His easy promise sounded too hollow. "How about freedom? I was in Iran. I saw for myself."

"So, you want to exchange your homeland and your husband for freedom?" His lips took a sarcastic twist. He raised his voice. "What's that? A rented apartment and a low-paying job?"

"At least what I have is real and belongs to me," I answered in perfect calm.

He could boast all he wanted, but he could not offer me what my home country denied me—freedom! Freedom gave me the rights to work for a new life. It gave me alternatives. I chose who I was and how I looked. Freedom gave me self-confidence to challenge obstacles. It helped me find my lost identity.

Shoja's face turned red. His eyes, once filled with adulation for me, burned with contempt. He was defeated in what he could offer me. He took a few deep breaths and regained his composure.

"Very well, then. Hold on to your precious life! I can't force you to return. In fact, I'm fed up with this farce marriage. Do you hear me? As of now, you are free. I need a wife who could be waiting for me at the end of a long day. A wife who really loves me," he said bitterly.

His words cut into me like a sword. Tears swelled in my eyes. All those lonely years of waiting, longing, and fighting the world raced through my mind. I had been in the inferno because of my husband. In the center of the inferno, Shoja's face appeared. My whole existence became a struggle to prove his innocence, redeem his reputation, and hasten his freedom. These things I accomplished! My unconditional love for him tormented me, transformed me, and destined me to exile. And now he doubted me? Who was I? His wife, who wanted to be treated as an equal by him and by the society in which I lived. I thought he understood. Was this the man to whom I had given every inch of my heart, my body, and soul?

Whoever he was, I knew I had to end this perpetual struggle before the exhaustion of accusations and his demeaning coldness completely ruined me. The love was still there in my heart, but the man I loved was lost. He no longer belonged to me. I braced myself for the frustration inside me.

"Shoja, apparently, we have nothing further to discuss. Just leave me, please."

For a few seconds, Shoja stared at me, then with a determined stride, he walked out of my life. I remained motionless.

I had kept my promise to my children. I had remained the epitome of the ever faithful wife. Had I waited too long?

EPILOGUE

On July 18, 1988, the Iranian government finally agreed to end one of the bloodiest wars of the century. The Iran-Iraq War had been terminated.

Less than a year later, the Islamic Republic mourned the death of Ayatollah Khomeini—the magnetic leader of the Iranian Revolution. Iranians entered a new era.

In America, unlike so many tedious years, time raced past me. Days, weeks, and months merged in a blink. The children had left home to start new lives. Yet, there was a new child in my life—my first grandchild—Kayvan! To me, he was a perfect miracle, the miniature image of my daughter!

As captivating as he was, Kayvan provided no motivation to Shoja to move to the States. He was busy with his private practice and rebuilding his life in Iran.

Early in January, 1990, the Iranian divorce court requested my presence at a hearing in Tehran. Shoja's legal justification for the divorce? "The wife's refusal to return to her husband."

It was senseless to contest the divorce. The Iranian court would never rule in my favor. Besides, Shoja had already announced his plans to get married again. His future bride? How ironic! She happened to be the woman Shoja's parents had chosen for him many years ago! He did not marry her; instead, he chose to marry me. Why her now? Was she one of Shoja's reasons for staying in Iran? What karma! This woman would gain the man she always wanted!

In the months to come, I worked myself endlessly to blot out Shoja from my mind, and to put together the pieces of my life. In the mornings, I rushed out to my job at the library, a perfect distraction among my books. At nights, I searched through my memories for the scattered fragments of my life, and for the right words and phrases to weave them together. I reflected and I wrote. Of course, from time to time, my attempts at writing my story proved to be difficult. Re-living the past was painful. However, in an odd way, writing my story helped me understand the inevitable factors that changed my life forever. Shoja and I were both victims of a Revolution!

My occasional visits with my two little grandsons—Kayvan and his recently born brother, Kamron—were my only joys. Those precious children were my true connections to the future.

Late in February of 1992, after twenty-six months, the divorce papers arrived. My marriage of thirty-five years had been legally dissolved. Thirteen long, tumultuous years of waiting for my husband had come to an official end. I had lost the man I loved to a Revolution that took away my homeland!

Clasping the papers, I felt a sudden urge to scream with all my might. My mouth opened, but to my shock, I could not make a sound. There was no scream, but a coughing attack so severe that my breathing almost failed. My lungs heaved. I gasped for air to live.

Half an hour later, my exhausted body received oxygen in the Emergency Room. I was still clutching the divorce papers.

There is a different view through my window in the States: a vista of clear blue sky, no mountains, no boundaries, **no walls!**

From its perch in a high tree, a robin celebrates the spring with its beautiful melody. Now Ruz, the new year that starts with the spring, is here.

I have emerged out of the abyss. What do I have now? A fresh beginning...

About the Author

Azar Aryanpour was born to an old, prominent Iranian family of literary men and women. Graduating from high school with the highest honors, Azar received a scholarship to continue her education abroad. She and her new husband left for the United States in 1957 to further their education.

After studying English Literature at Western Reserve University in Cleveland, the author later attended the University of Pennsylvania and completed her studies with a degree in education from the University of Akron.

Ms. Arynapour returned to Iran and taught children's literature and philosophy of education at the College of Shemiran and the National University. She also worked as a freelance writer and translated both How Man Became a Giant and part of The Ascent of Man from English to Farsi. She received considerable acclaim for her command of both languages. The author is also the compiler of several children's stories and a book of lyrics entitled Songs from Four Continents.

Disrupted from her work toward a Ph.D. in Persian Literature at Tehran University in 1978 when the revolution in Iran broke out, Azar managed to escape to the United States where she and her three children started a new life.

The author returned to school, received her M.L.S. degree at Rutgers University in New Jersey and became the librarian at the Center for Urban Policy Research. Her children have also been successful: Roxana is a Ph.D. candidate in Education: Ramin is the president of a general contracting company; and Babak is an orthopaedic surgeon. Ms. Aryanpour also has three grand children: Kayvan, Kamron, and Kimya.